NEW

COMMUNITARIAN

THINKING

*Persons, Virtues,*

*Institutions, and*

*Communities*

# CONSTITUTIONALISM AND DEMOCRACY

## KERMIT HALL AND DAVID O'BRIEN, EDITORS

Kevin T. McGuire
*The Supreme Court Bar: Legal Elites in the Washington Community*

Mark Tushnet, ed.
*The Warren Court in Historical and Political Perspective*

David N. Mayer
*The Constitutional Thought of Thomas Jefferson*

F. Thornton Miller
*Juries and Judges versus the Law: Virginia's Provincial Legal Perspective, 1783–1828*

Martin Edelman
*Courts, Politics, and Culture in Israel*

Tony Freyer
*Producers versus Capitalists: Constitutional Conflict in Antebellum America*

Amitai Etzioni, ed.
*New Communitarian Thinking: Persons, Virtues, Institutions, and Communities*

# NEW COMMUNITARIAN THINKING

*Persons, Virtues,*

*Institutions, and*

*Communities*

EDITED BY

*AMITAI ETZIONI*

UNIVERSITY PRESS OF VIRGINIA

*Charlottesville and London*

# THE UNIVERSITY PRESS OF VIRGINIA

Copyright © 1995 by the Rector and Visitors
of the University of Virginia

*FIRST PUBLISHED 1995*

Library of Congress Cataloging-in-Publication Data
New communitarian thinking : persons, virtues, institutions, and
   communities / edited by Amitai Etzioni.
       p.   cm. — (Constitutionalism and democracy)
     Includes bibliographical references and index.
     ISBN 0-8139-1564-3. — ISBN 0-8139-1569-4 (paper)
     1. Social ethics.   2. Community.   3. Liberalism.   4. Democracy.
   I. Etzioni, Amitai.   II. Series.
   HM216.N44   1995
   303.3'72—dc20                                          94-30415
                                                              CIP

PRINTED IN THE UNITED STATES OF AMERICA

# CONTENTS

Acknowledgments    vii

Introduction    1

Old Chestnuts and New Spurs
AMITAI ETZIONI    16

**Political Theory: The Communitarian Challenge**

1    Communitarian Liberalism
THOMAS A. SPRAGENS, JR.    37

2    The Communitarian Critique of Liberalism
MICHAEL WALZER    52

3    Moral Argument and Liberal Toleration:
Abortion and Homosexuality
MICHAEL J. SANDEL    71

4    Community: Reflections on Definition
ROBERT BOOTH FOWLER    88

**Human Nature, Social Theory, and the Moral Dimension**

5    The Communitarian Individual
JEAN BETHKE ELSHTAIN    99

6    Personhood and Moral Obligation
PHILIP SELZNICK    110

7    Human Nature and the Quest for Community
ALAN WOLFE    126

**Virtue in a Constitutional Democracy**

8    Virtue, the Common Good, and Democracy
DAVID HOLLENBACH, S.J.    143

**9**    The Virtues of Democratic Self-Constraint
AMY GUTMANN    154

**10**    Institutions as the Infrastructure of Democracy
WILLIAM M. SULLIVAN    170

**The Institutional Requirements of Constitutional Democracy**

**11**    Liberal Politics and the Public Sphere
CHARLES TAYLOR    183

**12**    Free Speech and Free Press: A Communitarian Perspective
JEFFREY ABRAMSON AND ELIZABETH BUSSIERE    218

**Citizenship in America: Two Views**

**13**    American Conceptions of Citizenship and National Service
ROGERS M. SMITH    233

**14**    Immigration and Political Community in the United States
DANIEL J. TICHENOR    259

Notes    283
About the Authors    310
Index    311

# ACKNOWLEDGMENTS

Chapter 2, Michael Walzer's "The Communitarian Critique of Liberalism," appeared previously in *Political Theory* 18 (Feb. 1990): 6–23 and is reprinted by permission of Sage Publications, Inc..

Chapter 3, Michael J. Sandel's "Moral Argument and Liberal Toleration: Abortion and Homosexuality," appeared previously in the *California Law Review* 77 (1989): 521–38.

Chapter 6, "Personhood and Moral Obligation," is adapted from Philip Selznick, *The Moral Commonwealth: Social Theory and the Promise of Community* (Berkeley and Los Angeles: University of California Press, 1992), pp. 193–206, 215–19, by permission of the press and the Regents of the University of California.

Chapter 11, Charles Taylor's "Liberal Politics and the Public Sphere," appeared previously in *Transit. Europäische Revue* 5 (Winter 1992/93).

The editor gratefully acknowledges the support of the Lilly Endowment, which helped fund the development of this volume.

The editor would also like to thank W. Bradford Wilcox for providing a lion's share of the drafting work for the Introduction.

NEW

COMMUNITARIAN

THINKING

*Persons, Virtues,*

*Institutions, and*

*Communities*

# Introduction

Communitarian thought has been dismissed as, at best, little more than a corrective to the excesses of liberalism and, at worst, as a form of "old-fashioned collectivism." By surveying a range of discrete and theoretical issues in social and political thought, this volume aims to provide an account of communitarian thought which answers charges such as these while establishing communitarian philosophy as a robust theory in its own right.[1] Sections on political theory, human nature and the moral dimension, virtue and the public sphere, the institutional requirements of constitutional democracy, and citizenship show how communitarian conceptions offer incisive answers to some of the most important contemporary and classic problems confronting us. This is not to say that communitarian philosophy is of a piece. As with other approaches, communitarian thought attracts scholars with a range of commitments from Christianity to egalitarianism; accordingly, the authors in this volume take disparate stances on such issues as human nature, the efficacy of state-sponsored attempts to inculcate virtue, and the value of religious faith.

## Political Theory:
## The Communitarian Challenge

The first section of this volume represents an effort to respond to the definitional questions that have plagued communitarian thinking from the start. Not surprisingly, attempts at definition are divided into the two most prominent schools of communitarian thinking: namely, a school arguing that communitarian thinking is a source of reform for contemporary liberalism, and a school which emphasizes the ways in which communitarian thinking offers an altogether distinctive approach to political theory. Nevertheless, the contributors to this section share common concerns as demonstrated by their commitment to exploring the ways in which contemporary political theory can better address questions of community, virtue, and moral discourse in the public square.

The conventional debate between liberalism and communitarianism induces "schizophrenia" in Thomas A. Spragens, Jr., the author of the first essay in this section (chap. 1, "Communitarian Liberalism"). He finds himself "both deeply committed to the fundamental verities of liberalism but also profoundly sympathetic to communitarian claims and concerns." Spragens thinks that part of the problem is that the debate has presented a caricature of liberalism.

By exploring the emergence of liberalism through the eyes of three of its founders—John Locke, Condorcet, and John Stuart Mill—Spragens aims to recover and rehabilitate liberal theory by showing that the liberal tradition is characterized by more "moral traditionalism and moral complexity," including a concern for the common good, than its opponents are wont to admit. He also aims to show the ways in which the two strains of contemporary liberalism—libertarianism and egalitarianism—have remained all too agnostic when it comes to issues of the good life. By arguing that liberty and equality are important but limited goods, Spragens dedicates much of his essay to exploring the ways in which a robust communitarian liberalism can attend to issues of virtue and community without lapsing into antiliberalism.

Michael Walzer might also be counted as a communitarian liberal of sorts. In his essay (chap. 2, "The Communitarian Critique of Liberalism") Walzer sees communitarian thought as an eternally recurring corrective to liberalism. The communitarian critique, in his view, may be powerful, but it is also parasitical, in that it only arises in response to liberalism and cannot sustain itself as an independent vision of social and political life.

He acknowledges that communitarianism is right to claim that liberalism, and the personal and social mobilities it legitimates, generates a "sense of loss" as settled convictions, relations, and ways of life constantly face erosion. But Walzer takes a stoic view of the essentially tragic character of liberalism. He argues that we must accept the "principle that communities must always be at risk" because liberalism is our tradition, and a popular tradition at that. Seeing no other way but liberalism, he offers a few communitarian suggestions for ways in which the fragile social relationships of liberal societies can be strengthened. The fate, then, of communitarianism is to offer periodic corrections to liberalism's disassociative tendencies so that liberalism itself can remain strong.

Michael J. Sandel does not seek to redeem or correct liberalism. In an essay (chap. 3, "Moral Argument and Liberal Toleration: Abortion and Homosexuality") which confronts two of the most fractious moral issues of contemporary life, Sandel aims to displace the principle of liberal toleration. To make his point, he suggests that proponents and opponents of abortion and homosexuality often advance a "naive view under cover of the sophisticated [view]." What he means is that both camps often claim they are defending or opposing the legal prohibition of these practices on the basis of general norms of toleration or democracy—the sophisticated view—when in fact their stance is rooted in a moral conviction about the permissibility of the practice under question—the naive view.

For instance, he argues that the Supreme Court's decision in *Roe v. Wade* (1973) was disingenuous in offering the sophisticated argument that abortion need be tolerated until the third trimester because it is not the state's place to decide when life begins. By allowing abortions until viability outside the womb, the Supreme Court implicitly endorsed the naive argument that life did not begin until viability. In his view this is one example of how liberalism only fools itself when it claims in the name of toleration that questions of the good life can be "bracketed" from public discussion and regulation. Accordingly, Sandel argues that in public debates about the legal status of abortion and homosexuality, we must acknowledge that the "justice (or injustice) of laws against abortion and homosexual sodomy depends, at least in part, on the morality (or immorality) of those practices." Only such a communitarian acknowledgment will generate the kind of "substantive moral discourse in political and constitutional argument" we require.

Robert Booth Fowler reflects in chapter 4 on contemporary efforts to define community. Three disparate kinds of community—communities of ideas, crisis, or memory—predominate in current discussions of community in American political thought, according to Fowler. Intellectuals appear preoccupied with communities of ideas: namely, participatory communities based upon talk and republican community predicated on public virtue and spiritedness. Communities of crisis aim at overcoming the social and ecological crises of the day through, respectively, tribal and global communities of purpose. Communities of memory are the domain of those who are concerned about what they see as the precarious state of traditional beliefs and virtue, or who would like to see a particular faith in God serve as the basis of communal renewal.

Fowler is well aware that there are those who worry about the "tyrannical possibilities of community," whatever form community takes. But he warns them they "also need to fear the tyrannical dangers of the desiccation of community." He therefore seeks a communal via media between those who would ignore community and those who would lose themselves and their peers in totalistic communities. In his view the quest for community must be chastened by a form of "existential watchfulness." The latter half of his essay is dedicated to describing what that means and the ways in which some of our contemporary theories of community do not measure up to existential watchfulness.

## Human Nature, Social Theory, and the Moral Dimension

Since the initial communitarian challenge to liberalism, the divide that once seemed to separate communitarian and liberal theories of human nature has begun to close. Liberals such as Amy Gutmann have argued that liberalism does not necessarily rule out a social theory of human nature; communitarians (Charles Taylor being a leading one) acknowledge as much. Nevertheless, even if some liberals are willing to admit that persons are shaped by their social environment, they still believe that environment should tilt, in Rawlsian fashion, toward autonomy and a universalistic ethic of individual justice. The first two essays of this section stress the limits of such an approach by detailing the ways in which the social environment should be attentive to the human need for connectedness and for particularistic communities. The last essay suggests that any effort to cultivate particular values must be tempered by a recognition of the importance of respecting individual capacities.

Jean Bethke Elshtain strives to transcend the panegyrics associated with the liberal-communitarian debate in the first article in this section (chap. 5, "The Communitarian Individual"). She does this by turning one of liberalism's archetypes—autonomous individualism—on its head, stressing that the communitarian individual is tied to her family, community, and past in ways that liberalism cannot account for. Elshtain believes that this form of contractarian individualism comes at a high price of detachment and offers an alternative model better suited to the communitarian individual: "a world framed by a social compact." This compact aims to validate and acknowledge those relationships—be they familial or otherwise—stretching between and beyond generations which are not a matter of choice but rather constituent elements of the "thick" self. This self "acknowledges that he or she has many debts and obligations and that one's history and the history of one's society frames one's own starting point." Yet Elshtain does not think that the communitarian individual is so embedded that she does and must reflect any single moral order; rather, the communitarian individual recognizes "the moral conflicts of our age" and attempts to negotiate them as best she can. Elshtain ends by sketching out the kinds of communities where her communitarian individual might feel at home.

Philip Selznick, a liberal communitarian, also recognizes that the self's ability to sustain a meaningful sense of autonomy is dependent upon the self's ability to maintain a home "within a framework of bonding to other persons and to person-centered activities." Hence, a univeralistic ethic directed toward all individuals—regardless of their beliefs, practices, or social status—should never serve as the primary basis for a social ethic. Rather, a particularistic ethic grounded in "genuinely other-regarding" commitment, care, and concern for specific persons in concrete settings has to be the foundation for any decent social order. Selznick takes this essential insight and applies it in intriguing ways in chapter 6: he reminds us that the Christian ethic of brotherly love must be first directed to one's neighbor and not mankind in general and that welfare programs applied in universal fashion can be profoundly alienating, no matter how fair, if they are impersonal.

This is not to say that particularism is perfect or that we can live without universalism, according to Selznick. The particularistic evils of intolerance, group egotism, and atavism "must be disciplined by a universalistic ethic" which ensures no one is robbed of their due. Nevertheless, Selznick's essay would suggest he is convinced that we can best recognize and attend to the needs of individuals and the communities to which they belong when we acknowledge the particularistic obligations and opportunities of those institutions. In such communities the person (he thinks this is a better word than *individual*) recognizes that "self-determination is the freedom to find one's proper place within a moral order, not outside it."

While Alan Wolfe is interested in communal efforts to shape human nature, his essay (chap. 7, "Human Nature and the Quest for Community") focuses on the extent to which natural and ecological models provide sound empirical and normative bases for a communitarian vision of human nature. "Just about every major innovation in social theory—including liberalism, conservatism, and Marxism—" Wolfe points out, "has been accompanied by a set of ideas of what is natural and what is not." Communitarian thinking is no different, he argues, in asserting that humans are "sociable by nature." This assertion often borrows from an ecological theory of human behavior which assumes persons are naturally inclined to specific social arrangements, much as animals are suited to particular habitats and behaviors. This theory paves the way for three claims: that persons need and seek community, that community interests take priority over individual needs, and that community ought to be cultivated paternalistically.

However, the usefulness of the ecological approach, in Wolfe's view, is limited by the fact that persons are more than the sum of their social environments. Rejecting the claims of sociobiology and structuralism (not to mention Tory conservatism), Wolfe writes that human ecologies "contain individuals who are active agents in transforming and understanding the environment in which they exist." Not only are persons different from animals in cognitive and relational terms, but they are also so complex that biology cannot fully explain human behavior: this is why proponents of particular viewpoints on topics ranging from mother-infant bonding to homosexuality should treat biology as destiny arguments with care (especially, he notes, since they generally flip-flop on the role of genetics in the two aforementioned examples). Wolfe concludes on a note reminiscent of the social theories explored at the beginning of his essay: that is, he provides an indeterminate vision of human nature, one that he believes will provide a better basis for the kind of "inclusive and open society" to which communitarian philosophy, in his view, should aim.

### Virtue in a Constitutional Democracy

There is a nominalist strain among contemporary liberals like John Rawls and Bruce Ackerman when it comes to public virtues besides the minimalist virtues of toleration and fairness. Concerned that public virtue could only be maintained—given the profound pluralism of modern democracies—by authoritarian tactics, they shy away from discussions of public virtue or publicly generated virtue. The authors of this section believe that such a tack, while understandable, would prove fatal to contemporary democracies. Chapter 8 argues that the centrifugal cultural and economic tendencies of the current era make the pursuit of a public, common good integral to social survival. Democracy requires specific virtues of deliberation, nonrepression, and nondiscrimination, and they can be defended on terms internal to democracy itself, contends chapter 9. Chapter 10 argues that public and private virtues only take shape in supportive institutions, and that this necessitates a turn away from an instrumental approach to institutions.

The individualistic and privatistic strains "in American culture today need to be transformed by more communal and solidaristic sensibilities," writes David Hollenbach (chap. 8, "Virtue, the Common Good, and Democracy"). While he calls for political and social changes that would undercut some of liberalism's most cherished concerns, Hollenbach avoids the temptation of painting liberalism as a theory preoccupied only with the freedom of autonomous individuals. He is well aware that liberalism was as much a reaction to the overweening character of the ancien régime as it was a theory of individualism. But Hollenbach thinks that efforts to privatize visions of the good—rooted in liberalism's concern about the state and the contemporary fact of deep disagreement about the good—in order to protect the open and free society we live in will prove contradictory.

Political alienation and increasing economic fragmentation—not to mention the culture wars—mean that many Americans are retreating from the public realm. Ironically, this comes just as large structural forces related primarily to the state and market bring us closer together. If citizens do not make some effort to cultivate the public virtue of solidarity, "large domains of social existence [may] slip from the control of human freedom or . . . fall under the direction of powerful elites." Liberals are concerned that communitarians will seek to generate solidarity through the state; Hollenbach offers an alternative: civil society, by which he means churches, universities, charities, the media. This third way is consistent with his Catholic tradition's commitment to subsidiarity. But he argues, in an interesting turn, that subsidiarity is not enough. Citizens cannot just retreat to their own communities. They have to cultivate the virtue of solidarity. This means engaging other communities and voluntary institutions to create common ground to deal with common problems. Coalitions such as these can generate "new standards of political rationality"—as they did with civil rights and environmentalism—that will provide new bases for the kind of "public reason" Rawls takes as a prerequisite for decent, liberal societies.

Reason, or more accurately the criterion of reasonableness, also figures heavily in Amy Gutmann's essay (chap. 9, "The Virtues of Democratic Self-Constraint"). Reasonableness is important insofar as democracies are deliberative, which she argues they should be. For deliberation generates the kind of open and responsible discourse that enables every citizen to have a stake in the political process. Deliberation also, in dialectical fashion, depends on and generates democratic virtues such as honesty, tolerance, and nonviolence. Finally, given America's pluralistic cast, deliberation "makes a virtue out of a necessity" in providing citizens with a means of addressing and deciding public issues even in the face of deep disagreement.

Deliberation is complemented by two other necessary democratic virtues: nonrepression and nondiscrimination, which guarantee everyone a voice in the process. In Gutmann's provocative formulation, nonrepression is not a negative virtue; it is a positive virtue which requires the state to "cultivate the capacity for political deliberation among all future citizens." Admitting that this conception is "not neutral" to all ways of life, she argues that this capacity entails "respect toward different ways of life" so long as such points of view are reasonable. She acknowledges this may prove objectionable to parents—particularly religious parents who do not want their children to develop respect for other views—but she argues that the parents' interest in their children's education must be balanced by the state's interest in their role as future deliberative citizens. This move is justified, in her view, because a deliberative democracy must be willing "to take its own side in an argument about the public reasonableness of politically relevant reflection." For democracy, according to Gutmann, is not a means but a political ideal, one that secures the free and equal political standing of its citizens with the virtues of deliberation, nonrepression, and nondiscrimination.

The kinds of virtues—be they solidarity or deliberation—democracy requires do not just appear ex nihilo. It is within the context of institutions that virtues take on moral meaning and are fostered in men and women, contends William M. Sullivan (chap. 10, "Institutions as the Infrastructure of Democracy"). Tragically, America's instrumental and individualistic bent has contributed to the eclipse of institutions: "From the family to the law, institutions have been reduced to an instrumental status." Why? As Americans increasingly have seen their lives as exercises in self-assertion, they have come to see institutions as objects of hindrance or aid to be avoided or used as they realize their own personal values. The ironic consequence is that the social fabric that supports individuals is worn thin, with difficult consequences for individual and society alike.

In what might be considered a gentle rebuke to some of his fellow communitarians and to cultural conservatives, Sullivan argues that renewed appeals for personal responsibility are destined to founder unless they also acknowledge the institutional logic that is at work. The reconstitution of virtues, from personal responsibility to civic engagement, is really a twofold project. First, Sullivan argues that persons must begin to see how the practices that develop within institutions—be they parenting, voting, or lawyering—have "goods intrinsic to the practices themselves." Being a good lawyer, for instance, should not just be about racking up billable hours, it should also be about practicing the law with precision and integrity. Second, society must provide material, personal, and organizational support to institutions and the social environments where they thrive or fail. For example, community policing in inner cities—which focuses on building citizen associations (crime watches), creating relationships between officers and residents, and providing a safe environment for families and businesses—can generate "a slow spiral of more social cohesion" in fragile urban environments. Sullivan concludes by arguing that a vigorous effort to launch a project of institutional renewal is the best way to halt "social entropy."

### Institutional Requirements of Constitutional Democracy

The modern temptation, arguably, is to focus on political institutions and practices as the primary locus of social life. But constitutional democracies are profoundly shaped in ways that are not explicitly political. The public sphere—the realm of newspapers, businesses, voluntary institutions, and the arts (not to mention individuals)— is one realm that lies to a large degree outside the direct control of the state. Paradoxically, as the two essays in this section argue, this realm is both shaped by and shapes the state. The extra political character of the public sphere and its functions in a liberal democracy are the subject of the first essay. The second essay explores the ways in which communitarian thinking might offer a vision of the First Amendment which is more public-spirited and less expressivist in its thrust.

Charles Taylor is concerned about three questions in the section's first essay (chap. 11, "Liberal Politics and the Public Sphere"): What is distinct about liberal society? What makes it work? and What dangers does it face? He answers these questions by focusing on the public sphere where multiple associations "operate as a whole outside the ambit of the state." One of the most essential differences between premodern and contemporary societies is that "the opinion of mankind" reflected in the discourse of the public sphere is no longer received: it is the product of reflection, dialogue, and the active participation of the populace as a whole, and this discourse takes place outside of the direct control of the state. But since the legitimacy of the state is integrally tied to public opinion in a liberal society and since democracies place such a priority on self-rule, the operations of the extrapolitical realm have important consequences for the success of liberal politics.

One of the problems facing liberal societies, though, is that the public sphere, capacious as it is, can tend toward hypercentralization and/or a mass character: that is, powerful media institutions or currents of opinion can crowd out smaller institutional voices or alternative opinions. This is dangerous insofar as democracies maintain their legitimacy by securing the voices and/or the participation of their participants. If they do not, Taylor argues that they can become paralyzed by a form of "soft despotism" where citizens are fragmented and alienated, "less and less bound to their fellow citizens in common projects and allegiances." Taylor is worried that America is fast approaching such a fate, torn as it is by class and cultural fragmentation. He argues that the best way to keep the public sphere functioning is to encourage what might best be described as principled decentralization. That is, communities, institutions, and individuals have a responsibility to cultivate a variety of different venues so that alternative voices are expressed. At the same time these venues must maintain open frontiers with one another and with the larger public sphere. In this way pragmatic coalitions can be built around common goals where an overlapping consensus has been established. Without such a commitment decentralization can only lead to Babel and, ultimately, Balkanization.

Jeffrey Abramson and Elizabeth Bussiere are also concerned with the role that expression takes in a democracy in the second essay of this section (chap. 12, "Free Speech and Free Press"), although they lean toward a greater political role than does Taylor. In their view a libertarian ethic favoring market and expressivist modes of expression, combined with a firm requirement that the state remain neutral in regulating speech, has gained ascendancy in the judiciary and in recent Republican administrations. They argue that this ethic, which prioritizes individual over social interests, represents a "break with the classical defenses of free speech as an instrument of democracy." Taking up participatory and republican strains of recent political thought, they argue that a communitarian ethic of free expression would be more attentive to public concerns relating primarily to civic practices and virtues, and to the common good.

They focus on two areas to see whether government should "restrict pure individual rights of expression" to further important social goods. Turning first to public campaigns, they argue that recent Supreme Court decisions protecting the rights of political action committees to buy unlimited amounts of political speech are based upon a "thin" vision of democracy that views the political realm as little more than a sphere of competing interests. They argue the Court should have given Congress more room to "close the gap between the speech available to the haves and the have-nots," thereby promoting democracy's interest in having citizens equally influential on the political process. Second, Abramson and Bussiere explore ways in which government can stimulate a more "rich and robust public debate" by ensuring that telecommunications giants do not have sole purchase on mass media. In their view, despite new technologies and market expansion in the media realm, media conglomerations still exercise a disproportionate influence on what is aired, particularly on cable television, and limit the ability of citizens to express their views. Public access requirements, combined with interactive technologies, might be a way of reversing this trend, allowing citizens, associations, and governments the opportunity to engage one another over public issues. They conclude on a theoretical note, arguing that their communitarian vision of free speech is one that acknowledges the necessarily communal context of speech and the ways in which liberty—defined as self-government rather than expression—can be served by government intervention.

### Citizenship in America: Two Views

While communitarians seek a renewed commitment to public purposes and social institutions, the extent to which they attach primacy to public or private communities has a marked influence on their prescriptive vision of citizenship. Proponents of public community—republican, participatory, and strong democracy theorists—tend to have a "thick" view of citizenship; citizens are supposed to contribute to and find meaning within political institutions of which they play a part in shaping through their own involvement. Proponents of private community—conservatives, religious thinkers, and liberal theorists—argue for a "thin" view; they believe transcendent, traditional, or civil institutions are more important than public ones, and hence, that citizenship should be circumscribed so as to allow persons the opportunity to serve and be served by these private institutions. The essays in the final section of the book are dedicated to exploring the meaning of citizenship in America.

In the first essay in this section (chap. 13, "American Conceptions of Citizenship and National Service"), Rogers M. Smith argues that the advocates who cluster around the public ("strong democratic") or private ("liberal") constellations of citizenship fail to take into account the integral role that the cultural ethic of Americanism has played in shaping the character of citizenship in the United States. Stepping away from those who argue that Americanism is essentially a form of civic religion, bringing all Americans into a common project predicated upon liberty and equal opportunity, Smith argues that Americanism is based upon ascriptive characteristics that have systematically devalued or denied social—not to mention civic—participation, including service, to minorities. Americanism, then, has often taken hierarchical forms that deny a place at the table to blacks, Native Americans, other ethnic minorities, religious minorities, women, and now homosexuals. But Americanism has continued to occupy such a strong role through much of American history because Americans find thin, liberal conceptions or thick, democratic citizenship insufficient. They want the national project, not to mention their lives, "validated by more transcendent historical, natural, and divine standards."

According to Smith, national service programs—be they military, educational, or otherwise—have reflected the competing strands of liberalism, strong democracy, and Americanism in their design and operation. He points particularly to the ways in which Americanist notions have served to maintain patterns of social hierarchy—as with the historic pattern of military racial segregation. The tide begins to change with the Progressive era and leaders like John Dewey, Horace Kallen, and Randolph Bourne who sought to "minimize the importance of American national identity" and give greater warrant to smaller social groups and mutual tolerance. But the Progressives were divided, at the communal level, on whether they wanted to encourage traditional or democratic practices and, at the public level, on whether tolerance required integrated public institutions or particularistic institutions. As the nation builds a fledgling national service program, these issues continue to haunt us. Smith concludes by offering his own provocative program for the future. He argues that while the government should not aim to transform communities, it should aim to promote integration at the public level, with young persons serving communities with which they are not necessarily familiar. His hope is that this will rework the narrative of traditional Americanism into one where people are working to reshape their own communities in line with more voluntaristic and egalitarian ideals. In taking this turn, interestingly enough, Smith appears to link his new Americanism with the tradition of strong democracy he described at the beginning of his essay, a tradition dedicated to using the civic arena to "bring the social constituents of our lives under more conscious collective control."

Daniel Tichenor argues that the liberal tradition—not the strong democratic one—has shaped our recent approach to citizenship vis-à-vis immigration. Despite a dramatic rise in legal and illegal immigration over the last decade and a half which would have typically resulted in restrictive immigration measures, America found itself with "stunning" immigration reform measures in 1986 and 1990 that resulted in "expanded alien rights and increased migration to the United States although the original impetus for policy change was restrictionist." The reason: civil libertarians and free-market expansionists deployed the language and practice of rights-based liberalism—for markedly different reasons—to convince Congress and the courts to open the gates to immigrants.

Tichenor is of a double mind about the liberalization of immigration policy. On the one hand, he thinks America compares favorably to western European nations—traditionally lauded by Progressives for their generous welfare measures—because it has been more open to immigrants with divergent racial, cultural, and national backgrounds. On the other, he thinks that the way that the debate centered around the rights of immigrants and employers forestalled any "meaningful deliberation" of how immigration affects the common good, particularly the plight of African-Americans who often compete with immigrants in the labor pool. He is also concerned about the way in which immigrants are not being integrated as full citizens in American life. Partly as a consequence of the fact that juridicial liberalism has secured them virtually all the legal rights that citizens enjoy, immigrants are now less inclined to seek the citizenship that can secure their political status in the community.

Tichenor suggests that immigration policy makers need to pay greater attention to the impact of immigration on the public interest. For one thing, the rights-based reforms have generated an anti-immigration backlash from local communities that feel exciuded from the Washington-based decision-making process and unnecessarily burdened by the result of that process. For another, current immigration policy has only increased boundaries between race and income in

America by allowing large numbers of immigrants to compete with African-Americans in the labor force. Accordingly, Tichenor concludes by arguing that immigration policy now needs to focus more on including the concerns of local communities and integrating immigrants into the political process, thereby balancing the individual interests of immigrants with the public good of the nation. This, then, is an appropriate ending point for the volume. For it is just this kind of balancing effort that marks the communitarian enterprise.

# Old Chestnuts and
# New Spurs

Liberals are often preoccupied with protecting individual liberties from the ominous state.[1] They often ignore or give short shrift to the communitarian concern: the social preconditions that enable individuals to maintain their psychological integrity, civility, and ability to reason. When community (social webs carrying moral values) breaks down, the individual's psychological integrity is endangered, and a vacuum is generated which invites the state to expand its role and power; when community is properly cultivated, by contrast, the kind of citizen liberals take for granted flourishes. In this sense, liberal treatises, and above all their elaboration of individual rights, presume a communitarian foundation.

Initial sections of this essay deal with the issues that arise out of membership in community, the link between individual rights and social responsibilities, and the dangers of majoritarianism; they also detail the ways in which a communitarian vision of political theory helps to sustain the American experiment in ordered liberty. I argue that the relationship between the individual and the community is more nuanced than the simple opposition of the individual versus the overarching collectives generally posited by liberals. Essentially, I assume as the cornerstone of this discussion that individuals and communities are constitutive of one another, and their relationship is, at one and the same time, mutually supportive and tensed. The mutual character of the relationship between individuals and communities also suggests that any effort to advance one at the expense of the other is likely to undermine the important benefits that arise from keeping these two essential factors in proper balance.[2]

In the latter half of the essay, I turn to look at the ways in which our concepts of community and of social values, as well as the study of human nature, can incorporate this communitarian perspective. I confront definitional and functional issues related to the concept of community because communitarians have previously been charged with relying on a "thin" and indeterminate theory of community (see Robert Booth Fowler in chap. 4). Sections on community definition, deliberation, the source of overarching values, and human nature address these challenges.

Specifically, I suggest that community is a shared set of social bonds or a social web, as distinct from one-to-one bonds. These bonds, which are in and of themselves morally neutral, carry a set of shared moral and social values. I also examine the scope of community (that is, the reach and character of the social and moral bonds established by communities) by addressing the tensions between particularism and universalism. In my discussion of deliberation, I argue that true communal values cannot be imposed by an outside group or an internal elite or minority but must be generated by the members of community in a dialogue which is open to all and fully responsive to the membership. Values transmitted from generation to generation are often the starting point for such a give-and-take, but they need to be constantly adjusted as changes in circumstances and membership pose new issues.

Regardless of the nature of the process used to reach communal values, these values must be assessed at some level for their legitimacy. In my view, communal values are only legitimate insofar as they are not in tension with overarching core values; for reasons elaborated below, I take here a sharp leave from those communitarians who hold that as long as a community has agreed on a set of values, these are the ultimate criteria as to what is morally appropriate.

Whatever values a community adheres to, human nature must be taken into account as a major constraint. I argue that communities must not extend their reach too far because individuals—no matter how much they are conditioned by social influences—have universal attributes that cannot be extinguished by an overzealous community or state. We might compensate for them (as we do for people who are disabled at birth) or adjust to them (as we do to the fact that in every sizable society there are going to be some sociopaths), but we can never ignore the effects of the underlying human nature.

### The I&We

Some communitarians, Markate Daly points out, take "community rather than the individual as their basic concept."[3] Liberals, of course, tend to ignore community or assign it secondary status as a derivative, the result of an aggregation of individual choices or transactions.[4] This seems an unnecessary opposition. True, individuals are socially embedded rather than freestanding. However, it is equally valid that communities are composed of members who, at least in modern times, have varying degrees of individuality. Hence, it makes just as much sense to say that communities are composed of individual members as to say that individuals must be seen as members of communities. The concept of membership is the cardinal one: it might be defined as a person who is an integral part of a community yet not consumed by it or submerged within it. Like hammer and nail, neither is more essential; they require one another.

Our thinking may well progress if we embellish this view to explicate a somewhat more complex concept. Namely, we should make our basic starting point (one that all philosophies require) the notion of a person who is a member within a community even as there is a congenital yet frequently creative tension between the two. That is, persons are shaped by and oriented toward their communities even as they are more than the sum of the social influences that inform their behavior, character, and thoughts. To the extent that they have an identity independent of the community's role, persons often seek to expand their realm of unprescribed behavior (as well as to change the community to reflect more fully their values and interests). At the same time the community generally tries to sustain its social/moral prescriptions and reformulate individuals more in line with its values and needs.

Following Martin Buber's term "the I and Thou,"[5] I use the notation the *I&We* to capture the tense but close bond between individuals and communities. While the tension can be excessive and burdensome (in the sense of high social and personal costs) or even fractious (excessive conflict), up to a point the tension is creative. The uncommunitized parts of personhood are sources of creativity and change for the community and personal expression for the person. The communitized part of the person is a source of effective psychological stability and one source of personal and social virtue.

By way of analogy, the role of bricks in an arch is instructive. There is little sense in asking which is more basic. Without the arch the bricks are a pile of rubble. And without bricks there is no arch. A proper relation among the bricks ensures that a sufficient level of tension will maintain the bond. If there is too much or too little tension, the arch will come apart and the bricks will scatter.

This primary concept of the I&We needs to be placed within a historical context.[6] Granted, in all communities there are centrifugal forces that seek to pull members out of their socially prescribed roles and duties toward their personal projects and centripetal forces that seek to absorb ever more psychic energy, time, and resources into collective pursuits. Nevertheless, at any stage in history one can determine where forces are more powerful in one direction than another and in which direction they are tilting. Thus, totalitarian societies clearly tilted far in the collectivist direction, while it is often argued that the contemporary American society is leaning excessively in the opposite direction.

If one accepts that communities and individuals do best when these two forces are well in balance, it follows that the role of those who are able to discern such tilts (because they themselves are not swayed by them) is to seek to argue for balance and urge fellow citizens, leaders, and policy makers to take the needed measures to restore balance. This is the role of social critics, such as intellectuals, the fourth estate, and civic leaders. This is the reason communitarians in the United States, who see excessive individualism, call for a return to community. It is not that community is in principle more basic than the individual but that the American I&We is out of balance after decades in which self-interest and expressive individualism have prevailed.[7]

The quest for balance and the historical duty of intellectuals and their fellow critics is also the reason that John Locke, Adam Smith, and other classical liberals focused on individualism: they were writing in a period when community was overpowering, and they were fighting for space for individual interests, expression, and rights (rather than holding that community in principle is not a basic element or has a secondary moral standing). In short, while neither community nor individuals have an ontological or normative primacy, the historical context guides us as to which needs to be nourished within a given period and culture.

### The Link between Rights and Responsibilities

For the same basic reasons a civil society requires attention to both centrifugal and centripetal social forces, it seems unnecessarily polarizing to suggest that while liberals are preoccupied with individual rights (which they most assuredly are), communitarians should concern themselves only with social responsibilities. Communitarians are in the business of defining and promoting societal balances. They recognize that most individual rights have a social responsibility which is their corollary. For these rights it makes little sense and it is morally indefensible to posit them without attending to the other side of the coin: the responsibilities that ensure respect for them. But attending to these responsibilities is not to diminish or ignore rights; on the contrary, in the longer run, cultivation of social responsibilities is the only way to ensure the societal conditions that rights require. Such attention becomes urgent when it has been long neglected, in a society which stressed individualism to begin with because its founders escaped societies that were excessively duty-imposing.

As Justice Frank Iacobucci of the Canadian Supreme Court has written, "Legal rights and freedoms cannot properly be understood without appreciating the existence of corresponding duties and responsibilities."[8] It is for this reason that Dallin Oaks warns us that "no society is so secure that it can withstand continued demands for increases in citizen rights and decreases in citizen obligations."[9] Take the right to be tried before a jury of one's peers if one is suspected of having committed a crime. If one claims that there is no duty to serve as a juror, yet one demands a jury of one's peers, then one is demanding an untenable social and political condition: that one is entitled to benefit from communal services or institutions but not need not contribute to them. First, a jury of one's peers will not exist if the peers will not serve, and, further, it is morally indefensible to continuously seek to draw on the commons but refuse to contribute to it.

One can grant some exceptions: it is said that animals and even sand have rights,[10] and they are unable to reciprocate or assume responsibilities. For this reason others prefer to think about our concern for animals and the environment but refrain from viewing them as carriers of rights. Either way, these are exceptions to the rule. Most times there is a symmetry. Those who are the beneficiaries of rights are also expected to assume responsibilities. That many Americans believe they are entitled to ever more government services but are opposed to government is thus a major symptom of the disjunction between individual rights (to services) and social responsibilities (to serve, say, as a volunteer or pay higher taxes) that results when a society tilts toward excessive individualism. This is the kind of tilt President Kennedy's oft-cited line tried to correct by suggesting that one should give to one's country (meaning society at large) rather than asking incessantly what the country will do for oneself.

Once one grants the basic complementarity of individual rights and social responsibilities, one can turn to a number of challenging issues that arise, ranging from the question of whether those who have been disadvantaged for a long time have entitlements but should be exempt (forever?) from social responsibilities to the question of under what conditions community needs (which often prescribe social responsibilities) take priority over some limited individual rights (e.g., should those who drive school buses be obliged to submit to drug tests?).[11]

There are some who would suggest that any turn toward responsibility necessarily entails a diminution of rights. Nadine Strossen, president of the American Civil Liberties Union (ACLU), for one, argues that communitarian thinking equals a decline in rights: "We're not against community, but are we willing to sacrifice our individual rights?"[12] Ironically, an excessive reliance on rights—of the kind advocated by civil libertarian groups such as the ACLU—deprives those social and political institutions of the very mechanisms that communities require to protect individual rights.

Without a language and practice of social responsibilities, as Mary Ann Glendon observes, we are left with the "unexpressed premise that we roam at large in a land of strangers, where we presumptively have no obligations toward others except to avoid the active infliction of harm."[13] Here the discussions of individual rights and social responsibilities and the membership nature of persons find their deeper connection. Psychologists and sociologists indicate that individuals who are typically cut off from social bonds (the isolated, prototypical actors in the liberal world of rights) are unable to act freely, while they find that individuals who are bonded into comprehensive and stable relationships and into cohesive groups and communities are much more able to make reasoned choices, to render moral judgments, and to be free.

Indeed, the greatest danger for rights (and liberty more generally) arises when the social moorings of individuals are severed. The atomization of individuals, the dissolution of communities into mobs, the loss of attachments and social commitments, cause individuals to lose competence, the capacity to reason, and self-identity. This is a societal condition which, it has been widely observed, has preceded the rise of totalitarian movements and governments, although it is not necessarily the only cause.[14] As Alexis de Tocqueville argued, the best protection against totalitarianism is a pluralistic society laced with communities and voluntary associations, rather than a society of highly individualized rights carriers.

### No Majoritarianism Here

Communitarians are occasionally charged with opening the door to majoritarianism. The argument is something to the effect that by seeking a more secure place for the needs of the community in determining the course of social and political policies, individual and minority rights will be automatically or necessarily disregarded.[15] For instance, Ira Glasser, executive director of the ACLU, claims: "Communitarians really means majoritarians. The tendency is to make the constitutional rights responsible for the failure to solve social problems."[16] Elsewhere, Charles Derber writes, "'Consensual' values are, in reality, the voice of one part of the community—usually the majority or an elite minority—against the others."[17] Others fear that the community would, for example, ban books that the majority dislikes from public and school libraries. Note that the concern here is not that some local goon or national tyrant would take over, but that ordinary citizens would instruct their duly elected city council or school board to institute policies that violated basic rights.

Actually, American society has both constitutional and moral safeguards against majoritarianism that communitarians should very much respect. These safeguards basically work by *differentiation*, by defining some areas in which the majority has not had and ought not have a say and those in which it does and should. We are not a simple democracy but a constitutional one. That is, some choices, defined by the Constitution, are declared out of bounds for the majority.

Clearest among these is the Bill of Rights, which singles out matters that are exempt from majority rule, from typical democratic rule making, and in which minority and individual rights take precedence. The First Amendment, which protects the right of individuals to speak freely whether or not the majority approves of what they have to say, is a prime example of an area explicitly exempt from majority rule or consensus building. (A person's expressions are not as a rule subject to community rulings.) Similarly, the majority may not deny any opposition group the right to vote; even Communists were not banned in the United States during the period when they were most hated and feared. All citizens are entitled to a trial by jury of their peers, whether they are members of the majority or the minority. And so on.

The Constitution and our legal traditions and institutions clearly indicate, however, that other matters are subject to majority rule. Thus, all Americans must pay their taxes, drive with a license, and refrain from abusing children. It is inconceivable, and there is no moral or legal support for the notion, that everybody would be allowed to decide for himself whether or not he wished to obtain a license, how much taxes he would choose to pay, and so on. (On still other matters, we require a special majority, say, a two-thirds vote; these are matters that are not so fully set aside as individual and minority rights but are more weighty than routine policy matters, such as overriding a presidential veto or amending the Constitution.)

There is more here than meets the eye. This constitutional differentiation between the realms of minority and individual rights and where the majority is to rule is not merely a matter of legal provisions. They are backed up by a set of settled convictions that many Americans hold. That is, differentiation is not merely upheld in courts of law but, most times, also underwritten by community consensus. Thus, when in the early nineties about 130 universities moved to ban racial slurs and thereby limit free speech, very few of the challenges to this approach found their way into the courts. The primary voices of opposition to any such codes were raised by editorial writers, authors (such as Arthur M. Schlesinger, Jr., in *The Disuniting of America* and Dinesh D'Souza in *Illiberal Education*),[18] columnists (from George Will to Nat Hentoff), and many others who together comprise the main opinion leaders of America. They evoked a moral claim: we must continue to allow free expression of ideas, words, and sentiments even if it hurts the feelings of minorities and women. The majority ought not to decide what can be said; it is the right of each individual to speak freely. They carried the day most of all in the court of public opinion. The so-called hate codes did not spread to most universities; several were canceled, and those that are in place are rarely enforced.

In short, restoring community and enhancing social responsibilities—after both have been neglected—does not entail a penetration of the areas in which individual and minority rights are held to govern. On the contrary, only a well-functioning community can provide the social and psychological conditions that ensure that rights are fully respected. At the same time there is no reason, in those areas so designated, that the majority should not govern.

### Communitarian Query:  Which Community?

I have addressed the ways in which ordered liberty requires communitarian foundations. But critics complain that we have portrayed the essential foundation, community, in a fuzzy manner. They ask for a clear definition of the concept. Communities are webs of social relations that encompass shared meanings and above all shared values.[19] Families may qualify as minicommunities. Villages often are, although not necessarily so. Some neighborhoods in cities (such as Little Havana in Miami, Chinatown in New York City) constitute communities. Well-integrated national societies may be said to be communities. Communities need not be geographically concentrated. One may speak of, say, a Jewish community in a city even if its members are dispersed among the population and maintain their social-normative web around core institutions such as a synagogue and private schools. (Benedict Anderson's concept of "imagined communities" and the sociological concept of communities as reference groups deserve further consideration in this context.)

True communities are not automatically or necessarily places of virtue. Many traditional communities that were homogenous if not monolithic were authoritarian and oppressive. And a community may lock into a set of values that one may find abhorrent, say a lynching-prone Afrikaner village. (See below on criteria for judgment.) Communitarians such as Michael Sandel who automatically sanctify whatever is a community do leave communitarianism open to the kind of criticism leveled by Steven Holmes, who argues that "members of the Ku Klux Klan, too, have a 'commonality of shared self-understanding.' "[20]

However, contemporary communities tend to be "New Communities" that are part of a pluralistic web of communities.[21] People are at one and the same time members of several communities such as those at work and at home. They can and do use these multimemberships (as well as the ability to choose one's work and residential communities) to protect themselves from excessive pressure by any one community.

What are the boundaries or scope of communities? It is best to think about communities as nested, each within a more encompassing one. Thus, neighborhoods are parts of more encompassing suburbs or cities or regional communities. These, in turn, often intersect or are part of larger ethnic or racial or professional communities. And many communities are contextuated by the national society. Ultimately, some aspire to a community which would encapsulate all people. Other communitarians object to such universalism and suggest that the strong bonds and the moral voice—which are the essence of communities—are to be found mainly in relatively small communities in which people know one another at least to some extent, as in many stable neighborhoods. This in turn may reduce the moral scope of our commitment and will lead us to be more concerned with our best friends and closest neighborhoods rather than with those who are most in need.[22]

Most people are able to maintain a commitment both to their immediate community and to more encompassing ones (see Philip Selznick's essay, chap. 6). Indeed, a strong case can be made that what might be called upward shifting of moral commitments, to ever more encompassing communities, is the earmark of a community which is most progressive. Such a community is likely to be more committed to widely shared values, such as peace and social justice. However, both the empirical aspects of this question (e.g., does internationalism drain local commitments?) and the moral issues involved are far from settled even among communitarians.

## Deliberative Polity or Community in Action?

Once we have a community and the proper bulkhead to block majoritarianism, we still need to ask how do communities evolve shared
directions, policies, and above all values. Both liberals and political scientists, who played key if not dominant roles in the liberal-
communitarian debate in the 1980s, have often referred to individuals
as "citizens" and viewed their coming together in the image of a town
meeting, in which reasonable people *deliberate* to reach an agreed-
upon course of action. Communitarians tend to refer to members of a
community who *act* to embody values in their daily practices and
projects. To cite but a few of the very numerous examples that could be
given: Stephen L. Elkin calls for political institutions that are "formative of the sort of citizenry that is necessary if a commercial republic
is to flourish";[23] Samuel H. Beer writes about "government by discussion" where preexisting private preferences would be transformed
into public policies.[24] When Mark Blitz tries to summarize what
he believes communitarians do, he maintains his noncommunitarian
lenses, suggesting that communitarians "emphasize that individuals
are not primarily discrete entities but are citizens who are members of
a body politic."[25] Harry Boyte joins this issue explicitly when he writes,
"Renewal of the larger commonwealth dimensions of politics cannot
be very effectively accomplished except through a political process by
means of which citizens forge the connections between their particular
interests and the public weal on their own terms."[26] As I see it, much of
what Boyte calls politics is actually the work of communities and their
institutions. The action-space of the community is much more encompassing than that of the polity.

   This elementary but also often overlooked point applies especially
to the sterile debate about the relative merits of regulating things via
the state or allowing the market to reign. Aside from the fact that all
social systems are mixed (and thus, the correct questions are how
much market and how much state are desired and how best to combine
the two), the opposition between market and state completely ignores
the enormous amount of shared projects that individuals carry out in a
third realm, the community. It further inaccurately assumes that if the
government is going to do less, say, provide less welfare, the only or
even main alternative is the market; rather, community institutions can

step into the breach, for instance, attending to the social, cultural, and a significant part of the economic needs of new immigrants.

Once the richness of the community realm is recognized, we must further note that it has numerous ways of organizing and expressing itself, of which the polity is but one. Voluntary associations are well known, but so are informal communications, local press, group meetings in schools, and churches. The image of a Greek polis in which the citizens spend their days deliberating in town meetings is often held up as a model. It ignores that this model assumed slaves, serfs, and women would do much of the other stuff of daily life. In our society all members must attend to nonpolitical institutions, or community needs will not be served.

The tendency to look at course settings of communities chiefly through political lenses is even more detrimental when it comes to the romanticization of deliberation. This tendency is directly derived from the notion that individuals are rational, in the sense that they are able to collect and process the information needed for a reasoned decision and can process that information in an empirically logical manner. I have demonstrated elsewhere that there are mountains of data to show that this is an erroneous claim.[27] The less discussed question is how do members of community work out their different value commitments, presumptions about the nature of the world, favored public policies, and so on through processes that are only in part deliberative. Grassroots leadership, influence of opinion leaders, expression of affect, and mobilization of power all play a key role in community decisions, and not via cognitive channels.

The recognition that people behave mainly and first not as members of an Oxford debating club (although there, too, nonreasonable factors play an important role) need not distress us. Once we are more open to accepting the ways that members of communities actually work out their differences, we can turn to the question of how to ensure that these only partially deliberative processes become as democratic, morally substantive, and empirically sound as possible. (By empirically sound, I mean that arguments include empirical arguments, where relevant. For instance, a particular community considering the moral arguments for and against the death penalty may also wish to take into account whether or not it actually has an effect on crime rates.)

### A Challenge: Contextuating Values

Regardless of how just communities develop a shared set of values, we require criteria to establish whether these values are morally appropriate. In my opinion, communities are free to follow whatever value consensus they achieve, provided that their decisions are arrived at via the proper consensus-building processes, but only so long as they do not violate a basic set of overarching values. Not all communitarians have made it quite clear that they endorse such a position.[28] Robert Nisbet, for instance, has written that we need a "new philosophy of laissez faire" that will "hold fast to the ends of autonomy and freedom of choice; one that will begin not with imaginary, abstract individuals but with the personalities of human beings as they are actually given to us in association."[29] Similarly, Clint Bolick (who happens to be a libertarian) has argued that when communities "adopt rules or values that are contrary to government regulation, a constitutional presumption in favor of liberty would force government to justify such restrictions, thereby protecting communities against government."[30] Such a statement fully appreciates that individuals are members of communities rather than freestanding, but it does not address at all the question of whether or not associations are the ultimate arbiters of what is right or wrong for their members.

Amy Gutmann's article on "The Virtues of Democratic Self-Constraint" (chap. 9) provides a systematic treatment of this question when she argues in effect that a community may follow any course it seeks as long as it does not violate two cardinal principles: nondiscrimination, which secures the equal moral and political standing of all citizens in the public realm, and nonrepression, which ensures that civil liberties are guaranteed and that "the capacity for political deliberation" is cultivated among citizens. Others will recognize additional sets of values that communities must abide by, from living peacefully with one another to fulfilling obligations for more affluent communities to assist less fortunate ones.

The challenging questions are what is the source of these overarching, context-setting values, and, above all, what provides them with special standing? It is not sufficient to determine that, say, American society received certain values engendering a commitment to the public welfare from Britain (or contemporary Russian communities from the West). The pressing question that requires a response is what provides these values (and some but not others that also lay a claim) with the power to set aside what communities chose to seek, even if that consensus was reached in the most open, deliberative, free, and otherwise legitimate manner?

Some find the answer in religion. Prescriptions that are in the Old or New Testament, the Koran, or other such holy texts are taken as so authoritative and compelling that no community may set them aside. Others suggest that there is a Natural Law, a principle which sets out general standards of right-minded conduct for all communities. But these are sources that many others do not find compelling and that in themselves may require further accounting. Some look for an answer in values that they claim anthropological studies show are universally respected (such as Thou shalt not kill), but these offer a moral foundation which is insecure (many values are not universally endorsed) and rather meager at that (surely burning books, and even killing their authors, is quite valued in some communities, as in contemporary Iran). Others see the answer in deontological claims, the idea being that certain moral duties present themselves to us as binding and incontestable.[31] I find the deontological position the most satisfactory, which is not to suggest that it is free from all challenges. Surely it is more compelling than utilitarian/consequentialist approaches, according to which values change as circumstances alter the calculus of harm. Nor does it trouble me particularly that to state that certain moral values present themselves to us as compelling does not allow one to go beyond that point. All logical, scientific, philosophical, ideological, and religious systems of belief and thinking have at least one such primary term that cannot be explicated from inside the system and must be taken for granted for it to work (for religion, it is God; for neoclassical economists, it is the assumption of a rational individual). Deontology does not stand out as particularly deficient in comparison. To put it most simply, when someone argues that under most circumstances truth telling is morally superior to lying, it seems to invite very little need for further elaboration. Does anyone serious argue that the opposite is true?

Others use the presence of a strong public or societal interest as the guideline that informs us when shared values should take precedent over community ones. Two recent court cases illustrate the issue. In 1987 the town of Hialeah, Florida, a suburb of Miami, passed an ordinance prohibiting animal sacrifice after the Church of Lukumi

Babalu—which sacrifices chickens and other animals as part of its Santeria faith—sought permission to open a church in the town. The town argued that the law was designed to protect public sanitation and the interests of animals, which the sacrifices violated. The church challenged this act as an infringement of its constitutional right to free exercise of religious belief, noting that the regulation was not applied to others (such as restaurants or rodent control companies).

Across the continent, in Oregon, the state employment division refused to grant unemployment benefits to two men who had been dismissed from their jobs for using the peyote that was part of their Native American Church service. The state office argued that the men were not entitled to benefits because peyote is an illegal hallucinogenic in Oregon. But the men who had lost their benefits invoked the First Amendment religious liberty guarantee, arguing that they deserved an exemption from the law because their church required the sacramental use of peyote.

While these two cases (and others like them) are often discussed in terms of the balance between two societal values—freedom of religious expression versus secular societal values such as avoiding cruelty to animals and the control of hallucinogenics—they may also properly be viewed as illuminating the relationship between community values (of the two religious groups, the Santeria church and the Native American faith in Oregon) and the encompassing American society.

The Supreme Court ruled in the case of *Lukumi Babalu Aye v. Hialeah* (1993) that the town had acted unconstitutionally by targeting a religious practice which would have been otherwise permissible. But in the latter case, *Employment Division v. Smith* (1990), the Court ruled 6–3 that the Oregon Employment Division had acted properly because the Oregon drug laws were neutral insofar as they were not aimed at any particular religion.

For the communitarian these cases are important not because they illuminate the extent to which a particular law is neutral toward a particular religious practice.[32] Rather, these cases illustrate the ongoing tension between the values of particular communities and those of the American society. From a communitarian perspective particular communities should be given as much latitude as possible unless the national community can demonstrate a compelling interest in prohibiting or otherwise limiting a practice which a particular community may endorse. In these terms the Supreme Court found that the action of the Santeria church did not sufficiently violate the society's norms against cruelty toward animals while the Native American use of peyote does violate the societywide opposition to the use of these kinds of drugs.

One may argue that the Court was unduly restrictive, that it is possible to allow limited use of controlled substances in religious services (the way we allow some medicinal use of marijuana). But one cannot deny that we must draw a societal line between permissible and impermissible group practices. For instance, it is hard to imagine an American court which would permit a group of African immigrants to practice clitoral circumcision on their daughters just because this procedure was valued and consensual in their community. We all realize that certain overarching values take priority, but which values and on what grounds remain subjects of considerable and unresolved discussion, especially at the margin.[33]

### A Cardinal Challenge: Human Nature

As Alan Wolfe indicates in his article on "Human Nature and the Quest for Community" (chap. 7), every social theory and philosophy contains an implicit or explicit theory of human nature. Putting it in somewhat different words, liberals assume that people are basically good by nature and reasonable, and hence, they urge the government not to interfere with the choices of individuals and to allow them to set the collective and personal course on their own. They typically blame the social structure for deviant behavior exhibited by criminals, drug addicts, and rioters. Their most recommended treatment is to change society (rather than "blame the victim"). Individuals need to be informed and empowered because they are inherently inclined to do what is right and beneficial for the commons.

In contrast, many social conservatives assume that people are, if not nasty and brutish, at least governed by impulses and other irrational forces. While social conservatives seek to indoctrinate people with values, they tend to assume that human nature cannot be perfected, and hence, there is a congenital need to "keep the lid on" by the use of public authorities, not least of all the police. Still other social philosophers and theories make different assumptions, but it is difficult to imagine doing without an underlying conception of human nature.

Presently, a range of postmodern philosophers argue that people are fully "constructed," that is, determined by their culture, or at least that our views of human nature reflect our assumptions and values (or those drummed into us, or implicit in our culture). These philosophers make the implicit assumption that human nature is extremely pliable. Richard Rorty has argued, for instance, that what "was needed and what the idealists [Kant and Hegel] were unable to envisage, was a repudiation of the very idea of anything—mind or matter, self or world—having an intrinsic nature to be expressed or represented."[34]

It is certainly true that our understanding of human nature is hindered by the fact that we encounter it only in specific cultural settings that most would agree significantly affect what we see reflected in human behavior. (Only those who assume that behind each specific behavior directly lies a specific gene may reach a fundamentally different position.) However, the fact that we can reach conclusions about human nature only indirectly does not mean that we cannot glean what it is and draw conclusions from what we are able to establish. For instance, when certain attributes repeat themselves in all cultures, they are more likely to be a reflection of human nature than of other factors. (I include here in human nature the parts of nature we share with animals. Thus, to be warm-blooded and a mammal is part of human nature. So is the potential to walk erect.)

Another way to proceed is to ask in what direction behavior is changing when societies' mechanisms of control (socialization and reinforcement) weaken or break down. Thus, the fact that in many societies and eras so many priests in religious institutions that prohibit sex do indulge in some form of sexual expression informs us about human nature. So does the fact that religion, magic, and culture proved irrepressible despite numerous attempts in Nazi Germany and the former USSR to repress them.

At the same time, as these lines are written, there is considerable opposition in circles that consider themselves progressive if not politically correct to acknowledge the existence of human nature. Some argue that once one draws on the concept that there is a generic human nature, the next step is to argue that there are particular attributes that differentiate people by their nature: for instance, that men have a different nature than women (or blacks from whites). This, in turn, opens the door to various discriminatory positions. For instance, if women are "naturally" mothers but men are not equally "natural" at being fathers, it is said, it will follow that women should be relegated to the chores of parenting, and so on. Thus, a feminist such as Alison Jaggar writes: "As Marx himself remarked, 'All history is nothing but a continuous transformation of human nature.' Socialist feminists . . . deny that there is anything especially natural about women's relationships with each other, with children or with men."[35] Hence, the argument that all human nature is constructed is supposed to protect a position from being vulnerable to discriminatory implications.

The problem with proceeding in this way is that human nature is presented in such a way as to be infinitely malleable, and hence, an assessment of human nature can play no role in value judgments or social criticism! As Iacobucci argues, "At its crudest expression, one finds the argument that as there is no objective reality outside the knower, it is impossible to agree on any objective standards. 'You have your opinion and I have mine . . . who's to say who is right and who is wrong?' "[36] If this is the case, there is no Archimedean point where we can criticize social practices—such as slavery or sexism—without being accused of ethnocentrism or insensitivity to the values of other communities.

As I see it, human nature is universal; we are—men and women, black, brown, yellow, white, and so on—all basically the same under all the layers that cultures foster and impose on us. I see a great deal of evidence that people of different eras, societies, and conditions show the same basic inclinations.[37] Hence, one certainly cannot find in human nature any justification for treating one group of people worse than another.

What does human nature inform us that bears on the liberal/communitarian debate? There is a strong accumulation of evidence that people have a deep-seated need for social bonds (or attachments) and that they have a compelling need for normative (or moral) guidance. The evidence also suggests that they are unable to fulfill any of the conditions that various liberal and libertarian models presume (such as the capacity to render rational choices or to separate many of one's preferences from those that are culturally endorsed).[38] The same findings further demonstrate that individuals have a capacity to distance (but not to fully liberate) themselves from their social and cultural context and thus pass judgments on what is fostered on them and even participate in attempts to change shared values and hence the directional signals of their social and moral context.

Building on this capacity leads one to observe that granting that human nature has certain attributes does not mean that we need to embrace them or approve of them. The fact, for instance, that people cannot make even a nearly rational decision may either lead us to seek systems that require less rational capacity, or provide equipment that will help them, or to argue that decisions should be made by those who are most rational (hardly my position).

How should we respond to the basic human need for attachment and for values? Neither is an unmixed blessing, but neither needs to be confronted head-on. The need for attachment and normative guidance is at the foundation of the family, neighborhoods, voluntary associations, community, and many of the institutions that basically enrich human life (and possibly ennoble it).[39] We need to guard against excesses (e.g., conformism, fads, or unjust notions that are implicit in the culture and that deserve open critical normative examination). However, none of these is severe enough or sufficiently resistant to amelioration that we should seek to do without these basic human features (even if we could). In short, the communitarian self— part member, part creative and critical—is a rather well empirically grounded concept and one on which a communitarian philosophy can build constructively.

POLITICAL THEORY:

THE COMMUNITARIAN

CHALLENGE

# 1 *THOMAS A. SPRAGENS, JR.*

# Communitarian Liberalism

One of the more common ways of characterizing communitarian theory is to depict it as a critical alternative to liberalism. On this account, communitarian thought is a twentieth-century legatee of the civic republican tradition, which can be contrasted in several respects with liberalism, at least if the latter is styled in a particular way. Contemporary debates between communitarians and rights-based liberals are therefore understood as a reprise of the eighteenth-century disputes between the republican country party in British politics and those adherents of a liberal society organized around markets and self-interest.

There is some plausibility to this way of conceiving communitarianism and its adversaries. In the first place, both of the central categories, *communitarianism* and *liberalism*, are rather loose groupings that admit of diverse renderings. Each can be construed in different ways, depending upon what is deemed central to each perspective and depending upon who is deemed to be their paradigmatic representatives. Some artistic license is legitimate, and in any case uneliminable, whenever ideal type categories are constructed; and the categories of liberal and communitarian are no exception to this rule.

The ideal-typical construction that underlies and sustains the interpretation of communitarianism as a departure from liberal doctrine might go as follows. The essence of liberalism as a normative doctrine is its focus upon the protection of rights as the central (perhaps even the only) purpose of political society. Its essence as a social theory is its focus upon autonomous and separate individuals as the sum and substance of society. A properly ordered society, therefore, is centered around contractual relationships among these individuals.

Set over against this construction of liberalism, the communitarian critique comes into quick relief. Communitarians, inspired by the republican insistence upon the necessity for "civic virtue," reject the normative focus of liberalism upon rights claims and instead insist upon the necessity of correlative or supervening responsibilities that a democratic citizen owes to society. Empirically, communitarians depart from liberalism's nominalist resolution of society into an aggregation of individuals, insisting instead upon the irreducible corporate features of any society. A properly ordered society, therefore, cannot be merely a congeries of contractual relationships among self-interested individuals. Instead, it must be at least in part the product of public-spirited behavior by citizens who possess the requisite capacities and self-restraint for cooperation and self-governance.

This stylized contrast between liberal individualism and republican communitarianism is not entirely off the mark. It does identify some of the genuine concerns and beliefs of most of those who look with favor on the communitarian critique of contemporary liberal societies. And one can find important political theories and recurrent themes of contemporary political rhetoric that reflect this conception of liberalism. Despite its prima facie plausibility, however, I want to argue that this stylized account is faulty and misleading. It takes a partial truth and converts it into the whole story. As a consequence, it perpetuates an inaccurate perception of the liberal tradition. And, in so doing, it results in a misunderstanding of communitarianism and its relationship to the liberal legacy.

Against this account, I want to offer a different interpretation of liberalism and to tell a different story. This different story, in turn, carries with it a different understanding of the historical and theoretical import of the communitarian movement. It is a story which has the advantage of relieving the schizophrenia that the more conventional account induces in me, since I find myself both deeply committed to the fundamental verities of liberalism but also profoundly sympathetic to communitarian claims and concerns. Thus, either I am deeply confused, or else the stylized opposition of liberal versus communitarian has something wrong with it. Not surprisingly, I think the latter is the case.

My story, then, runs like this. In its inception liberalism was a complex normative doctrine. As the etymology of the name suggests, liberty was the defining value of the liberal movement. But the axial role of liberty in liberalism's pantheon of political virtues must be understood in context. First, in historical context liberty was of central importance because it reflected the liberal rejection of some very specific oppressions and constraints: restraints on thought and expression, prohibitions on economic activity, compulsion in matters of religion. In this setting liberty stood for relief, not for the be-all and end-all of human existence. Moreover, not only were free trade and freedom of religion valued for their intrinsic relationship to human dignity, but they were also considered to be instrumentally valuable to other important goals, including greater equality, prosperity, social stability, and civic harmony. If liberty was the central liberal value, it was by no means the sole liberal value. Instead, liberty played the focal role within a liberal strategy which encompassed a complex range of aspirations including political equality, civic friendship, and individual development.

In its philosophical grounding, moreover, liberalism was also a complex amalgam. It was inspired by the spectacular intellectual achievements produced by the rise of modern natural science, and hence most liberals were attracted to the rationalist and empiricist views that rose in tandem with and were in some ways logically linked with these achievements. But like most revolutionaries, intellectual and otherwise, the original liberals were still in fundamental respects committed to moral and philosophical assumptions they inherited from the classical tradition. Even as they spoke the language of modernity, they took for granted some of the anthropological and moral assumptions of the very same intellectual ancestors they were rejecting. In this respect they closely resembled that paradigmatic figure of intellectual revolution, Copernicus, who often invoked ideas taken from classical physics and philosophy to refute criticism of his attempt to overturn classical cosmology.[1] This partially tacit carryover of assumptions rooted in classical philosophy had the consequence that early liberals were morally more traditional than is often appreciated. And it also meant that their philosophies were sometimes afflicted with tensions and a lack of coherence they did not fully appreciate.[2]

These twin features of moral traditionalism and moral complexity are amply evident in classic liberal thinkers who span the three centuries preceding our own. This point needs to be stated with some insistence, because these features of classic liberal theorists have often been obscured or denied by careless readers who anachronistically read twentieth-century premises into their theories or by interpreters whose own ideological proclivities can be promoted by construing seventeenth-century figures as proto-Social Darwinists or proto-post-modernists.[3] Consider briefly, for example, John Locke, Condorcet, and John Stuart Mill.

Locke's account of human knowledge was empiricist, and his account of human motivation incorporated hedonistic explanations. But he was neither a positivist nor a materialist in his moral and religious beliefs. His personal letters and his personal life confirm the sincerity of his theistic beliefs, which find expression in his moral and religious treatises. He believed in the reality of natural laws. He thought that education should be directed toward the cultivation of virtue; and although his conception of virtue may have reflected a bourgeois sensibility, it certainly was not the celebration of unadorned self-interest.[4]

Grounded in these traditional values, his political and economic individualism was, however genuine and important, seriously constrained by other values and obligations. He defended the rights of private property and derived them from our distinctive relationship to our own individual bodies and hence to the labor of these bodies. But he also insisted that we were ultimately God's property, and that meant that we could not take our own lives and that property holders are subject to the obligations of responsible stewardship. However important the protection of individual rights might be to him, moreover, they did not trump all other moral norms. They had to be exercised within the context of a commitment to "the common good, for which societies are instituted."[5] Locke was not a rights theorist *simpliciter*, then, but rather "a theorist seeking an equilibrium between contract and consent, natural law, and natural rights."[6] He was neither a libertarian nor an individualist in the usual contemporary sense of that label. Instead, he sought to achieve in his liberal society a complex mix of liberty, equality (moral and legal, not social and economic), social cooperation, and the promotion of virtue.

Writing a century or more after Locke, Condorcet and John Stuart Mill also exhibited an attachment to a relatively traditional account of human virtue, even though neither the anticlerical Condorcet nor the agnostic Mill grounded this account in theological beliefs. Both of them justified a liberal society on the grounds that it contributed to the moral advancement of its citizens. They were in agreement that one central feature of moral development was the avoidance of what the Greeks called *pleonexia*, that is, the disposition to claim for oneself more than one's proper share. Although neither conceived human rationality as axiological and erotic in the fashion of the ancient moralists, they were fully in accord with the traditional view that held reason's restraint upon the passions to be fundamental to moral behavior. Both considered sympathy and benevolence to be unquestionable human virtues. And both assumed that a commitment to truth seeking was both morally obligatory and a part of the human flourishing that characterized good societies. They may have departed from the mainstream "tradition of civility" in their secularism and in their optimism about the capacity of enlightenment to generate virtue. But they clearly stood within that moral tradition; they were neither moral skeptics nor moral relativists; and although Mill defended diversity and valued autonomy in the choice of a "plan of life," neither would have given credence to the notion that all plans of life stood on a moral par.

Against the backdrop of this continuity with the moral tradition, the liberalisms of both Condorcet and Mill were devoted to the attainment of a complex cluster of human goods. Both were authentically liberal in their emphasis on the centrality of political, civil, and economic self-determination. But these human liberties were valued not only as good in themselves but also because they were held to be causally efficacious in the creation of other human goods. Among these goods were greater social equality, prosperity, and moral development. It is also fair to say, I think, that both of these liberal theorists believed strongly that liberal policies would enhance social solidarity and the sense of community. In Condorcet's case this would occur because of "those habits of an active and enlightened benevolence, of a fine and generous sensibility which nature has implanted in the hearts of all whose flowering waits only upon the favorable influences of enlightenment and freedom."[7] In Mill's case this would happen because mental advance went hand in hand with moral advance and because it would be expected to produce much greater unanimity on moral questions and an increased appreciation of social interdependence.

The general point here is this. The leading liberal theorists from the rise of liberalism in the seventeenth century until the middle of the nineteenth century depicted the norms and social goals of a good society as varied and complex. They did not endorse orienting a democratic regime around a single goal or value such as liberty or equality, nor even around these two central liberal norms as a pair. Instead, they aimed at a society which would be characterized by greater prosperity, stability, civic friendship, intellectual progress, and moral advance than any previous society. Liberty and equality they considered as goods in themselves—under the guise of autonomy and justice—but also as the most efficacious means of generating these other social goods. The optimism that is widely and not inaccurately perceived as a distinguishing trait of liberal thought stemmed from their conviction that these multiple goods were not only compatible but mutually reinforcing. They also were not in any fundamental sense moral radicals. Their conception of human virtue was more bourgeois and less aristocratic than that of earlier eras. But their innovations were preponderantly empirical and strategic ones. In their view maximizing civil liberty and political equality was the most effective way of creating a flourishing social union as well as a way of dismantling old oppressions and inequities.

In the late nineteenth century, however, to resume our story, this picture began to change. Philosophical developments and cultural changes eroded much of the moral traditionalism that had informed the beliefs and goals of the early liberals. And political and economic shifts cast into question the compatibility of some of the multiple values and aims that had guided liberalism in its inception. The result has been a twentieth-century liberalism which is divided into competing ideological wings and is largely divorced from its original moral culture.

The philosophical trends that have leached out most of the moral assumptions informing early liberalism encompass a variety of familiar isms. Darwinism undermined the sense of a fixed nature that had kept even the more subversive philosophers, such as David Hume, circumscribed by relatively traditional views about a universal morality. Relativism and historicism abandoned the residual belief in a natural order and natural rights that had inspired the liberalism of Jefferson and Paine. Positivism and emotivism called into question the cognitive meaningfulness of all moral claims whatever. Existentialism in its more radical forms construed the choice of one's plan of life as an act of wholly unbounded will. And postmodernism espouses the view that all social norms are, in words that have become almost a mantra, "politically constructed, arbitrary, and contingent."

Contemporary liberalism thus resides within and is suffused by a culture very different from the one that nurtured and constrained earlier liberalism. Contemporary liberalism, to state the obvious, is vastly more secular and arguably more materialistic than earlier liberalism. It is much more agnostic regarding what constitutes the good life and human virtue. And, to make a point which is particularly pertinent to the concerns of communitarianism, it has transformed and radicalized the whole conception of political individualism. From its outset, liberalism has embraced individualism, in the sense that it prized autonomy and demanded compelling warrant for any governmental restriction of individual freedom. But the individual in Locke, Mill, Adam Smith, and Condorcet enjoyed his or her freedom only within the context of complementary obligations, deriving from communal attachments and responsibilities, from the restraints of a valid moral order, and from the force of human sympathy. No early liberal would have ever defended the buccaneer individualism of a Herbert Spencer or ever even conceived of an individual like Sartre's Orestes, who finds "nothing left in heaven, no right or wrong, or anyone to give me orders" and concludes that he is to live by "no other law but mine."[8]

The major split in twentieth-century liberalism resulted from the consequences of the Industrial Revolution and the dynamics of advanced capitalism. Condorcet and Adam Smith both clearly assumed that a market-oriented economy would produce considerably greater social and economic equality. Condorcet, for example, wrote that "wealth has a natural tendency to equality and any excessive disproportion could not exist or at least would rapidly disappear if civil laws did not provide artificial ways of perpetuating and uniting fortunes" and if these same laws did not artificially restrain free commerce in other respects as well.[9] And well into the nineteenth century Mill could champion increased political, social, and economic equality at the same time as he wrote his famous defense of liberty and individuality. It became clear in the later nineteenth century, however, that the enterprises of maximizing liberty and maximizing equality were in some respects in tension with each other. If the onset of laissez-faire eroded some established inequalities by eliminating the political and legal restrictions that perpetuated them, laissez-faire policies in advanced capitalism generated concentrations of economic power and increased the gap between the commercial elite and the average worker. Twentieth-century liberals, therefore, have faced some necessity of prioritizing the classic liberal norms of liberty and equality.

The consequence has been a liberal culture divided into libertarian and egalitarian encampments. Both camps are individualistic and rights-oriented. But they begin from different moral premises and hence construe rights claims they would defend in contrasting ways. Libertarian liberals construe rights claims as entitlements that must be ascribed to individuals whenever they have not infringed the rights of others, an orientation paradigmatically expressed in recent years by Robert Nozick.[10] And they insist, with Milton Friedman, that "one cannot be both an egalitarian . . . and a liberal."[11] Egalitarian liberals, on the other hand, conceive all valid rights as constrained by a dominant norm of equality. Liberty is an important human good for them, but specific liberties are permissible only where they do not result in compromising the life chances of the disadvantaged members of society.[12]

Neither the libertarians nor the egalitarians, it might be noted, give much attention either to the problem of human virtue or to the goal of community. As for human virtue, Milton Friedman argues that liberalism "is not an all-embracing ethic" and it is indeed "a major aim of the liberal to leave the ethical problem for the individual to wrestle with."[13] And egalitarians generally insist that each individual's plan of life should be deemed as valuable as any other.[14] (Earlier liberals would also have opposed imposing conceptions of the good life on liberal citizens, for a variety of reasons. But they thought they had some reliable knowledge about the human good, and they drew upon those convictions in shaping the goals and policies of their ideal regimes.) Community is not ignored altogether as a value. But it receives only a tepid, secondary, and very fragile role in the libertarian and egalitarian schemes. Libertarians, for example, often offer as one of the virtues of a market-oriented society that it reduces social friction by not forcing majoritarian decisions on the allocation of social goods. Therefore, they accord community some implicit value by boasting that their system would at least not contribute to its disruption. Most liberal egalitarians also, I believe, have some appreciation of the value of community. Indeed, one of the reasons that equality can be valued is that it eliminates artificial barriers to civic friendship. Because egalitarians accord only peripheral attention and subordinate value to community, however, they generally provide flawed or inadequate accounts of what creating community entails; and they often support policies that damage communal ties.[15]

Space does not permit me to develop any serious or sustained critique of libertarianism or liberal egalitarianism here. But I would nonetheless contend that neither wing of contemporary liberalism provides a complete or compelling account of the good society. Each is committed to an important value, and each possesses important insights. But both have only a part of the truth, and when they offer this part as a sufficient and comprehensive blueprint for social policy, their blind spots lead us astray. Each side, indeed, has a rather good grasp of the other's weaknesses. But both of their critiques of the other side are more compelling than their own constructive accounts. For the purely market-driven society of the libertarians' dreams would produce a society rife with profound inequalities, deep divisions, social tensions, and selfish preoccupations, whereas the inevitably statist regime required to achieve the full goals of egalitarianism would be profoundly coercive, deleterious to excellence and efficiency, and productive of other forms of group hostility.

At the theoretical level libertarianism and egalitarianism share a common flaw: they both extract a single element of the good society from its context and offer it as the dominant if not exclusive goal of political organization and policy. Proceeding in this way creates normative visions marked by clarity and consistency. But they are also predictably simplistic and one-sided visions that lose sight of important dimensions of a well-ordered society.

When wrenched out of context in this fashion, liberty and equality make rather peculiar candidates for the role of dominant social good in another sense. For liberty, at least in the Anglo-American context, is a negative state of affairs, and equality is a relative state of affairs. Liberty is, in Hobbes's phrase, the "absence of impediment." And although it is obvious why people would like to escape impediments, it is not altogether clear how the absence of anything can function as the substantive telos of social organization. Similarly, a purely relative condition such as equality seems equally inadequate as the constitutive end of social action. The only rational response to the query "Don't you prize being equal?" is "Equal to what?" Prima facie, of course, one would prefer being equal to being on the lower side of a social inequality. But only those who make a fetish of equality would not prefer occupying a marginally lower position in a free, prosperous, and congenial society to being a full equal in a land of poverty, mutual hostility, and procrustean uniformity.

Seen against the background of this story, the communitarian project takes on a somewhat different appearance from that accorded to it by the conventional account. Rather than being some kind of incursion against the liberal tradition or a revolution within it, communitarianism is more an effort of reformation and recovery. It represents an attempt to recapture some of the normative complexity and the moral depth that was lost as a result of the philosophical shifts and political divisions that liberalism has encountered during its several-hundred-year history.

The task of recovering the complexity and depth of liberalism cannot, of course, be accomplished by an act of mere resuscitation. It would be both foolish and futile to urge that contemporary liberal societies simply repair once more to the alleged verities of earlier liberal sages like Locke or Mill. Admonitions to that effect would be inappropriate for two major reasons. First, the erosion of these earlier forms of liberalism was not a matter of accident or mere forgetfulness. Even apart from particular weaknesses or lacunae in earlier liberal theories, they suffered from internal tensions and incoherencies generated by the attempt to blend traditional moral doctrine with new epistemologies, ontologies, and anthropologies.[16] Moreover, quite obviously, both the philosophical landscape and the political environment have changed greatly since the inception of liberalism. Any revisionist liberal doctrine that hopes to be viable must address—even if it need not accede to—an intellectual world suffused with modes of thought, such as scientific naturalism and post-Nietzschean historicism, that earlier liberals did not have to contend with and that are not entirely hospitable to liberal values. Likewise, any persuasive liberal theory must come to terms with political, economic, and sociological developments that earlier liberals did not confront; it must explain, for example, how its norms and policies represent relevant and constructive responses to the dynamics of industrial capitalism in a global economy, of mass democracy, and of extensive social pluralism. For all these reasons, therefore, the attempt that I am endorsing to deepen and complexify contemporary liberal theory—and hence to bring it more in concert with what I have argued was the thrust of the liberal tradition at its inception—will have to be a highly creative undertaking.

Clearly, this challenging endeavor of creative reconstruction is not one to be accomplished here. I shall conclude, however, by suggesting what general direction this endeavor might take. And, in doing so, I trust that it will become apparent why I think that the perceptions and concerns of communitarianism are quite pertinent to the task at hand.

First, a reformed liberalism could recapture some of the normative complexity of earlier liberalism by insisting upon the importance of all of the three goals of its Enlightenment predecessors: liberty, equality, and fraternity. This recommendation may seem rather jejune, but the fact is that the dominant variants of liberal ideology have tended to become problematic precisely because of their fixation upon either liberty or equality as the ne plus ultra of political life. *Fraternity* in this context should be understood as standing for "civic friendship within a flourishing community." And against this backdrop, liberal individualism would be understood not as a kind of empirical or normative atomism but simply as an insistence upon the moral autonomy of each liberal citizen and upon the crucial value of personal development.

Fraternity in this expanded sense should in fact, I would argue, be construed as the capstone goal of a liberal society. For that reason, my preferred version of liberalism is quite properly characterizable as communitarian. But what makes this normative theory genuinely liberal at the same time is the insistence that civic friendship cannot be attained without extensive equality and that communities cannot flourish without extensive liberties. This recognition distinguishes communitarian liberalism from both conservatism and socialism and their own distinctive modes of community. Both conservativism and socialism have, with some degree of justification, criticized liberal societies for allegedly unraveling the social bonds among its citizens. Both Carlyle and Marx, from their opposing vantage points, chastised liberalism for reducing the ties between human beings to a mere "cash nexus." But the form of community that conservatism nostalgically embraced was essentially hierarchical, ignoring the valid claims of human equality. And the solidarity that socialism espoused seemed clearly—despite occasional rhetorical insistence to the contrary—to relegate individual liberties to the back burner or to a systematically elusive future.

A reformed liberalism should also seek to reacquire the moral dimension that was ubiquitous in early liberalism but has tended to disappear in the fastidious moral neutralism of much contemporary liberal theory. A robust liberalism must, I would argue, escape the thrall of moral emotivism and the genial form of nihilism it generates. It is true that no authentically liberal theory can privilege a specific doctrine of human perfection, for in doing so it would fail to maintain the epistemological humility that is one of its essential features. And the liberal state must likewise maintain neutrality among the comprehensive moral and religious doctrines that hold the allegiance of its citizens. But this does not mean that liberal theory or the liberal state cannot properly discriminate between sociopaths and good citizens. Any form of society, including a liberal polity, depends upon certain sustaining capacities, behaviors, and attitudes of its members. As John Stuart Mill reminded us in his *Considerations on Representative Government*, liberal democracies depend for their viability upon citizens who exercise some degree of self-restraint, accept and support the rule of law, respect the rights of others, and are willing to lend their energies to common endeavors. These attributes of mind and heart can be thematized as the liberal civic virtues, and liberal societies should, as William Galston has argued, recognize and encourage them.[17] Moreover, again following Mill's insistence that the measure of good government is its contribution to the "mental and moral advance" of its citizens, liberal societies should not be reticent in recognizing character formation—creating good people—to be one of its aspirations. To do this, liberal regimes need not embrace any comprehensive or sectarian doctrine of the human good. Instead, it can fashion its conception of "moral advance" from the attributes of good democratic citizenship and from the "overlapping consensus" (to borrow Rawls's term) of its members regarding the elemental features of the moral life. By the latter, I mean nothing very complicated or contentious, only the kinds of important precepts that most of us learn in kindergarten. Liberal regimes must leave it to individuals to decide whether their ultimate goal is to become a "strong poet," a sanctified believer, or just a good old boy. But that very proper reticence does not require liberal theory or liberal states to be completely neutral or indifferent about the rudiments of a good human life.

A more communitarian version of liberalism, then, would permit liberalism to recapture some of the normative complexity and moral weight that characterized its inception. And this theoretical reorientation would carry with it implications for policy and social organization. I conclude by noting a few of these implications in summary fashion.

First, a liberal democracy attuned to communitarian concerns would be very attentive to the health of the institutions of its civil society, as contrasted with the institutions of the marketplace or of the government proper. Libertarian liberals have characteristically focused on the market as the central institution of their ideal society, understandably so because markets are constituted by the consensual transactions of self-interested individuals that libertarians see as the essence of legitimate social interaction. Egalitarians, on the other hand, have for equally understandable reasons concentrated on the welfare state as the engine of social equality. Without denigrating for a moment the importance of state and market, communitarian liberals insist upon the crucial role of local communities, families, neighborhoods, churches, educational institutions, and civic associations in creating a productive environment for human development and happiness. Good social policies, therefore, should seek to bolster the health of these civic institutions. Strong markets and strong governments can crowd out or undermine the role of these institutions, and a wise liberal society would take steps to mitigate this tendency.[18] Indeed, it is the serious decline in familial and educational institutions during the past couple of decades in this country that more than anything has provided the impetus for communitarian ideas.

Communitarian liberals will also seek to design social institutions and policies in ways that promote civic friendship and a sense of common purpose. Libertarians would seem for all practical purposes content to have citizens be strangers as long as they are free. And egalitarians tend either to ignore the conditions of civic friendship or to conceive them in very abstract and implausible ways. Moreover, they have in recent years often championed in the name of diversity policies and ideals that, whatever their putative virtues, threaten to deepen social divisions. Communitarians can recognize that pluralism is both a fact of life and—as a derivative of autonomy and authenticity—a valid norm. But they also are aware that societies devoid of

moral consensus or a sense of common purpose have numerous difficulties governing themselves, and they recognize that achieving the
necessary minima in these respects cannot be taken for granted except
in the most homogeneous and compact polities. Accordingly, they will
be attracted to policies and undertakings that offer the prospect of
fostering bonds across the usual fissures of class, race, ethnicity, and
religion; this is one reason that communitarians tend to like the idea of
a national service program, for example. They will seek to promote
institutions, such as the public schools, that bring people from different backgrounds together in common endeavor. And they will
champion a public rhetoric of common identity and inclusiveness.

Communitarian liberals recognize the importance of individual
rights in protecting liberal citizens against majoritarian oppression.
But they are doubtful that a good society or a good policy process can
be constructed exclusively out of individual rights bearers who confront each other adversarially. Communitarians will be inclined to
believe that a society which makes juridical combat its paradigmatic
form of political interaction will be unnecessarily acrimonious and
divided. They will therefore want to promote political modes of mediation, reconciliation, and compromise that seek creative syntheses
from different interests and divergent moral concerns.[19]

For similar reasons, communitarian liberals will seek to maintain a
vital public sphere and to encourage a deliberative policy-making
process. Like Tocqueville, communitarians worry that the dynamics of
liberal democracy can result in an excess of privatism and an eclipse of
the public realm and public spiritedness. And the correlate tendency is
for deliberation among citizens directed toward the common good to
dissipate into straightforward bargaining among private interests. So
communitarians will respond with great sympathy to the recommendations of theorists like James Fishkin and Benjamin Barber about
ways to encourage more deliberative decision making throughout the
political system.[20]

Finally, communitarian liberals will seek to promote a robust conception of citizenship within liberal democracy, to the effect that democratic citizens should not perceive themselves or behave as mere
passive recipients of government protection and largesse. Strong democracies require active citizens, ones who participate in civic affairs
and who shoulder responsibilities for the common good. Recognizing
that the creation of a responsible citizenry is largely a matter of social

ethos that cannot be dictated, communitarians will nonetheless seek to encourage those kinds of civic education and public rituals that contribute to this goal.

I hope that it is clear from this cursory survey of communitarian concerns that nothing in them is at odds with the fundamental elements of the liberal tradition. Communitarians are as committed as anyone to representative government, legitimacy through consent, the rule of law, civil rights, and civil liberties. They simply flesh out this liberal framework with a conception of the good society which challenges the market utopia of the libertarians and the welfare utopia of the egalitarians. And when all of these ideals are juxtaposed with the classical liberal texts of Locke, Smith, Mill, Condorcet, and others, it should be clear that communitarians have as much right as their competitors to lay claim to the liberal tradition and that they should conceive themselves as reformers rather than as revolutionaries or as aliens.

## 2

*MICHAEL WALZER*

# The Communitarian

# Critique of Liberalism

Intellectual fashions are notoriously short-lived, very much like fashions in popular music, art, or dress. But there are certain fashions that seem regularly to reappear. Like pleated trousers or short skirts, they are inconstant features of a larger and more steadily prevailing phenomenon, in this case, a certain way of dressing. They have brief but recurrent lives; we know their transience and accept their return. Needless to say, there is no afterlife in which trousers will always be pleated or skirts forever short. Recurrence is all.

Although it operates at a much (infinitely?) higher level of cultural significance, the communitarian critique of liberalism is like the pleating of trousers: transient but certain to return. It is a consistently intermittent feature of liberal politics and social organization. No liberal success will make it permanently unattractive. At the same time no communitarian critique, however penetrating, will ever be anything more than an inconstant feature of liberalism. Someday, perhaps, there will be a larger transformation, like the shift from aristocratic knee breeches to plebeian pants, rendering liberalism and its critics alike irrelevant. But I see no present signs of anything like that, nor am I sure that we should look forward to it. For now, there is much to be said for a recurrent critique, whose protagonists hope only for small victories, partial incorporations, and when they are rebuffed or dismissed or co-opted, fade away for a time only to return.

Communitarianism is usefully contrasted with social democracy, which has succeeded in establishing a permanent presence alongside of and sometimes conjoined with liberal politics. Social democracy has its own intermittently fashionable critics, largely anarchist and libertarian in character. Since it sponsors certain sorts of communal identification, it is less subject to communitarian criticism than liberalism is. But it can never escape such criticism entirely, for liberals and social democrats alike share a commitment to economic growth and cope (although in different ways) with the deracinated social forms that growth produces. Community itself is largely an ideological presence in modern society; it has no recurrent critics of its own. It is intermittently fashionable only because it no longer exists in anything like full strength, and it is criticized only when it is fashionable.

The communitarian critique is nonetheless a powerful one; it would not recur if it were not capable of engaging our minds and feelings. In this essay I investigate the power of its current American versions and then offer a version of my own, less powerful, perhaps, than the ones with which I begin but more available for incorporation within liberal (or social democratic) politics. I do not mean (I hardly have the capacity) to lay communitarianism to rest, although I would willingly wait for its reappearance in a form more coherent and incisive than that in which it currently appears. The problem with communitarian criticism today—I am not the first to notice this—is that it suggests two different, and deeply contradictory, arguments against liberalism. One of these arguments is aimed primarily at liberal practice, the other primarily at liberal theory, but they cannot both be right. It is possible that each one is partly right—indeed, I insist on just this partial validity— but each of the arguments is right in a way which undercuts the value of the other.

## Liberalism: The First Critique

The first argument holds that liberal political theory accurately represents liberal social practice. As if the Marxist account of ideological reflection were literally true, and exemplified here, contemporary Western societies (American society especially) are taken to be the home of radically isolated individuals, rational egotists, and existential agents, men and women protected and divided by their inalienable rights. Liberalism tells the truth about the asocial society that liberals create, not, in fact, ex nihilo as their theory suggests but in a struggle against traditions and communities and authorities that are forgotten as soon as they are escaped, so that liberal practices seem to have no history. The struggle itself is ritually celebrated but rarely reflected on. The members of liberal society share no political or religious traditions; they can tell only one story about themselves, and that is the story of ex nihilo creation, which begins in the state of nature or the original position. Each individual imagines himself absolutely free, unencumbered, and on his own and enters society, accepting its obligations, only in order to minimize his risks. His goal is security, and security is, as Marx wrote, "the assurance of his egoism." And as he imagines himself, so he really is, "that is, an individual separated from the community, withdrawn into himself, wholly preoccupied with his private interest and acting in accordance with his private caprice. . . . The only bond between men is natural necessity, need, and private interest."[1] (I have used masculine pronouns in order to fit my sentences to Marx's. But it is an interesting question, not addressed here, whether this first communitarian critique speaks to the experience of women: are necessity and private interest their only bonds with one another?)

The writings of the young Marx represent one of the early appearances of communitarian criticism, and his argument, first made in the 1840s, is powerfully present today. Alasdair MacIntyre's description of the incoherence of modern intellectual and cultural life and the loss of narrative capacity makes a similar point in updated, state-of-the-art, theoretical language.[2] But the only theory that is necessary to the communitarian critique of liberalism is liberalism itself. All that the critics have to do, so they say, is to take liberal theory seriously. The self-portrait of the individual constituted only by his willfulness, liberated from all connection, without common values, binding ties, customs, or traditions—sans eyes, sans teeth, sans taste, sans everything—need only be evoked in order to be devalued: it is already the concrete absence of value. What can the real life of such a person be like? Imagine him maximizing his utilities, and society is turned into a war of all against all, the familiar rat race, in which, as Hobbes wrote, there is "no other goal, nor other garland, but being foremost."[3] Imagine him enjoying his rights, and society is reduced to the coexistence of isolated selves, for liberal rights, according to this first critique, have more to do with "exit" than with "voice."[4] They are concretely expressed in separation, divorce, withdrawal, solitude, privacy, and political apathy. And finally, the very fact that individual life can be described in these two philosophical languages, the language of utilities and the language of rights, is a further mark, says MacIntyre, of its incoherence: men and women in liberal society no longer have access to a single moral culture within which they can learn how they ought to live.[5] There is no consensus, no public meeting of minds, on the nature of the good life, hence the triumph of private caprice, revealed, for example, in Sartrean existentialism, the ideological reflection of everyday capriciousness.

We liberals are free to choose, and we have a right to choose, but we have no criteria to govern our choices except our own wayward understanding of our wayward interests and desires. And so our choices lack the qualities of cohesion and consecutiveness. We can hardly remember what we did yesterday; we cannot with any assurance predict what we will do tomorrow. We cannot give a proper account of ourselves. We cannot sit together and tell comprehensible stories, and we recognize ourselves in the stories we read only when these are fragmented narratives, without plots, the literary equivalent of atonal music and nonrepresentational art.

Liberal society, seen in the light of this first communitarian critique, is fragmentation in practice; and community is the exact opposite, the home of coherence, connection, and narrative capacity. But I am less concerned here with the different accounts that might be provided of this lost Eden than I am with the repeated insistence on the reality of fragmentation after the loss. This is the common theme of all contemporary communitarianisms: neoconservative lamentation, neo-Marxist indictment, and neoclassical or republican hand-wringing. (The need for the prefix *neo* suggests again the intermittent or recurrent character of communitarian criticism.) I should think it would be an awkward theme, for if the sociological argument of liberal theory is right, if society is actually decomposed, without residue, into the problematic coexistence of individuals, then we might well assume that liberal politics is the best way to deal with the problems of decomposition. If we have to create an artificial and a historical union out of a multitude of isolated selves, why not take the state of nature or the original position as our conceptual starting point? Why not accept in standard liberal fashion the priority of procedural justice over substantive conceptions of the good, since we can hardly expect, given our fragmentation, to agree about the good? Michael Sandel asks whether a community of those who put justice first can ever be more than a community of strangers.[6] The question is a good one, but its reverse form is more immediately relevant: if we really are a community of strangers, how can we do anything else but put justice first?

## Liberalism: The Second Critique

We are saved from this entirely plausible line of argument by the second communitarian critique of liberalism. The second critique holds that liberal theory radically misrepresents real life. The world is not like that, nor could it be. Men and women cut loose from all social ties, literally unencumbered, each one the one and only inventor of his or her own life, with no criteria, no common standards, to guide the invention: these are mythical figures. How can any group of people be strangers to one another when each member of the group is born with parents, and when these parents have friends, relatives, neighbors, comrades at work, coreligionists, and fellow citizens, connections, in fact, which are not so much chosen as passed on and inherited? Liberalism may well enhance the significance of purely contractual ties, but it is obviously false to suggest, as Hobbes sometimes seemed to do, that all our connections are mere "market friendships," voluntarist and self-interested in character, which cannot outlast the advantages they bring.[7] It is in the very nature of a human society that individuals bred within it will find themselves caught up in patterns of relationship, networks of power, and communities of meaning. That quality of being caught up is what makes them persons of a certain sort. And only then can they make themselves persons of a (marginally) different sort by reflecting on what they are and by acting in more or less distinctive ways within the patterns, networks, and communities that are willy-nilly theirs.

The burden of the second critique is that the deep structure even of liberal society is in fact communitarian. Liberal theory distorts this reality and, insofar as we adopt the theory, deprives us of any ready access to our own experience of communal embeddedness. The rhetoric of liberalism—this is the argument of the authors of *Habits of the Heart*—limits our understanding of our own heart's habits and gives us no way to formulate the convictions that hold us together as persons and that bind persons together into a community.[8] The assumption here is that we are in fact persons and that we are in fact bound together. The liberal ideology of separatism cannot take personhood and bondedness away from us. What it does take away is the sense of our personhood and bondedness, and this deprivation is then reflected in liberal politics. It explains our inability to form cohesive solidarities, stable movements and parties, that might make our deep convictions visible and effective in the world. It also explains our radical dependence (brilliantly foreshadowed in Hobbes's *Leviathan*) on the central state.

But how are we to understand this extraordinary disjunction between communal experience and liberal ideology, between personal conviction and public rhetoric, and between social bondedness and political isolation? That question is not addressed by communitarian critics of the second sort. If the first critique depends on a vulgar Marxist theory of reflection, the second critique requires an equally vulgar idealism. Liberal theory now seems to have a power over and against real life that has been granted to few theories in human history. Plainly, it has not been granted to communitarian theory, which cannot, on the first argument, overcome the reality of liberal separatism and cannot, on the second argument, evoke the already existing structures of social connection. In any case, the two critical arguments are mutually inconsistent; they cannot both be true. Liberal separatism either represents or misrepresents the conditions of everyday life. It might, of course, do a little of each—the usual muddle—but that is not a satisfactory conclusion from a communitarian standpoint. For if the account of dissociation and separatism is even partly right, then we have to raise questions about the depth, so to speak, of the deep structure. And if we are all to some degree communitarians under the skin, then the portrait of social incoherence loses its critical force.

### Facing Up to Liberalism

But each of the two critical arguments is partly right. I will try to say what is right about each, and then ask if something plausible can be made of the parts. First, then, there cannot be much doubt that we (in the United States) live in a society where individuals are relatively dissociated and separated from one another, or better, where they are continually separating from one another, continually in motion, often in solitary and apparently random motion, as if in imitation of what physicists call Brownian movement. Hence, we live in a profoundly unsettled society. We can best see the forms of unsettlement if we track the most important moves. So, consider (imitating the Chinese style) the Four Mobilities:

1. Geographic Mobility. Americans apparently change their residence more often than any people in history, at least since the barbarian migrations, excluding only nomadic tribes and families caught up in civil or foreign wars. Moving people and their possessions from one city or town to another is a major industry in the United States, even though many people manage to move themselves. In another sense, of course, we are all self-moved, not refugees but voluntary migrants. The sense of place must be greatly weakened by this extensive geographic mobility, although I find it hard to say whether it is superseded by mere insensitivity or by a new sense of many places. Either way, communitarian feeling seems likely to decline in importance. Communities are more than just locations, but they are most often successful when they are permanently located.

2. Social Mobility. This chapter does not address the arguments about how best to describe social standing or how to measure changes, whether by income, education, class membership, or rank in the status hierarchy. It is enough to say that fewer Americans stand exactly where their parents stood or do what they did than in any society for which we have comparable knowledge. Americans may inherit many things from their parents, but the extent to which they make a different life, if only by making a different living, means that the inheritance of community, that is, the passing on of beliefs and customary ways, is uncertain at best. Whether or not children are thereby robbed of narrative capacity, they seem likely to tell different stories than their parents told.

3. Marital Mobility. Rates of separation, divorce, and remarriage are higher today than they have ever been in our own society and probably higher than they have ever been in any other (except perhaps among Roman aristocrats, although I know of no statistics from that time, only anecdotes). The first two mobilities, geographic and social, also disrupt family life, so that siblings, for example, often live at great distances from one another, and later as uncles and aunts they are far removed from nephews and nieces.

But what we call "broken homes" are the product of marital breaks, of husbands or wives moving out, and then, commonly, moving on to new partners. Insofar as home is the first community and the first school of ethnic identity and religious conviction, this kind of breakage must have countercommunitarian consequences. It means that children often do not hear continuous or identical stories from the adults with whom they live. (Did the greater number of children ever hear such stories? The death of one spouse and the remarriage of the other may once have been as common as divorce and remarriage are today. But, then, other sorts of mobility have to be considered: both men and women are more likely today to marry across class, ethnic, and religious lines; remarriage will therefore often produce extraordinarily complex and socially diverse families, which probably are without historical precedent.)

4. Political Mobility. Loyalty to leaders, movements, parties, clubs, and urban machines seems to decline rapidly as place and social standing and family membership become less central in the shaping of personal identity. Liberal citizens stand outside all political organizations and then choose the one that best serves their ideals or interests. They are, ideally, independent voters, that is, people who move around; they choose for themselves rather than voting as their parents did, and they choose freshly each time rather than repeating themselves. As their numbers increase, they make for a volatile electorate and hence for institutional instability, particularly at the local level where political organization once served to reinforce communal ties.

The effects of the Four Mobilities are intensified in a variety of ways by other social developments that we are likely to talk about in the common metaphor of movement: the advance of knowledge, technological progress, and so on. But I am concerned here only with the actual movement of individuals. Liberalism is, most simply, the theoretical endorsement and justification of this movement.[9] In the liberal view, then, the Four Mobilities represent the enactment of liberty and the pursuit of (private or personal) happiness. And it has to be said that, conceived in this way, liberalism is a genuinely popular creed. Any effort to curtail mobility in the four areas described here would require a massive and harsh application of state power. Nevertheless, this popularity has an underside of sadness and discontent that are intermittently articulated, and communitarianism is, most simply, the intermittent articulation of these feelings. It reflects a sense of loss, and the loss is real. People do not always leave their old neighborhoods or hometowns willingly or happily. Moving may be a personal adventure in our standard cultural mythologies, but it is as often a family trauma in real life. The same thing is true of social mobility, which carries people down as well as up and requires adjustments that are never easy to manage. Marital breaks may sometimes give rise to new and stronger unions, but they also pile up what we might think of as family fragments: single-parent households, separated and lonely men and women, and abandoned children. And independence in politics is often a not-so-splendid isolation: individuals with opinions are cut loose from groups with programs. The result is a decline in "the sense of efficacy," with accompanying effects on commitment and morale.

All in all, we liberals probably know one another less well, and with less assurance, than people once did, although we may see more aspects of the other than they saw and recognize in him or her a wider range of possibilities (including the possibility of moving on). We are more often alone than people once were, being without neighbors we can count on, relatives who live nearby or with whom we are close, or comrades at work or in the movement. This is the truth of the first communitarian argument. We must now fix the limits of this truth by seeking what is true in the second argument.

In its easiest version the second argument—that we are really, at bottom, creatures of community—is certainly true but of uncertain significance. The ties of place, class or status, family, and even politics survive the Four Mobilities to a remarkable extent. To take just one example, from the last of the Four: It remains true, even today in this most liberal and mobile of societies, that the best predictor of how people will vote is our knowledge of how their parents voted.[10] All those dutifully imitative young Republicans and Democrats testify to the failure of liberalism to make independence or waywardness of mind the distinctive mark of its adherents. The predictive value of parental behavior holds even for independent voters: they are simply the heirs of independence. But we do not know to what extent inheritances of this sort are a dwindling communal resource; it may be that each generation passes on less than it received. The full liberalization of the social order, the production and reproduction of self-inventing individuals, may take a long time, much longer, indeed, than liberals themselves expected. There is not much comfort here for communitarian critics, however; while they can recognize and value the survival of older ways of life, they cannot count on, and they must have anxieties about, the vitality of those ways.

But there is another approach to the truth of the second critical argument. Whatever the extent of the Four Mobilities, they do not seem to move us so far apart that we can no longer talk with one another. We often disagree, of course, but we disagree in mutually comprehensible ways. I should think it fairly obvious that the philosophical controversies that MacIntyre laments are not in fact a mark of social incoherence. Where there are philosophers, there will be controversies, just as where there are knights, there will be tournaments. But these are highly ritualized activities, which bear witness to the connection, not the disconnection, of their protagonists. Even political conflict in liberal societies rarely takes forms so extreme as to set its protagonists beyond negotiation and compromise, procedural justice, and the very possibility of speech. The American civil rights struggle is a nice example of a conflict for which our moral/political language was and is entirely adequate. The fact that the struggle has had only partial success does not reflect linguistic inadequacy but rather political failures and defeats.

Martin Luther King's speeches evoked a palpable tradition, a set of common values such that public disagreement could focus only on how (or how quickly) they might best be realized.[11] But this is not, so to speak, a traditionalist tradition, a gemeinschaft tradition, a survival of the preliberal past. It is a liberal tradition modified, no doubt, by survivals of different sorts. The modifications are most obviously Protestant and republican in character, though by no means exclusively so: the years of mass immigration have brought a great variety of ethnic and religious memories to bear on American politics. What all of them bear on, however, is liberalism. The language of individual rights— voluntary association, pluralism, toleration, separation, privacy, free speech, the career open to talents, and so on—is simply inescapable. Who among us seriously attempts to escape? If we really are situated selves, as the second communitarian critique holds, then our situation is largely captured by that vocabulary. This is the truth of the second critique. Does it make any sense then to argue that liberalism prevents us from understanding or maintaining the ties that bind us together?

It makes some sense, because liberalism is a strange doctrine, which seems continually to undercut itself, to disdain its own traditions, and to produce in each generation renewed hopes for a more absolute freedom from history and society alike. Much of liberal political theory, from Locke to Rawls, is an effort to fix and stabilize the doctrine in order to end the endlessness of liberal liberation. But beyond every current version of liberalism, there is always a superliberalism, which, as Roberto Unger says of his own doctrine, "pushes the liberal premises about state and society, about freedom from dependence and governance of social relations by the will, to the point at which they merge into a large ambition: the building of a social world less alien to a self that can always violate the generative rules of its own mental or social constructs."[12] Although Unger was once identified as a communitarian, this ambition—large indeed!—seems designed to prevent not only any stabilization of liberal doctrine but also any recovery or creation of community. For there is no imaginable community that would not be alien to the eternally transgressive self. If the ties that bind us together do not *bind* us, there can be no such thing as a community. If it is anything at all, communitarianism is antithetical to transgression. And the transgressive self is antithetical even to the liberal community that is its creator and sponsor.[13]

Liberalism is a self-subverting doctrine; for that reason, it really does require periodic communitarian correction. But it is not a particularly helpful form of correction to suggest that liberalism is literally incoherent or that it can be replaced by some preliberal or antiliberal community waiting somehow just beneath the surface or just beyond the horizon. Nothing is waiting; American communitarians have to recognize that there is no one out there but separated, rights-bearing, voluntarily associating, freely speaking, liberal selves. It would be a good thing, though, if we could teach those selves to know themselves as social beings, the historical products of, and in part the embodiments of, liberal values. For the communitarian correction of liberalism cannot be anything other than a selective reinforcement of those same values or, to appropriate the well-known phrase of Michael Oakeshott, a pursuit of the intimations of community within them.

## Liberal Society: A Social
## Union of Social Unions

The place to begin the pursuit is with the liberal idea of voluntary association, which is not well understood, it seems to me, either among liberals or among their communitarian critics. In both its theory and its practice, liberalism expresses strong associative tendencies alongside its dissociative tendencies: its protagonists form groups as well as split off from the groups they form; they join up and resign, marry and divorce. Nevertheless, it is a mistake, and a characteristically liberal mistake, to think that the existing patterns of association are entirely or even largely voluntary and contractual, that is, the product of will alone. In a liberal society, as in every other society, people are born into very important sorts of groups, born with identities, male or female, for example, working-class, Catholic or Jewish, black, and so on. Many of their subsequent associations (like their subsequent careers) merely express these underlying identities, which, again, are not so much chosen as enacted.[14] Liberalism is distinguished less by the freedom to form groups on the basis of these identities than the freedom to leave the groups and sometimes even the identities behind. Association is always at risk in a liberal society. The boundaries of the group are not policed; people come and go, or they just fade into the distance without ever quite acknowledging that they have left. That is why liberalism is plagued by free-rider problems, by people who continue to enjoy the benefits of membership and identity while no longer participating in the activities that produce these benefits.[15] Communitarianism, by contrast, is the dream of a perfect free-riderlessness.

At its best the liberal society is the social union of social unions that John Rawls described: a pluralism of groups bonded by shared ideas of toleration and democracy.[16] But if all the groups are precarious, continually on the brink of dissolution or abandonment, then the larger union must also be weak and vulnerable. Or, alternatively, its leaders and officials will be driven to compensate for the failures of association elsewhere by strengthening their own union, that is, the central state, beyond the limits that liberalism has established. These limits are best expressed in terms of individual rights and civil liberties, but they also include a prescription for state neutrality. The good life is pursued by individuals, sponsored by groups; the state presides over the pursuit and the sponsorship but does not participate in either. Presiding is singular in character; pursuing and sponsoring are plural. Hence, it is a critical question for liberal theory and practice whether the associative passions and energies of ordinary people are likely over the long haul to survive the Four Mobilities and prove themselves sufficient to the requirements of pluralism. There is at least some evidence that they will not prove sufficient—without a little help. But, to repeat an old question, whence cometh our help? A few of the existing social unions live in the expectation of divine assistance. For the rest, we can only help one another, and the agency through which help of that sort comes most expeditiously is the state. But what kind of a state is it that fosters associative activities? What kind of a social union is it that includes without incorporating a great and discordant variety of social unions?

Obviously, it is a liberal state and social union; any other kind is too dangerous for communities and individuals alike. It would be an odd enterprise to argue in the name of communitarianism for an alternative state, for that would be to argue against our own political traditions and to repudiate whatever community we already have. But the communitarian correction does require a liberal state of a certain sort, conceptually though not historically unusual: a state which is, at least over some part of the terrain of sovereignty, deliberately nonneutral. The standard liberal argument for neutrality is an induction from social fragmentation. Since dissociated individuals will never agree on the good life, the state must allow them to live as they think best, subject only to John Stuart Mill's harm principle, without endorsing or sponsoring any particular understanding of what *best* means. But there is a problem here: the more dissociated individuals are, the stronger the state is likely to be, since it will be the only or the most important social union. And then, membership in the state, the only good that is shared by all individuals, may well come to seem the good that is best.

This is only to repeat the first communitarian critique, and it invites a response like the second critique: that the state is not in fact the only or even, for ordinary people in their everyday lives, the most important social union. All sorts of other groups continue to exist and to give shape and purpose to the lives of their members, despite the triumph of individual rights, the Four Mobilities in which that triumph is manifest, and the free riding that it makes possible. But these groups are continually at risk. And so the state, if it is to remain a liberal state, must endorse and sponsor some of them, namely, those that seem most likely to provide shapes and purposes congenial to the shared values of a liberal society.[17] No doubt, there are problems here, too, and I do not mean to deny their difficulty. But I see no way to avoid some such formulation, and not only for theoretical reasons. The actual history of the best liberal states, as of the best social democratic states (and these tend increasingly to be the same states), suggest that they behave in exactly this way, although often very inadequately.

Let me give three relatively familiar examples of state behavior of this kind. First, the Wagner Act of the 1930s. This was not a standard liberal law, hindering the hindrances to union organization, for it actively fostered union organization, and it did so precisely by solving the free-rider problem. By requiring collective bargaining whenever there was majority (but not necessarily unanimous) support for the union, and then by allowing union shops, the Wagner Act sponsored the creation of strong unions capable, at least to some degree, of determining the shape of industrial relations.[18] Of course, there could not be strong unions without working-class solidarity; unionization is parasitic on underlying communities of feeling and belief. But those underlying communities were already being eroded by the Four Mobilities when the Wagner Act was passed, and so the act served to counter the dissociative tendencies of liberal society. It was nevertheless a liberal law, for the unions that it helped create enhanced the lives of individual workers and were subject to dissolution and abandonment in accordance with liberal principles should they ever cease to do that.

The second example is the use of tax exemptions and matching grants of tax money to enable different religious groups to run extensive systems of day-care centers, nursing homes, hospitals, and so on: welfare societies inside the welfare state. I do not pretend that these private and pluralist societies compensate for the shoddiness of the American welfare state. But they do improve the delivery of services by making it a more immediate function of communal solidarity. The state's role here, beside establishing minimal standards, is to abate, since in this case it cannot entirely solve, the free-rider problem. If some number of men and women end up in a Catholic nursing home, even though they never contributed to a Catholic charity, they will at least have paid their taxes. But why not nationalize the entire welfare system and end free-ridership? The liberal response is that the social union of social unions must always operate at two levels: a welfare system run entirely by private, nonprofit associations would be dangerously inadequate and inequitable in its coverage; and a totally nationalized system would deny expression to local and particularist solidarities.[19]

The third example is the passage of plant-closing laws designed to afford some protection to local communities of work and residence. Inhabitants are insulated, although only for a time, against market pressure to move out of their old neighborhoods and search for work elsewhere. Although the market "needs" a highly mobile workforce, the state takes other needs into account, not only in a welfarist way (through unemployment insurance and job-retraining programs) but also in a communitarian way. But the state is not similarly committed to the preservation of every neighborhood community. It is entirely neutral toward communities of ethnicity and residence, offering no protection against strangers who want to move in. Here geographic mobility remains a positive value, one of the rights of citizens.

Unions, religious organizations, and neighborhoods each draw on feelings and beliefs that, in principle if not always in history, predate the emergence of the liberal state. How strong these feelings and beliefs are, and what their survival value is, I cannot say. Have the unions established such a grip on the imaginations of their members as to make for good stories? There are some good stories, first told, then retold, and sometimes even reenacted. But the narrative line does not seem sufficiently compelling to younger workers to sustain anything like the old working-class solidarity. Nor is it sufficient for a religious organization to provide life-cycle services for its members if they are no longer interested in its religious services. Nor are neighborhoods proof for long against market pressure. Still, communal feeling and belief seem considerably more stable than we once thought they would be, and the proliferation of secondary associations in liberal society is remarkable, even if many of them have short lives and transient memberships. One has a sense of people working together and trying to cope, and not, as the first communitarian critique suggests, just getting by on their own, by themselves one by one.

### The Role of the State

A good liberal (or social democratic) state enhances the possibilities for cooperative coping. John Dewey provided a useful account of such a state in *The Public and Its Problems*. Published in 1927, the book is a commentary on and a partial endorsement of an earlier round of communitarian criticism. Dewey shared with the critics of his time, who called themselves "pluralists," an uneasiness with the sovereign state, but he was not quite so uneasy as most of them were. He also shared an admiration for what he called "primary groupings" within the state, but he was more inclined than the pluralists were to qualify his admiration. Primary groupings, he wrote, are "good, bad, and indifferent," and they cannot by their mere existence fix the limits of state activity. The state is not "only an umpire to avert and remedy trespasses of one group upon another." It has a larger function: "It renders the desirable association solider and more coherent. . . . It places a discount upon injurious groupings and renders their tenure of life precarious . . . [and] it gives the individual members of valued associations greater liberty and security; it relieves them of hampering conditions. . . . It enables individual members to count with reasonable certainty upon what others will do."[20] These may seem like tasks too extensive for a liberal state, but they are constrained by the constitutional establishment of individual rights, which are themselves (on the pragmatic understanding) not so much recognitions of what individuals by nature are or have as expressions of hope about what they will be and do. Unless individuals act together in certain ways, state action of the sort that Dewey recommended cannot get started. When we recognize the "right of the citizens peacefully to assemble," for example, we are hoping for assemblies of citizens. If we then discriminate among such assemblies, we do so on limited grounds, fostering only those that really do express communities of feeling and belief and do not violate liberal principles of association.

It is often argued these days that the nonneutral state, whose activities I have made some attempt to justify, is best understood in republican terms. A revival of neoclassical republicanism provides much of the substance of contemporary communitarian politics. The revival, I have to say, is largely academic; unlike other versions of communitarianism in Dewey's time and ours, it has no external reference. There really are unions, churches, and neighborhoods in American society, but there are virtually no examples of republican association and no movements or parties aimed at promoting such association. Dewey probably would not recognize his "public," nor Rawls his "social union," as versions of republicanism, if only because in both these cases energy and commitment have been drained from the singular and narrowly political association to the more various associations of civil society. Republicanism by contrast is an integrated and unitary doctrine in which energy and commitment are focused primarily on the political realm. It is a doctrine adapted (in both its classical and neo-classical forms) to the needs of small, homogeneous communities, where civil society is radically undifferentiated. Perhaps the doctrine can be extended to account for a "republic of republics," a decentralized and participatory revision of liberal democracy. A considerable strengthening of local governments would then be required in the hope of encouraging the development and display of civic virtue in a pluralist variety of social settings. This indeed is a pursuit of the intimations of community *within* liberalism, for it has more to do with John Stuart Mill than with Rousseau. Now we are to imagine the nonneutral state empowering cities, towns, and boroughs; fostering neighborhood committees and review boards; and always on the lookout for bands of citizens ready to take responsibility for local affairs. [21]

None of this is any guarantee against the erosion of the underlying communities or the death of local loyalties. It is a matter of principle that communities must always be at risk. And the great paradox of a liberal society is that one cannot set oneself against this principle without also setting oneself against the traditional practices and shared understandings of the society. Here, respect for tradition requires the precariousness of traditionalism. If the first communitarian critique were true in its entirety, if there were no communities and no traditions, then we could just proceed to invent new ones. Insofar as the second critique is even partly true, and the work of communal invention is well begun and continually in progress, we must rest content with the kinds of corrections and enhancements—they would be, in fact, more radical than these terms suggest—that Dewey described.

### The Constitution of the Self

I have avoided until now what is often taken to be the central issue between liberals and their communitarian critics: the constitution of the self. [22] Liberalism, it is commonly said, is founded on the idea of a presocial self, a solitary and sometimes heroic individual confronting society, who is fully formed before the confrontation begins. Communitarian critics then argue, first, that instability and dissociation are the actual and disheartening achievement of individuals of this sort and, second, that there really cannot be individuals of this sort. The critics are commonly said in turn to believe in a radically socialized self which can never confront society because it is, from the beginning, entangled in society, itself the embodiment of social values. The disagreement seems sharp enough, but in fact, in practice, it is not sharp at all, for neither of these views can be sustained for long by anyone who goes beyond staking out a position and tries to elaborate an argument.[23] Nor does liberal or communitarian theory require views of this sort. Contemporary liberals are not committed to a presocial self but only to a self capable of reflecting critically on the values that have governed its socialization; and communitarian critics, who are doing exactly that, can hardly go on to claim that socialization is everything. The philosophical and psychological issues here go very deep, but so far as politics is concerned, there is little to be won on this battlefield; concessions from the other side come too easily to count as victories.

The central issue for political theory is not the constitution of the self but the connection of constituted selves, the pattern of social relations. Liberalism is best understood as a theory of relationship, which has voluntary association at its center and which understands voluntariness as the right of rupture or withdrawal. What makes a marriage voluntary is the permanent possibility of divorce. What makes any identity or affiliation voluntary is the easy availability of alternative identities and affiliations. But the easier this easiness is, the less stable all our relationships are likely to become. The Four Mobilities take hold, and society seems to be in perpetual motion, so that the actual subject of liberal practice, it might be said, is not a presocial but a postsocial self, free at last from all but the most temporary and limited alliances. Now, the liberal self reflects the fragmentation of liberal society: it is radically underdetermined and divided, forced to invent itself anew for every public occasion. Some liberals celebrate this freedom and self-invention; all communitarians lament its arrival, even while insisting that it is not a possible human condition.

I have argued that insofar as liberalism tends toward instability and dissociation, it requires periodic communitarian correction. Rawls's "social union of social unions" reflects and builds on an earlier correction of this kind, the work of American writers like Dewey, Randolph Bourne, and Horace Kallen. Rawls has given us a generalized version of Kallen's argument that America, after the great immigration, was and should remain a "nation of nationalities."[24] In fact, however, the erosion of nationality seems to be a feature of liberal social life, despite intermittent ethnic revivals like that of the late 1960s and 1970s. We can generalize from this to the more or less steady attenuation of all the underlying bonds that make social unions possible. There is no strong or permanent remedy for communal attenuation short of an antiliberal curtailment of the Four Mobilities and the rights of rupture and divorce on which they rest. Communitarians sometimes dream of such a curtailment, but they rarely advocate it. The only community that most of them actually know, after all, is just this liberal union of unions, always precarious and always at risk. They cannot triumph over this liberalism; they can only, sometimes, reinforce its internal associative capacities. The reinforcement is only temporary, because the capacity for dissociation is also strongly internalized and highly valued. That is why communitarianism criticism is doomed—it probably is not a terrible fate—to eternal recurrence.

# 3
*MICHAEL J. SANDEL*

# Moral Argument
# and Liberal Toleration
*Abortion and*

*Homosexuality*

$P$eople defend laws against abortion and homosexual sodomy in two different ways: some argue that abortion and homosexuality are morally reprehensible and therefore worthy of prohibition; others try to avoid passing judgment on the morality of these practices and argue instead that in a democracy political majorities have the right to embody in law their moral convictions.

In a similar way arguments against antiabortion and antisodomy laws take two different forms: some say the laws are unjust because the practices they prohibit are morally permissible, indeed sometimes desirable; others oppose these laws without reference to the moral status of the practices at issue and argue instead that individuals have a right to choose for themselves whether to engage in them.

These two styles of argument might be called, respectively, the *naive* and the *sophisticated*. The naive view holds that the justice of laws depends on the moral worth of the conduct they prohibit or protect. The sophisticated view holds that the justice of such laws depends not on a substantive moral judgment about the conduct at stake but instead on a more general theory about the respective claims of majority rule and individual rights, of democracy on the one hand and liberty on the other.

I try in this chapter to bring out the truth in the naive view, which I take to be this: the justice (or injustice) of laws against abortion and homosexual sodomy depends, at least in part, on the morality (or immorality) of those practices.[1] This is the claim the sophisticated view rejects. In both its majoritarian and its liberal versions, the sophisticated view tries to set aside or "bracket" controversial moral and religious conceptions for purposes of justice. It insists that the justification of laws be neutral among competing versions of the good life.

In practice, of course, these two kinds of argument can be difficult to distinguish. In the debate over cases like *Roe v. Wade*[2] and *Bowers v. Hardwick*,[3] both camps tend to advance the naive view under cover of the sophisticated. (Such is the prestige of the sophisticated way of arguing.) For example, those who would ban abortion and sodomy out of abhorrence often argue in the name of deference to democracy and judicial restraint. Similarly, those who want permissive laws because they approve of abortion and homosexuality often argue in the name of liberal toleration.

This is not to suggest that all instances of the sophisticated argument are disingenuous attempts to promote a substantive moral conviction. Those who argue that law should be neutral among competing conceptions of the good life offer various grounds for their claim, including most prominently the following:

1. the *relativist* view says law should not affirm a particular moral conception because all morality is relative, and so there are no moral truths to affirm;
2. the *utilitarian* view argues that government neutrality will, for various reasons, promote the general welfare in the long run;
3. the *voluntarist* view holds that government should be neutral among conceptions of the good life in order to respect the capacity of persons as free citizens or autonomous agents to choose their conceptions for themselves; and
4. the *minimalist*, or pragmatic, view says that, because people inevitably disagree about morality and religion, government should bracket these controversies for the sake of political agreement and social cooperation.

In order to bring out the truth in the naive way of arguing, I look to the actual arguments that judges and commentators have made in recent cases dealing with abortion and homosexuality. Their arguments, unfailingly sophisticated, illustrate the difficulty of bracketing moral judgments for purposes of law. Because their reasons for trying to be neutral among conceptions of the good life are drawn primarily from voluntarist and minimalist assumptions, I focus on these arguments. Finally, although much of my argument criticizes leading theories of liberal toleration, I do not think it offers any comfort to majoritarianism. The cure for liberalism is not majoritarianism but a keener appreciation of the role of substantive moral discourse in political and constitutional argument.

### Privacy Rights: Intimacy and Autonomy

In the constitutional right of privacy, the neutral state and the voluntarist conception of the person are often joined. In the case of abortion, for example, no state may, "by adopting one theory of life,"[4] override a woman's right to decide "whether or not to terminate her pregnancy."[5] Government may not enforce a particular moral view, however widely held, for "no individual should be compelled to surrender the freedom to make that decision for herself simply because her 'value preferences' are not shared by the majority."[6]

As with religious liberty and freedom of speech, so with privacy; the ideal of neutrality often reflects a voluntarist conception of human agency. Government must be neutral among conceptions of the good life in order to respect the capacity of persons to choose their values and relationships for themselves. So close is the connection between privacy rights and the voluntarist conception of the self that commentators frequently assimilate the values of privacy and autonomy: privacy rights are said to be "grounded in notions of individual autonomy," because "the human dignity protected by constitutional guarantees would be seriously diminished if people were not free to choose and adopt a lifestyle which allows expression of their uniqueness and individuality."[7] In "recognizing a constitutional right to privacy,"[8] the Court has given effect to the view "that persons have the capacity to live autonomously and the right to exercise that capacity."[9] Supreme Court decisions voiding laws against contraceptives "not only protect the individual who chooses not to procreate, but also the autonomy of a couple's association." They protect men and women "against an unchosen commitment" to unwanted children and "against a compelled identification with the social role of parent."[10]

In Supreme Court decisions and dissents alike, the justices have often tied privacy rights to voluntarist assumptions. The Court has thus characterized laws banning the use of contraceptives as violating "the constitutional protection of individual autonomy in matters of childbearing."[11] It has defended the right to an abortion on the grounds that few decisions are "more properly private, or more basic to individual dignity and autonomy, than a woman's decision . . . whether to end her pregnancy."[12] Justice Douglas, concurring in an abortion case, emphasized that the right of privacy protects such liberties as "the autonomous control over the development and expression of one's intellect, interests, tastes, and personality," as well as "freedom of choice in the basic decisions of one's life respecting marriage, divorce, procreation, contraception, and the education and upbringing of children."[13] Writing in dissent, Justice Marshall found a regulation limiting the hair length of policemen "inconsistent with the values of privacy, self-identity, autonomy, and personal integrity" that he believed the Constitution was designed to protect.[14] And four justices would have extended privacy protection to consensual homosexual activity on the grounds that "much of the richness of a relationship will come from the freedom an individual has to *choose* the form and nature of these intensely personal bonds."[15]

Although the link between privacy and autonomy is now so familiar as to seem natural, even necessary, the right of privacy need not presuppose a voluntarist conception of the person. In fact, through most of its history in American law, the right of privacy has implied neither the ideal of the neutral state nor the ideal of a self freely choosing its aims and attachments.

Where the contemporary right of privacy is the right to engage in certain conduct without government restraint, the traditional version is the right to keep certain personal facts from public view. The new privacy protects a person's "independence in making certain kinds of important decisions," whereas the old privacy protects a person's interest "in avoiding disclosure of personal matters."[16]

The tendency to identify privacy with autonomy not only obscures these shifting understandings of privacy; it also restricts the range of reasons for protecting it. Although the new privacy typically relies on voluntarist justifications, it can also be justified in other ways. A right to be free of governmental interference in matters of marriage, for example, can be defended not only in the name of individual choice but also in the name of the intrinsic value or social importance of the practice it protects. As the Court has acknowledged, "certain kinds of personal bonds have played a critical role in the culture and traditions of the Nation by cultivating and transmitting shared ideals and beliefs; they hereby foster diversity and act as critical buffers between the individual and the power of the State."[17] The Court's greater tendency, however, has been to view privacy in voluntarist terms, as protecting "the ability independently to define one's identity."[18]

### From the Old Privacy to the New

The right to privacy first gained legal recognition in the United States as a doctrine of tort law, not constitutional law. In an influential article in 1890, Louis Brandeis, then a Boston lawyer, and his onetime law partner Samuel Warren argued that the civil law should protect "the right to privacy."[19] Far from latter-day concerns with sexual freedoms, Brandeis and Warren's privacy was quaint by comparison, concerned with the publication of high society gossip by the sensationalist press and the unauthorized use of people's portraits in advertising.[20] Gradually at first, then more frequently in the 1930s, this right to privacy gained recognition in the civil law of most states.[21] Prior to the 1960s, however, privacy received scant attention in constitutional law.

Two members of the Supreme Court first addressed the right of privacy as such in 1961 when a Connecticut pharmacist challenged the state's ban on contraceptives in *Poe v. Ullman*.[22] Although the majority dismissed the case on technical grounds,[23] Justices Douglas and Harlan dissented, arguing that the law violated the right of privacy. The privacy they defended was privacy in the traditional sense. The right at stake was not the right to use contraceptives but the right to be free of the surveillance that enforcement would require. "If we imagine a regime of full enforcement of the law," wrote Douglas, "we would reach the point where search warrants issued and officers appeared in bedrooms to find out what went on. . . . If [the State] can make this law, it can enforce it. And proof of its violation necessarily involves an inquiry into the relations between man and wife."[24] Banning the sale of contraceptives would be different from banning their use, Douglas observed. Banning the sale would restrict access to contraceptives but would not expose intimate relations to public inspection. Enforcement would take police to the drugstore, not the bedroom, and so would not offend privacy in the traditional sense.[25]

Justice Harlan also objected to the law on grounds that distinguish the old privacy from the new. He did not object that the law against contraceptives failed to be neutral among competing moral conceptions. Although Harlan acknowledged that the law was based on the belief that contraception is immoral in itself and encourages such "dissolute action" as fornication and adultery by minimizing their "disastrous consequence,"[26] he did not find this failure of neutrality contrary to the Constitution. In a statement clearly opposed to the strictures of neutrality, Harlan argued that morality is a legitimate concern of government: "The very inclusion of the category of morality among state concerns indicates that society is not limited in its objects only to the physical wellbeing of the community, but has traditionally concerned itself with the moral soundness of its people as well. Indeed to attempt a line between public behavior and that which is purely consensual or solitary would be to withdraw from community concern a range of subjects with which every society in civilized times has found it necessary to deal."[27]

Though he rejected the ideal of the neutral state, Harlan did not conclude that Connecticut could prohibit married couples from using contraceptives. Like Douglas, he reasoned that enforcing the law would intrude on the privacy essential to the prized institution of marriage. He objected to the violation of privacy in the traditional sense, to "the intrusion of the whole machinery of the criminal law into the very heart of marital privacy, requiring husband and wife to render account before a criminal tribunal of their uses of that intimacy."[28] According to Harlan, the state was entitled to embody in law the belief that contraception is immoral but not to implement "the obnoxiously intrusive means it had chosen to effectuate that policy."[29]

Four years later, in *Griswold v. Connecticut*,[30] the dissenters prevailed. The Supreme Court invalidated Connecticut's law against contraceptives and for the first time explicitly recognized a constitutional right of privacy. Although the right was located in the Constitution rather than tort law, it remained tied to the traditional notion of privacy, as the interest in keeping intimate affairs from public view. The violation of privacy consisted in the intrusion required to enforce the law, not the restriction on the freedom to use contraceptives. "Would we allow the police to search the sacred precincts of marital bedrooms for telltale signs of the use of contraceptives?" wrote Justice Douglas for the Court. "The very idea is repulsive to the notions of privacy surrounding the marriage relationship."[31]

The justification for the right was not voluntarist but unabashedly teleological; the privacy the Court vindicated was not for the sake of letting people lead their sexual lives as they choose but rather for the sake of affirming and protecting the social institution of marriage. "Marriage is a coming together for better or for worse, hopefully enduring, and intimate to the degree of being sacred. It is an association that promotes a way of life . . . a harmony of living . . . a bilateral loyalty. . . . [I]t is an association for as noble a purpose as any involved in our prior decisions."[32]

Although commentators and judges often view *Griswold* as a dramatic constitutional departure, the privacy right it proclaimed was consistent with traditional notions of privacy going back to the turn of the century. From the standpoint of shifting privacy conceptions, the more decisive turn came seven years later in *Eisenstadt v. Baird*,[33] a seemingly similar case. Like *Griswold*, it involved a state law restricting contraceptives. In *Eisenstadt*, however, the challenged law restricted the distribution of contraceptives, not their use. While it therefore limited access to contraceptives, its enforcement could not be said to require governmental surveillance of intimate activities. It did not violate privacy in the traditional sense.[34] Furthermore, the law prohibited distributing contraceptives only to unmarried persons, and so did not burden the institution of marriage as the Connecticut law did.

Despite these differences, the Supreme Court struck down the law with only a single dissent. Its decision involved two innovations, one explicit, the other unacknowledged. The explicit innovation redescribed the bearers of privacy rights from persons qua participants in the social institution of marriage to persons qua individuals, independent of their roles or attachments. As the Court explained, "It is true that in *Griswold* the right of privacy in question inhered in the marital relationship. Yet the marital couple is not an independent entity with a mind and heart of its own, but an association of two individuals each with a separate intellectual and emotional makeup."[35]

The subtler, though no less fateful, change in *Eisenstadt* was in the shift from the old privacy to the new. Rather than conceiving privacy as freedom from surveillance or disclosure of intimate affairs, the Court found that the right to privacy now protected the freedom to engage in certain activities without governmental restriction. Al-though privacy in *Griswold* prevented intrusion into "the sacred pre-cincts of marital bedrooms,"[36] privacy in *Eisenstadt* prevented intru-sion into decisions of certain kinds. Moreover, as the meaning of privacy changed, so did its justification. The Court protected privacy in *Eisenstadt* not for the social practices it promoted but for the individ-ual choice it secured. "If the right of privacy means anything, it is the right of the *individual*, married or single, to be free from unwarranted governmental intrusion into matters so fundamentally affecting a per-son as the decision whether to bear or beget a child."[37]

One year later, in *Roe v. Wade*,[38] the Supreme Court gave the new privacy its most controversial application by striking down a Texas law against abortion and extending privacy to "encompass a woman's decision whether or not to terminate her pregnancy."[39] First with contraception, then with abortion, the right of privacy had become the right to make certain sorts of choices, free of interference by the state. The choice had also to be free of interference by husbands or parents. In *Planned Parenthood of Missouri v. Danforth*,[40] the Court struck down a law requiring a husband's consent, or parental consent in the case of unmarried minors, as a condition for an abortion. Since the state may not prevent even minors from having abortions in the first trimester, it cannot delegate to "a third party" such as a husband or parent the authority to do so.[41]

The voluntarist grounds of the new privacy found explicit state-ment in a 1977 case invalidating a New York law prohibiting the sale of contraceptives to minors under age sixteen.[42] For the first time, the Court used the language of autonomy to describe the interest privacy protects and argued openly for the shift from the old privacy to the new. Writing for the Court in *Carey v. Population Services International*, Justice Brennan admitted that *Griswold* focused on the fact that a law forbidding the use of contraceptives can bring the police into marital bedrooms.[43] "But subsequent decisions have made clear that the con-stitutional protection of individual autonomy in matters of childbear-ing is not dependent on that element."[44] Surveying the previous cases, he emphasized that *Eisenstadt* protected the "*decision* whether to bear or beget a child,"[45] and *Roe* protected "a woman's *decision* whether or not to terminate her pregnancy."[46] He concluded that "the teaching of *Griswold* is that the Constitution protects individual decisions in mat-ters of childbearing from unjustified intrusion by the State."[47]

Given the voluntarist interpretation of privacy, restricting the sale of contraceptives violates privacy as harshly as banning their use; the one limits choice as surely as the other. "Indeed, in practice," Brennan observed, "a prohibition against all sales, since more easily and less offensively enforced, might have an even more devastating effect upon the freedom to choose contraception."[48] Ironically, the very fact that a ban on sales does not threaten the old privacy makes it a greater threat to the new.

Later decisions upholding abortion rights also used the language of autonomy to describe the privacy interest at stake. The Court held in a recent opinion that "few decisions are . . . more properly private, or more basic to individual dignity and autonomy than a woman's decision . . . whether to end her pregnancy. A woman's right to make that choice freely is fundamental."

Despite its increasing tendency to identify privacy with autonomy, the Court refused, in a 5–4 decision, to extend privacy protection to consensual homosexual activity. Writing for the majority, Justice White emphasized that the Court's previous privacy cases protected choice only with respect to child rearing and education, family relationships, procreation, marriage, contraception, and abortion. "We think it evident," he held, "that none of the rights announced in those cases bears any resemblance to the claimed constitutional rights of homosexuals to engage in acts of sodomy."[49] He also rejected the claim that Georgia's citizens could not embody in law their belief "that homosexual sodomy is immoral and unacceptable."[50] Neutrality to the contrary, "the law . . . is constantly based on notions of morality, and if all laws representing essentially moral choices are to be invalidated under the Due Process Clause, the courts will be very busy indeed."[51]

Writing for the four dissenters, Justice Blackmun argued that the Court's previous privacy decisions did not depend on the virtue of the practices they protected but on the principle of free individual choice in intimate matters. "We protect those rights not because they contribute . . . to the general public welfare, but because they form so central a part of an individual's life. '[T]he concept of privacy embodies the "moral fact that a person belongs to himself and not others nor to society as a whole." ' "[52]

Blackmun argued for the application of earlier privacy rulings in the considerations of homosexual practices by casting the Court's concern for conventional family ties in individualist terms: "We protect the decision whether to have a child because parenthood alters so dramatically an individual's self-definition. . . . And we protect the family because it contributes so powerfully to the happiness of individuals, not because of a preference for stereotypical households."[53] Because the right of privacy in sexual relationships protects "the freedom an individual has to *choose* the form and nature of these intensely personal bonds,"[54] it protects homosexual activity no less than other intimate choices.

Defending the ideal of the neutral state, Blackmun added that traditional religious condemnations of homosexuality "give the State no license to impose their judgments on the entire citizenry."[55] To the contrary, the state's appeal to religious teachings against homosexuality undermines its claim that the law "represents a legitimate use of secular coercive power."[56]

Despite the Court's reluctance to extend privacy rights to homosexuals, the privacy cases of the last twenty-five years offer ample evidence of assumptions drawn from the liberal conception of the person. They also raise two questions about the liberalism they reflect: first, whether bracketing controversial moral issues is even possible; and, second, whether the voluntarist conception of privacy limits the range of reasons for protecting privacy.

### The Minimalist Case for Toleration:  Abortion

Unlike the voluntarist grounds for the neutral state, minimalist liberalism seeks a conception of justice that is political, not philosophical, that does not presuppose any particular conception of the person, autonomous or otherwise. It proposes bracketing controversial moral and religious issues for the sake of securing social cooperation in the face of disagreement about ends, not for the sake of such "comprehensive" liberal ideals as autonomy or individuality.[57] One objection to minimalist liberalism is that the case for bracketing a particular moral or religious controversy may partly depend on an implicit answer to the controversy it purports to bracket. In the case of abortion, for example, the more confident we are that fetuses are, in the relevant moral sense, different from babies, the more confident we can be in bracketing the question about the moral status of fetuses for political purposes.

The Court's argument in *Roe v. Wade*[58] illustrates the difficulty of deciding constitutional cases by bracketing controversial moral and religious issues. Although the Court claimed to be neutral on the question of when life begins, its decision presupposes a particular answer to that question. The Court began by observing that the Texas law against abortion rests upon a particular theory of when life begins. "Texas urges that . . . life begins at conception and is present through-out pregnancy, and that, therefore, the State has a compelling interest in protecting that life from and after conception."[59]

The Court then claimed to be neutral on that question: "We need not resolve the difficult question of when life begins. When those trained in the respective disciplines of medicine, philosophy, and theology are unable to arrive at any consensus, the judiciary . . . is not in a position to speculate as to the answer."[60] It then noted "the wide divergence of thinking on this most sensitive and difficult question" throughout the Western tradition and in the law of various American states.[61]

From this survey the Court concluded that "the unborn have never been recognized in the law as persons in the whole sense."[62] Accord-ingly, it argued that Texas was wrong to embody in law a particular theory of life. Since no theory was conclusive, it held that Texas erred in "adopting one theory of life . . . [which would] override the rights of the pregnant woman that are at stake."[63]

However, contrary to its professions of neutrality, the Court's deci-sion presupposed a particular answer to the question it claimed to bracket. "With respect to the State's important and legitimate interest in potential life, the 'compelling' point is at viability. This is so because the fetus then presumably has the capability of meaningful life outside the mother's womb. State regulation protective of fetal life after viabil-ity thus has both logical and biological justifications."[64]

That the Court's decision in *Roe* presupposes a particular answer to the question it purports to bracket is no argument against its decision, only an argument against its claim to have bracketed the controversial question of when life begins. It does not replace the Texas theory of life with a neutral stance but with a different theory of its own.

The minimalist case for neutrality is subject to a further difficulty: even given an agreement to bracket controversial moral and religious issues for the sake of social cooperation, what counts as bracketing may be controversial; and this controversy may require for its solution either a substantive evaluation of the interests at stake or the autonomous conception of agency that minimalist liberalism resolves to avoid. *Thornburgh v. American College of Obstetricians & Gynecologists,*[65] a 1986 abortion case upholding *Roe*, offers an example of this difficulty.

Writing in dissent, Justice White urged the Court in *Thornburgh* to overrule *Roe v. Wade* and "return the issue to the people."[66] He agreed that abortion was a controversial moral issue but argued that the best way for the Court to bracket this controversy was to let each state decide the question for itself. He proposed, in effect, to bracket the intractable controversy over abortion as Stephen Douglas proposed to bracket the intractable controversy over slavery, by refusing to impose a single answer on the country as a whole. "Abortion is a hotly contested moral and political issue," White wrote. "Such issues, in our society, are to be resolved by the will of the people, either as expressed through legislation or through the general principles they have already incorporated into the Constitution they have adopted."[67] For the Court to do otherwise is not to be neutral but to "impose its own controversial choices of value upon the people."[68]

Justice Stevens responded to White by arguing for a different way of bracketing. Given the controversial moral issues at stake, he urged that individual women, not legislatures, should decide the question for themselves. For the Court to insist that women be free to choose for themselves is not to impose the Court's values but simply to prevent local majorities from imposing their values on individuals. "No individual should be compelled to surrender the freedom to make that decision for herself simply because her 'value preferences' are not shared by the majority."[69] For Stevens the basic question is not which theory of life is true but "whether the 'abortion decision' should be made by the individual or by the majority 'in the unrestrained imposition of its own, extraconstitutional value preferences.' "[70]

What is striking is that both ways of bracketing are in principle consistent with minimalist liberalism: the practical interest in social cooperation under conditions of disagreement about the good offers no grounds for choosing one over the other. Even given agreement to bracket an intractable moral or religious controversy for the sake of social cooperation, it may still be unclear what counts as bracketing. Moreover, resolving that question—deciding between White's position and Stevens's—requires either a substantive view about the moral and religious interests at stake or an autonomous conception of the person such as the voluntarist view affirms. Both solutions, however,

would deny minimalist liberalism its minimalism; each would impli-
cate its putatively political conception of justice in precisely the moral
and philosophical commitments that it seeks to avoid.

### The Voluntarist Case for
### Toleration: Homosexuality

The dissenters' argument for toleration in *Bowers v. Hardwick*[71] illustrates the difficulties with the version of liberalism that ties toleration
to autonomy rights alone. In refusing to extend the right of privacy to
homosexuals, the majority in *Bowers* declared that none of the rights
announced in earlier privacy cases resembled the rights that homosexuals were seeking: "No connection between family, marriage, or procreation on the one hand and homosexual activity on the other has
been demonstrated."[72] Any reply to the Court's position would have
to show some connection between the practices already subject to
privacy protection and the homosexual practices not yet protected.
What then is the resemblance between heterosexual intimacies, on the
one hand, and homosexual intimacies, on the other, such that both are
entitled to a constitutional right of privacy?

This question might be answered in at least two different ways, one
voluntarist, the other substantive. The first argues from the autonomy
that the practices reflect, whereas the second appeals to the human
goods that the practices realize. The voluntarist answer holds that
people should be free to choose their intimate associations for themselves, regardless of the virtue or popularity of the practices they
choose so long as they do not harm others. In this view, homosexual
relationships resemble the heterosexual relationships that the Court
has already protected in that all reflect the choices of autonomous
selves.

By contrast, the substantive answer claims that much that is valuable in conventional marriage is also present in homosexual unions. In
this view, the connection between heterosexual and homosexual relations is not that both result from individual choice but that both realize
important human goods. Rather than rely on autonomy alone, this
second line of reply articulates the virtues that homosexual intimacy
may share with heterosexual intimacy, along with any distinctive virtues of its own. It defends homosexual privacy the way *Griswold*
defended marital privacy, by arguing that, like marriage, homosexual

union may also be "intimate to the degree of being sacred . . . a harmony in living . . . a bilateral loyalty," an association for a "noble . . . purpose."[73]

Of these two possible replies, the dissenters in *Bowers* relied wholly on the first. Rather than protect homosexual intimacies for the human goods they share with intimacies the Court already protects, Justice Blackmun cast the Court's earlier cases in individualist terms and found their reading applied equally to homosexuality because "much of the richness of a relationship will come from the freedom an individual has to choose the form and nature of these intensely personal bonds."[74] At issue was not homosexuality as such but respect for the fact that "different individuals will make different choices" in deciding how to conduct their lives.[75]

Justice Stevens, in a separate dissent, also avoided referring to the values that homosexual intimacy may share with heterosexual love. Instead, he wrote broadly of "the individual's right to make certain unusually important decisions" and "respect for the dignity of individual choice,"[76] rejecting the notion that such liberty belongs to heterosexuals alone. "From the standpoint of the individual, the homosexual and the heterosexual have the same interest in deciding how he will live his own life, and, more narrowly, how he will conduct himself in his personal and voluntary associations with his companions."[77]

The voluntarist argument so dominates the *Bowers* dissents that it seems difficult to imagine a judicial rendering of the substantive view. But a glimmer of this view can be found in the appeals court opinion in the same case.[78] The United States Court of Appeals had ruled in Hardwick's favor and had struck down the law under which he was convicted. Like Blackmun and Stevens, the appeals court constructed an analogy between privacy in marriage and privacy in homosexual relations. But unlike the Supreme Court dissenters, it did not rest the analogy on voluntarist grounds alone. It argued instead that both practices may realize important human goods.

The marital relationship is significant, wrote the court of appeals, not only because of its procreative purpose but also "because of the unsurpassed opportunity for mutual support and self-expression that it provides."[79] It recalled the Supreme Court's observation in *Griswold* that "marriage is a coming together for better or for worse, hopefully enduring, and intimate to the degree of being sacred."[80] And it went on to suggest that the qualities the Court so prized in *Griswold* could be present in homosexual unions as well: "For some, the sexual activity in question here serves the same purpose as the intimacy of marriage."[81]

Ironically, this way of extending privacy rights to homosexuals depends on an old-fashioned reading of *Griswold* as protecting the human goods realized in marriage, a reading the Court has long since renounced in favor of an individualist reading.[82] By drawing on the teleological dimension of *Griswold*, the substantive case for homosexual privacy offends the liberalism that insists on neutrality. It grounds the right of privacy on the good of the practice it would protect, and so fails to be neutral among conceptions of the good.

The more frequently employed precedent for homosexual rights is not *Griswold* but *Stanley v. Georgia*,[83] which upheld the right to possess obscene materials in the privacy of one's home. *Stanley* did not hold that the obscene films found in the defendant's bedroom served a "noble purpose," only that he had a right to view them in private. The toleration that *Stanley* defended was wholly independent of the value or importance of the thing being tolerated.[84]

In the 1980 case of *People v. Onofre*,[85] the New York Court of Appeals vindicated privacy rights for homosexuals on precisely these grounds. The court reasoned that if, following *Stanley*, there is a right to the "satisfaction of sexual desires by resort to material condemned as obscene," there should also be a right "to seek sexual gratification from what at least once was commonly regarded as 'deviant' conduct," so long as it is private and consensual.[86] The court emphasized its neutrality toward the conduct it protected: "We express no view as to any theological, moral or psychological evaluation of consensual sodomy. These are aspects of the issue on which informed, competent authorities and individuals may and do differ."[87] The court's role was simply to ensure that the state bracketed these competing moral views, rather than embodying any one of them in law.[88]

The case for toleration that brackets the morality of homosexuality has a powerful appeal. In the face of deep disagreement about values, it seems to ask the least of the contending parties. It offers social peace and respect for rights without the need for moral conversion. Those who view sodomy as sin need not be persuaded to change their minds, only to tolerate those who practice it in private. By insisting only that each respect the freedom of others to live the lives they choose, this toleration promises a basis for political agreement that does not await shared conceptions of morality.

Despite its promise, however, the neutral case for toleration is subject to two related difficulties. First, as a practical matter, it is by no means clear that social cooperation can be secured on the strength of autonomy rights alone, absent some measure of agreement on the moral permissibility of the practices at issue. It may not be accidental that the first practices subject to the right of privacy were accorded constitutional protection in cases that spoke of the sanctity of marriage and procreation. Only later did the Court abstract privacy rights from these practices and protect them without reference to the human goods they were once thought to make possible. This suggests that the voluntarist justification of privacy rights is dependent—politically as well as philosophically—on some measure of agreement that the practices protected are morally permissible.

A second difficulty with the voluntarist case for toleration concerns the quality of respect it secures. As the New York case suggests, the analogy with *Stanley* tolerates homosexuality at the price of demeaning it; it puts homosexual intimacy on a par with obscenity: a base thing which should nonetheless be tolerated so long as it takes place in private. If *Stanley* rather than *Griswold* is the relevant analogy, the interest at stake is bound to be reduced, as the New York court reduced it, to "sexual gratification." (The only intimate relationship at stake in *Stanley* was between a man and his pornography.)

The majority in *Bowers* exploited this assumption by ridiculing the notion of a "fundamental right to engage in homosexual sodomy."[89] The obvious reply is that *Bowers* is no more about a right to homosexual sodomy than *Griswold* was about a right to heterosexual intercourse. But by refusing to articulate the human goods that homosexual intimacy may share with heterosexual unions, the voluntarist case for toleration forfeits the analogy with *Griswold* and makes the ridicule difficult to refute.

The problem with the neutral case for toleration is the opposite side of its appeal; it leaves wholly unchallenged the adverse views of homosexuality itself. Unless those views can be plausibly addressed, even a Court ruling in their favor is unlikely to win for homosexuals more than a thin and fragile toleration. A fuller respect would require, if not admiration, at least some appreciation of the lives that homosexuals live. Such appreciation, however, is unlikely to be cultivated by a legal and political discourse conducted in terms of autonomy rights alone.

The liberal may reply that autonomy arguments in court need not foreclose more substantive, affirmative arguments elsewhere; bracketing moral argument for constitutional purposes does not mean bracketing moral argument altogether. Once their freedom of choice in sexual practice is secured, homosexuals can seek, by argument and example, to win from their fellow citizens a deeper respect than autonomy can supply.

The liberal reply, however, underestimates the extent to which constitutional discourse has come to constitute the terms of political discourse in American public life. While most at home in constitutional law, the main motifs of contemporary liberalism—rights as trumps, the neutral state, and the unencumbered self—figure with increasing prominence in our moral and political culture. Assumptions drawn from constitutional discourse increasingly set the terms of political debate in general.

## Conclusion

Admittedly, the tendency to bracket substantive moral questions makes it difficult to argue for toleration in the language of the good. Defining privacy rights by defending the practices that privacy protects seems either reckless or quaint; reckless because it rests so much on moral argument, quaint because it recalls the traditional view that ties the case for privacy to the merits of the conduct that privacy protects. But as the abortion and sodomy cases illustrate, the attempt to bracket moral questions faces difficulties of its own. They suggest the truth in the naive view, that the justice or injustice of laws against abortion and homosexual sodomy may have something to do with the morality or immorality of these practices after all.

## 4

*ROBERT BOOTH*
*FOWLER*

# Community

*Reflections on*

*Definition*

N o single version of community dominates present-day discussion, and my own work delineating some of these understandings of community has recognized the diversity and disagreement that exists. I argue that community in American political thought at present engages three kinds of community: (1) communities of ideas: for example, the participatory democratic and republican models, (2) communities of crisis: for example, the earth community born of the environmental crisis, and (3) communities of memory: for example, religious and traditional ideas of community.[1]

These categories are not exhaustive of contemporary intellectual views. Yet they include principal conceptions of community today and suggest how far from consensus we are on what community means.[2]

## Communities of Ideas

If we step into the contemporary intellectual debates over community, we encounter immediately, and perhaps too often, the ideals of participatory community and republican community. Their respective proponents dominate much of the professional political theory devoted to community in our time. There is no single version of participatory community as community, but its advocates emphasize the importance of people deciding together, face to face, conversing with, and respecting each other in a setting which is as equal as possible. As Benjamin Barber says, "at the heart of strong democracy is talk" that animates what is a "process of ongoing, proximate self-legislation and the creation of political community."[3]

Proponents believe that participatory community will encourage both greater individual self-confidence and public-spiritedness through increased communal unity and satisfaction.[4] There is little doubt that they have a high view of what humans in participatory circumstances can learn to do. For them, people have great unrealized capacity to think, to be informed, to debate, and to learn from discussion. They want to be more than selfish individuals and to join a public community. What they need is an opportunity.

A second conception of community which has had a major run in our time is republicanism. J. G. A. Pocock has been the most influential discoverer (or inventor, if you will) of the tradition, but many have followed in his wake.[5] While republican community comes in an array of hues, several features are common: republicans are noted for their support of public-regarding virtues among citizens roughly equal in their political and socioeconomic situations. They generally hold that public-spiritedness and public community have the potential to operate through a whole country and thus are not necessarily limited to the small, participatory community.[6]

Controversy swirls around every aspect of the republican image of community. There is argument over how republican the United States ever was. Did this vision of community dominate late colonial intellectual—or popular—opinion? If so, for how long?[7] Equally controversial is the nature of this model of community. How serious are its current advocates in their defense of public freedoms given their republicanism—with its stress on shared virtue and common law—and what are its possibilities for human tyranny?[8]

### Communities of Public Crisis

If we look directly at the public world around us and at intellectual perceptions that focus on grave crises that seem immanent, other images of community and public life arise. They are conceptions of community fashioned by the times more than by intellectual ideas, and the attention they receive is not necessarily a statement of approval.

An obvious case in point is the growing sign of "tribal communities" in the contemporary world—and in the United States in particular—that have drawn the attention of those concerned with community. Some analyses of the rise of communities based on nationalism, ethnicity, race, or other tribal concepts are provocative and fascinating.[9] But rarely are they sympathetic to this powerful version of public community. This resistance makes good sense to many American intellectuals today who observe with dismay the tide of ethnic, religious, national, or racial tribes or communities who wage wars for power, or for self-identity. No form of community is less open than these ethnic or racial ones; none is more insistent on its truth; none can be harsher to those who dissent—or do not belong to the tribe. The ugly reality of tyranny often hangs in this thin air.

Perhaps even more important as an idea of community and crisis is the concern for community within environmentalism today. Environmentalism is about achieving an earth community, and this can be obscured by the common avoidance of environmentalist thought in the insular academic worlds of political theory and philosophy.[10] Nonetheless, the ecosystem or global metaphor is already routine in our public discourse, and environmentalism is strongly committed to making it the dominant metaphor of public life.[11]

The spur for this use of community is the crisis of survival of the earth in our time. Again and again environmentalist literature warns of this crisis and demands that we adopt a global perspective which reflects the reality of nature's ecosystem. The public varieties of ecological community are many: some proponents stress world government, others advocate federations, still others seek cooperative participatory communities, and some stand by a drastically revised nation-state system. Whatever the form, the goal is public community among the world's peoples and with all nature.[12]

## Communities of Memory

Lingering behind the theoretical or crisis-driven considerations of public community are powerful conceptions of communities of memory. By communities of memory I mean current ideas of community that derive from long-established belief systems that link the present and the past, communities fashioned, above all, from tradition and religion. Advocates of communities of memory often see their ideal as something once embodied in history. To them, communities of memory are far more than the apple of intellectuals' eyes or the jerry-built conceptions of crisis-obsessed policy makers.

Traditionalists of all sorts have had hard going in our mostly liberal culture. Leo Strauss and some of his students, above all Allan Bloom, have developed a highly intellectual community of memory based on a certain reading of the political ideas developed in ancient Athens by Aristotle and Plato. Thus, while they have attacked the disrespect for tradition in our culture, they have been, perhaps ironically, deeply ambivalent about our particular traditions. We offer little commitment to the search for absolute truth and scarcely honor the wise who seek that which their classical tradition celebrates.[13]

For Bloom the neglect of tradition in the United States constitutes a sad story. It guarantees continued great difficulties in nurturing community: "America is experienced not as a common project but as a framework within which people are only individuals."[14] But our country, according to Bloom, may not be hopeless. Liberalism may not be ideal, but it is a good deal better than the failed tradition represented by Marxism, he says. We are "built on low but solid ground."[15]

But even this consolation is slipping away, as Bloom sees it, as the family fails in the United States. For Bloom, and indeed for a good many others, the greatest problem of community in the United States is the disintegrating family.[16] It no longer carries even the thin tradition of our thin culture. Its decline suggests that renewed community will be terribly difficult to achieve. At its best, the family is the essential community of memory, and yet today it provides fewer and fewer people with a stable, happy childhood. As family degenerates into a world of conflict, divorce, and often outright chaos, who can expect any commitment to community in public life or elsewhere?

While some might welcome the fall of the sometimes tyrannical family or tradition, other possibilities for tyranny may simultaneously be enhanced. Given a world where personal communities are few, the opportunities for the tyranny of the mob, the bully, elites, criminals—and governmental responses to each—surely can grow. Those who properly fear the tyrannical possibilities of community also need to fear the tyrannical dangers of the desiccation of community.

The strength of religion in our culture continues to confound students of the classic nineteenth-century sociologists such as Max Weber or Karl Marx. Religion is often associated with the concept of community that has been basic in almost all religions.[17] Religion and religious organizations often represent communities of memory today, but fortunately for them, they are not in the fatal position of being only communities of memory. They frequently demonstrate organizational and doctrinal flexibility.[18]

Religious communities today come in many forms; some are participatory and some are hierarchical; some are institutional and some are loosely bounded; some are comfortable in association with the state, and some are at war with the state; many skate uneasily between government and other social institutions of culture and their own ideals. Some focus on churches or denominations, others on small, more informal groupings, while still others see religious community within a national or international context.

What the many proponents of religious community in American life—people such as Robert Bellah, Stanley Hauerwas, Richard Neuhaus, or Rosemary Radford Ruether—share is twofold. They support religiously informed community(-ities) as an expression of their basic religious faith: a community in creation under God. They also share their sense that community in the United States is in deep trouble today and that a revival of religious community in our damaged and vulnerable culture could help reverse the trend away from community building.[19]

While there is rarely any assumption that enhanced religious community will be a path to perfection,[20] the feeling that its strengthening will help revive national public community rests on the assumption that religion celebrates community and challenges in principle the individualistic, not to say disintegrative, sides of American life.

How to turn this impulse toward religious community into practice is not obvious, though if there is a model today, it is working from the bottom up, from the local level, from the small community forward. It has not proved easy when tried, but few religious writers about community find that surprising. They uniformly see community as a hard and rough path.[21]

## Toward Definition, the Issue of
## Tyranny, and Another View

My argument is that what community means in contemporary intellectual life in the United States is twofold. It is sharing in the public realm that is at least partly affective in nature. But it is also the forms and examples of that sharing; it is about how community is modeled, about the examples that contemporary intellectuals advance and argue about.

Critics of contemporary understandings of community continue to fault much community talk as impractical, often sunk in irrelevant nostalgia, and disappointingly antipolitical.[22] Above all, there remains the question of how freedom and diversity can fit together with community. Pleasant reassurances on this matter are, of course, worthless and may compound the danger by ignoring it. How to constitute a public community and ensure that tyranny does not overwhelm it remains an important question.

To guard against tyranny, the current chastened mood of much community thinking must continue, and the prospects look good. Michael Walzer's conception of community, restrained, pluralistic, and hostile to even a hint of tyranny, is widely and rightly admired.[23] Others wisely warn of the danger of conceiving community in terms of direct face-to-face relations among people with no protective barriers between them; or of community as uninhibited personal expressiveness with no form and no rules; or of community when advanced without a sense of its mixed historical record and the folly of thinking about perfection in regard to community.[24]

The chastened mood is not always the reality, for romance and nostalgia still weave strong threads through many discussions of community. Yet there are indications that nostalgia is on the wane; the glow is off republicanism as the distance back to republican moments in American history looks long; the traditions of the American or Greek pasts do not seem likely to be revived; and participatory democrats increasingly realize that the 1960s have passed.

A second step for celebrants of community must be the acceptance of the legitimacy of politics and all the messy disagreements that are intrinsic to politics and political freedom. Community cannot be defined in theory or in practice as public consensus or the absence of disputes. If it is, then we may suspect that community has become a substitute for politics, and tyranny may indeed lie right around the corner.

How to institutionalize a public community which is chastened in its expectations and accepting of politics is not obvious, but it is essential. Casual clichés about the need for checking institutions are not enough, as James Madison knew long ago.[25] In the end there is no sure protection from tyranny in any publicly constituted community, no matter how noble its forms or how sensible its rhetoric. My counsel is to continue exploring what structures and attitudes may help, but community must always be approached, advanced, and limited by what I call *existential watchfulness*.

Existential watchfulness welcomes community's potential joys but insists that any community is fraught with paradox, including the paradox that it can end—and has ended—in tyranny. From this perspective, community is an aspiration, one to be nourished, but not an ideal likely to be fully realized, since we are "not capable of community—not, at least, in any full and stable form."[26] Nor is community an ideal whose goods are guaranteed to be unmixed. Community will vary in theory and practice in every setting, and so will our efforts toward community. In the end what will matter is not whether somehow a community is achieved, but whether human sharing advances and does so unsullied by lost creativity and abandoned freedoms.[27] Existential watchfulness is commitment to the quest for community and to vigilance, determined not to grasp for community as an "all-consuming public spirit such as ancient Greek citizenship or revolutionary republicanism with its Jacobin fervor."[28]

What will count above all is character, the development of character or, as other ages said, virtue. Knowingly or not, the model is at the end of book 9 of Plato's *Republic*. There Plato articulates the view that his polis (community) can be built in the human soul. Its achievement anywhere else is welcome but not to be expected.[29]

From such a perspective there are no guarantees, and those who offer them are enemies, not friends, of community. Thus, there must be caution toward some proclaimed friends of community, especially those still beguiled in an enduring and embarrassing "unrealistic optimism" about achieving community.[30] Such a view is both groundless and dangerous. It can turn community into a sort of construction project, something to be achieved by a certain date, as if community could ever be finished. In the process it can paint ordinary politics as a lower form of life, an impediment to the triumph of public community, or even lead to the fatal suggestion that no cost is too great to attain community.

Dubious friends also include those who share the interest of many contemporary community supporters in identity but, like Iris Marion Young, turn it to reductionist directions in which group identities and communities overwhelm all else. In such worlds the self literally disappears, and tyranny looms, the precise nightmare feared by an existentialist perspective on community.[31] The search for a public community is not about how to realize a dream but rather a restless and endless exploration of a worthy but elusive reality. In the process we may reach toward community, but only if we simultaneously step back from its potential for tyranny.

# HUMAN NATURE,

# SOCIAL THEORY, AND

# THE MORAL DIMENSION

# 5 JEAN BETHKE ELSHTAIN

# The Communitarian

# Individual

**W**e are a society riven by conflict. Our terms of political debate all too often rigidify rather than clarify that conflict. One example is the pitched battle between those called (or labeled) "individualists" and those called (or labeled) "communitarians." At times each side traffics in fearsome and ill-humored characterizations of the positions of those on the wrong side of the conceptual and rhetorical divide. As with most stereotypical formulations, there is always some truth to the matter. Individualists, no doubt, are right to see constraints against "rights talk" lurking in the communitarian positions. Communitarians, no doubt, are right to see one-sided antipathy toward anything that smacks of tradition and appeals to duty or obligation in ultra-liberal panegyrics. For the purpose of this essay, such positioning of each side in relation to the other is rather beside the point. What I propose to do is to sketch a picture of the communitarian individual, stressing both the communitarian and the individual registers in this complex composite.

Three books—one a sociological and ethical ethnography of inter-familial relations, the second a text in moral philosophy, and the third a powerful and rather frightening novel—help me to situate my argument. I begin with the novel *The Children of Men* by P. D. James.[1] The novel is set in Britain in the year 2021. No children have been born—none at all—on planet Earth since the year l995. In that year, for reasons no one understands, all males became infertile. The world, quite literally, is dying. People are despondent, chagrined, violent. "Western science had been our god," writes the protagonist, Theodore Faron, an Oxford historian and a cousin to the dictator of Great Britain. He "shares the disillusionment" of one whose god has died. Now overtaken by a "universal negativism," the human race lurches toward its certain demise. Because there will be no future, "all pleasures of the mind and senses sometimes seem . . . no more than pathetic and crumbling defences shored up against our ruins." Children's playgrounds are dismantled. People disown commitments and responsibilities for one another save for whatever serves some immediate purpose: what is chosen by contrast to what is given. A cult of pseudo-births emerges as women take broken dolls and even baby kittens to be baptized in pseudo-ceremonies.

People thought they had eliminated evil, Faron notes, and all churches in the 1990s "moved from the theology of sin and redemption" to a "sentimental humanism." In the name of compassion, the elderly, no longer needed or wanted, are conducted to a ceremony (state sponsored, of course) of group suicide called the Quietus. Faron concludes that we are "diminished," we humans, if we live without knowledge of the past and without hope of the future. The old prayer "That I may see my children's children and peace upon Israel" is no more, and without the possibility of that prayer and the delicate imbrication of all our lives with such fructifying possibility, the world, quite literally, ceases to be. For in a world with no future, a world barren and forlorn, a world in which birth has ceased and death is managed and staged, "the very words 'justice,' 'compassion,' 'society,' 'struggle,' 'evil,' would be unheard echoes on an empty air." To be sure, we can "experience nothing but the present moment," but our understanding of that moment is profoundly shaped and given meaning by our ability to "reach back through the centuries for the reassurance of our ancestry." This rich ancestry, for individuals and entire cultures, in turn loses its meaning "without the hope of posterity . . . without the assurance that we being dead yet live." For whom do we build? In whose behalf do we dream? All our generative urges and the compassion and care this generates, at least some of the time, has no point if we are merely spinning our wheels until the end. The past, then, takes on shimmering vitality and importance only insofar as it is connected through the present to the future. This is something the communitarian individual recognizes and to which she gives explicit articulation.

The text in moral philosophy is Mary Midgley's *Can't We Make Moral Judgements?*[2] Midgley, a feisty and fascinating moral philosopher, takes on the Kantians, with their strenuous and categorical universalisms, the simpler sorts of utilitarians, and the even simpler relativists with their blithe endorsements of "whatever works" or "whatever you say." She eschews both harsh judgmentalism and nonjudgmental platitudes proffered in the name of "tolerance." How odd, she notes, that we have come to such a sorry pass in our civic life that we are even enjoined not to make anyone "uncomfortable" with our arguments and our claims. We seek "value clarification" without values, an incoherent enterprise to say the very least. Dogmatic skepticism is as indefensible as dogmatic certainty. Freedom matters, she insists, but so does knowledge, and if we engage in serious thinking about modern society and its many discontents, we come to understand that freedom can neither matter nor be defended if we disarticulate its endorsement from a wider social surround, a tangled web of "ways of relating to those around us."

We do interfere, all the time, in the affairs of one another. We cannot consistently be solipsists or hyperindividualists. The question is how we mark that which is yours and that which is mine and that which we share between us, the very sharing of which alone helps us to sort out the public and private dimensions to our lives and the life of our society. Society, contra J. S. Mill, is not a giant personification of a separate entity, "standing over against all individuals and actively oppressing them."

This way of talking gives a peculiar horror to the notion of conventionality, since it portrays conventional people not as making their own mistakes but as being zombified, possessed by an alien demon which has taken over their consciences and is now directing them, using them as its mere puppets or automata. That is the sense in which they lose inner freedom. This is silly, Midgley claims, and leads to a great deal of "humbug" along the lines of "blaming Society" rather than taking or accepting responsibility. For freedom and social continuity, individual integrity and social decency go together, not in some happy harmony but in a necessary, mutually constitutive relationship. This is something the communitarian individual recognizes and to which she gives explicit articulation.

Third, and finally, the ethical ethnography on what I called, in a lapse into sociologese, "interfamilial relations." Better, suggest Arthur Kornhaber and Kenneth L. Woodward, in *Grandparents/Grandchildren*, to be concrete and specific, acknowledging those many connections we do not choose but which, instead, may be said to have "chosen" us.[3] The story the authors tell is gripping, alternately tender and dismal. They point out that every time a child is born, a grandparent comes into being. Their book is "about the emotional attachments between grandparents and grandchildren. More precisely, it is about the loss of these attachments and the effects of this loss on children, on older people and, to a more limited extent, on the generation in between." Children, no dummies, know that they are grandchildren. Grandparents, similarly astute, know they are grandparents. How does our society help or hinder, sustain or sever, this "vital connection"? For in the long view of history, cutting the connection between grandparents and grandchildren is a relatively recent event. Perhaps that is progress. Perhaps it represents a salutary advance in individual freedom. Perhaps kids, especially, are better off if they don't have to negotiate lots of complex, intense relationships.

Not so, claim our authors, and they empty a bushel basketful of evidence on the table drawn from in-depth interviews from three different groups of grandparents and grandchildren: those with close contact, those with sporadic contact, and those with no contact. These groups encompassed three hundred grandchildren/grandparent pairings. In the grandchildren with sporadic or no contact, they found a sense of "loss, deprivation, abandonment." Children in these two groups were more likely to express bitterness and cynicism about old people in general. The grandchildren with no contact were especially troubled and troubling. "All we found," they write, "was a wound where, the children felt, a grandparent ought to be." Such children drew grandparents as shadowy figures or ugly caricatures. These children did represent a grandparent, but as a malign, wizened, and untrustworthy "old person." Not a happy situation.

By contrast, the grandchildren with close contact with grandparents told a variety of very specific, concrete stories about their particular grandparents. They, unlike the no-contact group, could in fact muster a sense of a future as older people; they had some inkling of a life cycle. For the children who had known grandparents well and lost them through death, "their grandparents lived on as constant objects, fixed forever as large and compelling, almost 'heroic' figures in their minds." Of course, many of these grandchildren did some complaining about a grandparent's eccentricities, but they were quite specific complaints about a quite specific individual being, not hazy images of disgusting old people. Alas, our authors continue, the pressures of contemporary American culture encourage grandparents to sever ties with grandchildren, whether voluntarily and in the name of not interfering with their children's lives or involuntarily and often bitterly when their child divorces his or her mate and the grandchildren are taken away. The current social contract mandates detachment; old and young alike pay the price. This is something the communitarian individual recognizes and to which she gives explicit articulation.

What form do this recognition and this articulation take? What sort of individual gives voice to, and lives within a frame of, communitarian imperatives: imperatives that are less than dogmatic rules but more, much more, than sentimental puffery. Here is the way I would parse the matter with our three texts behind us but kept in mind. First, I would distinguish between the ultraliberal world of our contemporary social contract by contrast to the chastened and tempered liberalism of a world framed by a social compact. I begin with the individualist social contract of the sort implicated in the nightmarish scenario of James's futuristic novel, the inadequate ethics of Midgley's utilitarian and relativist protagonists, and the real human costs of radical disconnection in Kornhaber and Woodward's worlds of grandparents and grandchildren.

The contract model has its historical roots in seventeenth-century social contract theory, and it incorporates a vision of society as constituted by individuals for the fulfillment of individual ends. The central feature of this tradition is the primacy of rights even as one denies any similar status to principles of belonging or obligation. Primacy-of-rights theory has been one of the most important formative influences on the political consciousness of the West; indeed, we are so immured in the world this notion has wrought that most of us most of the time grant individual rights prima facie force. Lurking behind rights talk is a view of humans as self-sufficient choosers whose good lies in the concatenation of rationalistic choices. There was much that was liberating in classical liberalism, including the notion of free individuals constructing new social forms. But this bracing vision of the free individual, antecedent to social conditions, is subject to particular forms of deformation and dissolution. Some have called this the notion of "possessive individualism." Whether one opts for that formulation or not, the crux of the matter is that individuals more and more see themselves as "owners" of their own person. Fused with market images, the terms under which individuals act in public get construed as wholly instrumental: as getting what one wants and translating that "want" into a "right."

Within a world of choice-making Robinson Crusoes, disconnected from essential ties with one another, any constraint on individual freedom is seen as a burden, most often an unacceptable one. For example, within the world of this social contract, the family does not fare very well. Liberal voluntarism and family, kin, and communal ties have never made for an easy mix. Even the world of children and childhood is redescribed in individualist terms, with a paternalistic bureaucracy lurking in the background to sustain and support "children's rights"! Women and children are to join ranks with an ideal of the sovereign male subject, for the ultraliberal can see in women's lingering links to birth and nurturing only the vestiges of our pre-enlightened history and origins. Briefly, then, the contractual frame exudes a politics of self-interest undertaken by a freely choosing, rational agent who, within the present order, is reborn as a sovereign consumer. In the world of this social contract, it is difficult to accommodate the family as something other than a "nonbinding commitment" (the modern oxymoron). No institution grounded in obligation or deep and often unchosen connection can be granted weightiness, hence the unbearable lightness of (contemporary) liberalism. For extreme liberalism would effect a break with all precontractual tradition.

I recognize, of course, that this ideal type, set up for heuristic purposes, is subject to much fine-tuning and counterclaiming. But it is a model felt in the bone and blood of real human beings, like those grandparents who see themselves as fulfilling the terms of this contract by getting out of their grandchildrens' lives or those truly luckless grandparents who are forced out precisely because the contract more readily sustains disconnection than connection if that connection puts pressure on the tacit terms of contractual understanding. People are more and more free but feel empty. There is a reason and it has nothing to do with an insufficiently raised individualist conscious-ness, it has to do with the fact that we human beings are not cut to the pattern the individualist social contract proffers, that of a wholly autonomous subject whose freedom lies solely in the voluntaristic choices she makes.

No, we are rather more complex than that. The alternative social compact ideal I will sketch recognizes that complexity and honors it. What images of the human self, what values and notions, does my alternative call forth? The issues at stake between the more rooted social and historical beings of the social compact and their contrac-tually understood opposites are serious and go very deep. Beings who see themselves primarily through the social compact idea do not find at all self-evident the atomistic starting point in primacy of rights and the making of choice an absolute. In contrast to the standpoint of extreme individualism, with its thin view of the self, the compact self is "thick," more particularly situated, a historical being who acknowl-edges that he or she has many debts and obligations and that one's history and the history of one's society frame one's own starting point. Chastening detachment and rights possession as primarily defining the self and moral life, the compact being—dare I say the "commu-nitarian individual"?—understands and believes that if she cuts her-self off from the past, she deforms present relationships. This, then, is a real-life story not unlike the scary tale P. D. James' tells of a future in which the present is utterly deformed and the past utterly irrelevant—to all persons, not just those who want children but cannot have them—in a world in which there are no more births, no more human possibilities, when nothing new is any longer a moment of yearning and hope. For the old and the new are intertwined, hopelessly, power-fully, and forever as long as any recognizably human society exists and persists.

My point is not a claim along the lines that the compact self is totally embedded within and defined by particular ties and identities; rather, she recognizes that without that beginning, there is no beginning at all. The world of the social compact is in tension with the rights-dominant surround, and it must be supple enough to provide for rebellion and dissent from within. Tradition is not of a piece. The past presents itself as the living embodiment of vital conflicts. Rebellion against one's particular place is one way to forge an identity with reference to that place. But there is little space in the compact frame for rebellion to take the form of an utter and remorseless severing of social ties and relations insofar as the individual thus chooses. The "thick" sociality of the social compact cannot be understood from the stand-point of contract theory. The compact ideal bears within it notions of what is good not reducible to functionalist or instrumental criteria. In the contract model, for example, women's traditional historical roles and identities are devalued. Within the social compact women's iden-tities as wives, mothers, community benefactors, and activists are not sealed off and shoved into a bin called "unchosen" and thus devalued.

Because I have constructed my prototypical communitarian indi-vidual as a woman, I will persist with this essay's preoccupation with familial and gendered understandings for a moment or two longer. The contract model leaves little space for those contributions of women that have been linked to the human life cycle, to the protection and nurturance of vulnerable human existence. In contractarian con-struals, women become individuals only when they, too, join ranks with the sovereign-self ideal. In the rights-absolutist climate of opin-ion, women are likely to be seen as victims or suckers if they fail to join the "separated" celebration with anything less than total enthusiasm. Interestingly, Kornhaber and Woodward found that the more grand-parents "describe their relationships with their grandchildren in terms of a contract," the more disconnected they become. Social compact grandparents used the language of mutuality, aid, a sense of "people-hood." Lurking just beneath the surface for contractarian grandpar-ents, especially for the grandmothers, was an uneasy sense that some-thing somehow wasn't quite right. They felt cheated, oddly bereft. The grandfathers sometimes talked bitterly about the emotional price they paid for their dutiful commitment to work, for that is what "men did for their families." Yet they couldn't see a way out of the terms of the contract, for they were central parties to it, often subjugating their own best feelings (and selves) to a notion that a "higher standard of living" and maximum freedom for all concerned meant they should get out of the way and let the young folks be "free."

Segregation by race is a well-known blot on the history of American society. Segregation by generation often goes unmarked, but it is striking, and unlike racial segregation it seems a part of, rather than in opposition to, the "American dream." Young and old alike are sacri-ficed when our tacit system of age segregation is upheld.

Any ongoing way of life must have in its number an important segment devoted to the protection and nurturance of vulnerable human beings, young and old. Historically, that was the mission of women. The pity is not that women embodied this ethic but that the public world of contractarian construals has so little use for such an ethic. It is also true that family and community were enormously constraining and burdensome for women in particular ways. It seems meet and right, therefore, to insist here that the compact family ideal can no longer be one in which the work of care is exclusively "women's work" or is seen as such even when the men do it, as men have always done, by teaching their children crafts and skills, by encouraging their achievement, by providing for them. Neither this male contribution nor, certainly, that of women can be understood and appreciated in all its complexity within a contract frame.

By contrast, the compact ideal is built up on such recognitions. The contemporary compact ideal—the home, so to speak, of the communitarian individual—is not comprised of do-gooders who sentimentalize the old ways. In modernity there can be no assent, without ambivalence, to a single scheme of things. We are all marked by the moral conflicts of our age. "My body, myself" is a necessary corrective when communities overwhelm the individual and stifle the self. That slogan (one, alas, that has grown banal from overuse) expressed an important truth about embodied dignity and the fact that there is a deep indignity at work if the individual has little say over what uses her body is to be put to. Surely the most fundamental right of all, one each individual shaped by the history and traditions of the West, including the legacy of liberalism, must respect, is freedom from bondage. That freedom begins with my right to embodied dignity. But to move from the solemnity of that recognition to an obsession with an utterly untrammeled self requires that more and more areas of social life be subjected to decisions along the lines of a narrowly construed "policy science" even as families and the remnants of communities are compelled to fall in line or struggle mightily not to succumb entirely to the terms of the social contract. In the world of the social compact, human beings are ends in themselves, not means, and no one is in a position to assign value to the human life of another, for that value is a given.

I know, of course, what the next question will be: do any communities approximate this vision of the social compact? The answer is not a simple one, no more than the question. There are pieces of such communities in small-town, rural, and urban America, in communities where people struggle to preserve their way of life against forces of dissolution. Often, religious communities aim explicitly to counter ultraindividualism and provide an institutional framework which nourishes alternatives. Harry Boyte, a populist, writes that "American history and tradition, like that of any nation, embodies contradictions between rapaciously individualist, democratic, and authoritarian elements. To reclaim the best in America's traditions and history is to rediscover the popular democratic heritage: our nation's civic idealism, our practices of mutual aid and self-help, our religious wellsprings of social justice."[4] What political theorist Sheldon Wolin has called "rejectionism" pervades our society. This is a form of rebellion which defies the terms of the wider social contract. We see such rejectionism in communities organized in the name of their common good against toxic waste or better schools or less violence and drugs or decent housing. The social compact inspiring such movements is local, bounded, grassroots; it is a community, not a state, and its ethos is preserving, not acquiring. Instead, they are organized to defend and sustain what remains of a way of life not permeated utterly by, and defined exclusively in, individualist or contractual terms.

I wish to convey the image of human relations that stand in opposition to the full sway of contractualism; of individuals who acknowledge and accept that they are social beings of a particular kind; of selves who commit themselves to responsibility for the future, either through rearing their own children or through other generative activities that link them to past and future beings and possibilities. Ties of family, friendship, and community constitute us and situate us as historical beings. But a communitarian politics requires something additional: entering the fray, engaging others, often those who hold a contractual view of things and who find other notions noxious or inexplicable. Let me reiterate that the communitarian individual is very much an individual. She is an individual who does not stand as an isolate but as a being emerging out of a dense social ground. She acknowledges that ground, with its rough edges and ill-defined boundaries, its ties that bind, its hold that paradoxically releases us into a wider world.

Nothing I have said, or argued, will convince a hard-nosed "power realist" or a committed ultraliberal whose hackles are raised by the mere suggestion of ties and tradition, of kith and kin, of communities and character. For if one's view of society and self commits one to the image of a world infused by power relations that can be curbed only by counterforce, my social compact will look like the concoction—or confection—of a starry-eyed optimist. I can only insist that this image does make contact with personal and political realities, as my own interviews with those I call "political mothers" makes clear to me over and over again.[5] What I hear repeated—in Argentina, in the Czech Republic, in Jerusalem, in Ramallah, in Booth Bay Harbor, Maine, in Chicago, in Nashville, in Los Angeles—is a steely determination to fight the forces of disintegration in the name of principles of loyalty, mutuality, concern, justice, in the name of all children, past, present, future. A contractarian must make a muddle of this by attempting to redescribe what the mothers so eloquently describe in terms that rip and trim and cut and tear to fit the individualist pattern. But this will not do. The communitarian individual hears voices whose animating ethos is not reducible to self-interest or self-fulfillment or self-maximization or all the other things contractarian selves are in thrall to. No, she can only remain open to a vision of mutual respect and the uncommon, quiet heroism of so many ordinary people. Yes, this is something the communitarian individual recognizes and to which she gives explicit articulation.

# Personhood and Moral Obligation

## The Primacy of the Particular

The findings of modern social science confirm the need for a stabilizing center in human life. For such a center to exist, there must be psychic autonomy within a framework of bonding to other persons and to person-centered activities. Such a self is not free-floating: it emerges from and is sustained by specific personal relationships. Only in and through such bonds—only if there is an embedded self—will the center hold.

This rich but parochial bonding—this particularity of association and symbolism—is a striking feature of the human condition. But what is its moral worth? The question brings us to a persistent ambivalence in both moral theory and moral experience. This is revealed in the competition between two basic forms of altruism: particularism and universalism.

Particularism is *bounded altruism*. It is an ethic of commitment to individuals who matter because of the special connections they have, not because of their general characteristics, whether as humans, children, voters, or consumers. The "other" to be regarded, for whom self-sacrifice is appropriate, belongs to one's own family or community. A classic expression of particularism is nepotism, hiring or doing business with relatives, friends, or other in-group members in preference to outsiders. A religion is particularist insofar as it is committed to maintaining the distinctive identity of a sacred community or chosen people.

Universalism is *inclusive altruism*. In defining objects of moral concern, the special interests of persons and groups are set aside. An impersonal standpoint is adopted and raised to the status of a prime virtue. People are classified according to objective criteria, such as age, need, talent, or achievement, in the light of general policies or purposes, without considering the special claims of kinship or group affiliation. This is the morality of fairness, the familiar logic of the rule of law.

Bounded and inclusive altruism are both responses to biosocial imperatives and opportunities. In its beginnings neither is a product of self-conscious choice. People do what is satisfying and convenient in their circumstances. As a result, over many generations, each form of altruism contributes to the evolution of moral ordering.

Of the two, particularism is the more secure and the more primordial. Parents often abuse, abandon, and even kill their children, to say nothing of how they treat their siblings or more distant relatives. Nevertheless, the biological bond, in humans as in other mammals, is a dependable source of motivation. (Just who will be considered a close relative, or ignored as kin altogether, is a matter of social definition; but all kinship systems are keyed to biologial affinity.) However, particularism does not require biological bonding. Identification with an in-group is a powerful impulse readily accounted for by the psychic sustenance it offers and the social power it yields. It may be said, indeed, that particularism is overdetermined, the product of many parallel and convergent causes, any one of which might be sufficient to sustain a fairly high level of commitment to kin, locality, and primordial community.

Universalism is more precarious, and more distinctively human. The impersonal standpoint is an outgrowth of (1) the capacity to reason and (2) the experience of cooperation and reciprocity. The ability to reason creates demands (from one's self as well as from others) for consistency and justification.[1] These become salient features of human interaction. As a result, moral argument pervades everyday life. It is everywhere an important part of the symbolic order we call culture.

When people are pressed to justify a claim and cannot close the discussion by resort to violence or by terminating the relationship, they are likely to apppeal to comprehensive interests and shared expectations: "When they are wronged, people suddenly understand objective reasons, for they require such concepts to press their resentment. That is why the primary form of moral argument is a request to imagine oneself in the situation of another person."[2] Little is really known about the natural history of justification, but we know enough to say that in the normal course of interaction, people very often feel compelled to offer reasons that transcend or justify their private interests.

Particularism and universalism are usefully understood as polar contrasts, that is, as quite different and even incompatible ways of relating to oneself and others.[3] They define different moralities and perhaps different ways of life. Universalism fits well with achievement-centered values and with instrumental rather than expressive modes of thought and action. Particularism, on the other hand, is the characteristic ethos of a traditional society: what counts is who you are, not what you can do or what purpose you serve.

Nevertheless, the two moralities coexist as well as compete. That is so in part because universalism is a natural accompaniment of the formation of communities. As opportunities for cooperation are enlarged and their benefits perceived, altruism is no longer limited to a small band of close relatives. Particularism is diluted as the community expands. More and more people are recognized, first as fellow creatures and then as colleagues or members of the same in-group. In the modern nation-state the particularist connotations of *citizen*, though far from lost, are greatly attenuated. The experience of citizenship encourages larger perspectives and undercuts primordial ties of family, tribe, religion, and locality. Patriotism and nationalism remain, however, as benign and virulent expressions of the particularist impulse.

A mix of both perspectives is guaranteed by the ordinary demands of group life. The ethos of particularism may be paramount in the family and in many communal groups, but it can never wholly satisfy the psychic needs of members or the requirements of effective social organization. In the division of labor and allocation of resources, conceptions of fairness are bound to arise even where primary bonding is strong; criteria of merit and achievement are too useful to be dispensed with altogether; rules and principles are framed because people expect consistency and demand justifications.

The moral worth of universalism has long been appreciated. The transition from kinship to polis, from the "significant other" to the "generalized other," from the "we" of affinity to the "we" of humanity, all are expressions of a quest for community which looks outward rather than inward. A crucial step is the embrace of strangers. When strangers are treated with the respect due members of an enlarged community, a moral watershed is reached. Every source of estrangement, of being divided from another part of humanity, is alien to the outward-looking aspect of community.

Furthermore, universalism is indispensable to critical or reflective morality. Without objective criteria of judgment there can be no basis for assessing a received morality. Without an ethic which transcends the personal and the parochial—without detachment, without a regime of rules—even conventional morality cannot be justly applied to competing claims and special circumstances. Insofar as justice matters, an impersonal standpoint must prevail.

And yet, despite these strong claims, the impersonal standpoint is not and cannot be embraced wholeheartedly. Judgment in the light of rule and principle has serious limitations from a moral point of view. That is so, fundamentally, because rule-centered judgment does not adequately appreciate the place of concreteness and particularity in moral experience. This criticism has existentialist overtones, as we have seen, but many who are not existentialists have had the same insight.

"There is no general doctrine," wrote George Eliot in *Middlemarch*, "which is not capable of eating out our morality if unchecked by the deep-seated habit of direct fellow-feeling with individual fellow-men."[4] This comment was stimulated by the author's account of one man's effort to find, in the cunning of Providence, a godly justification for his worldly transgressions. The lesson is that impersonal precepts must be tempered and assessed in the light of very specific human outcomes.

A contemporary moral and legal philosopher makes a similar point:

> It is plain that those most likely to abandon their moral beliefs when these are shown to have a subjective source are those whose moral sentiments have been formulated apart from concrete situations and kinds of conduct, and have become focused on general principles and theories or on the divine will or on

whatever is taken to be a general authoritative source of all moral right and wrong. . . . Conversely, those whose moral education or self-education has not led them into this mode of moral thinking and who find their moral reasons at the ground-floor level of particular concrete situations are least likely to be disturbed by the revelation that their moral practices, and the feeling of constraint and necessity that accompanies them, are reflections of concerns which lie deep in their character.[5]

Here again an empirical argument—an appeal to experience—purports to show that morality anchored in concrete situations, and in character, has greater depth and durability than one that looks to general principles and theories. A morality based on abstract ideals, and on the arguments that support them, is vulnerable to the challenge of fresh insights, new arguments, and revised convictions. If there are no surer touchstones for belief and conduct, morality easily becomes a sometime thing, superficial and transitory, and may be readily used, in systematic ways, to justify evil in the name of the good.

Even in a system of justice, rules and principles are not ends in themselves; they do not have intrinsic worth. They are judged according to the contribution they make to *substantive justice*, which is the ultimate criterion. Substantive justice is concrete, not abstract. It is fairness made good for particular litigants, taking all their circumstances into account. It is the just outcome, not the fair procedure.

In legal reasoning the search for a principle—reaching beyond a specific rule to some more general formula—is neither an academic exercise nor mainly a quest for consistency. It has the practical aim of cutting through the rigidity of rules the better to take account of particularity and concreteness. We discover principles, in the first instance, by looking for the reason behind a rule. When we know the purposes or policies the rule is meant to serve—when we know why, for example, students are required to take a certain number of courses in science and the humanities, or why a building permit is required for a remodeling project—we have a basis for making rational adjustments and exceptions.

A well-known paradox calls attention to the fact that as a community we may care more about the suffering of a few persons whose fate we confront directly than about many thousands for whom we may be more distantly responsible:

People who would be horrified by the idea of stealing an elderly neighbor's welfare check have no qualms about cheating on their income tax; men who would never punch a child in the face can drop bombs on hundreds of children; our government—with our support—is more likely to spend millions of dollars attempting to rescue a trapped miner than it is to use the same amount to install traffic signals which would, over the years, save many more lives. Even Mother Teresa, whose work for the destitute of Calcutta seems to exemplify so universal a love for all, has described her love for others as love for each of a succession of individuals, rather than "love of mankind, merely as such."[6]

If rationality is understood as a sharply focused calculus of costs and benefits, or of equally regarded preferences, then the most rational approach would be, as Peter Singer suggests, "to save as many lives as possible, irrespective of whether we do it by reducing the road toll or by saving specific, identifiable lives; and we would be no readier to kill children from great heights than face to face."[7]

But morality based on reason need not accept this rationalist premise. A different criterion is the effect of our choices on the construction of moral character, individual as well as social. From that standpoint it makes sense to hold on to the concreteness of persons and "the directness of fellow feeling" rather than risk attenuating that feeling by transforming everyone into an abstract individual. An important moral distinction must be drawn between an impersonal crime, such as some forms of embezzlement, and the more personal assaults and intrusions of burglary and robbery, even though the former may have greater consequences for the lives of the people affected. Similarly, there is an important moral difference between a government's failure to install traffic signals, which might decrease injuries and deaths, and its failure to respond when specific people are in distress. The consequences of the policy decision may be remote, contingent, and in part bound up with the responsibility of individuals for their own safety; there may be justifiable trade-offs in the use of resources. But palpable distress is a direct challenge to commitment and character.[8]

It is tempting to say that universalism has the greater claim to moral worth because (1) it is so closely bound up with human rationality, which is the receptacle of so many hopes for betterment; and (2) because in principle it may draw the boundaries of moral equality wide enough to include all humans and potentially other animals as well. But universalism need not go beyond baseline protection of all who are included as objects of moral consideration. Taken alone, therefore, it may serve only as an ethical minimum, much as equal protection of the laws, itself an expression of universalism, defines minimum constitutional safeguards.

Being impartial has undoubted worth if only because it shows respect for interests not our own. But respect is not the whole of morality. As Ronald Dworkin and others have emphasized, there is also *concern* or *caring*, which presumes a desire to further the interests of others, to make them whole if need be, not merely to give them the consideration they deserve as moral equals. An impersonal standpoint may lead to moral probity but not necessarily to moral enrichment. Only a context of commitment, where the unique person[9] really matters, generates full concern for the well-being of others. The idea of morality is impoverished when it is reduced to disinterestedness.

The alternative is to recognize the moral primacy of love over justice, over rationality, over any other abstract or judgmental way of deciding and relating. In love the claims of particularity are paramount. One does not truly love others without caring for specific persons and for their own sake. That is so not only in ordinary human relations but in the more subtle and demanding ideal of "neighborly love":

> Christian love does not mean discovering the essentially human underneath differences; it means detecting the neighbor underneath friendliness or hostility or any other qualities in which the agent takes special interest. The full particularity of neighborly love . . . should not be reduced to universal brotherhood or the cosmopolitan spirit. This is stoicism, not Christianity. . . . Love for men in general often means merely a bifocal "self-regarding concern for others," a selfish sociability, while love for neighbor *for his own sake* insists upon a single-minded orientation . . . toward *this* individual neighbor with all his concrete needs. Christian love . . . begins by loving "the neighbor," not mankind or manhood.[10]

Thus understood, neighborly love cuts through abstractions, well-intended or otherwise, to discover and embrace the person as a vividly realized organic unity.

A poignant example is George Orwell's encounter with a Fascist soldier during the Spanish Civil War:

> Early one morning another man and I had gone out to snipe at the Fascists in the trenches outside Huesca. . . . At this moment, a man . . . jumped out of the trench and ran along the top of the parapet in full view. He was half-dressed and was holding up his trousers with both hands as he ran. I refrained from shooting him. It is true that I am a poor shot and also that I was thinking chiefly about getting back to our trench. . . . Still, I did not shoot him partly because of that detail about the trousers. I had come here to shoot at "Fascists"; but a man who is holding up his trousers isn't a "Fascist," he is visibly a fellow-creature, similar to yourself, and you don't feel like shooting at him.[11]

This anecdote, said the author, proves "nothing very much, because it is the kind of thing that happens all the time in all wars." On the contrary, George Orwell's stayed hand is the stuff of which legends are made. It is testimony to his own humanity and to the resilience of neighborly love even under conditions of deprivation, hostility, and stress.

The primacy of the particular, from a moral point of view, derives from what it means to be—and what it takes to be—genuinely other-regarding. If the other is an abstraction, a unit within a category, as must be so for many purposes, other-regarding conduct loses direction, strength, and clarity. In welfare programs for the poor, in education, in schemes for protection of the environment, in medicine, in the administration of justice: the more impersonal the program or procedure, the more chance there is that the true object of moral concern may be poorly served or even lost from view. To be effectively other-regarding, we must, at some crucial point, where the fate of persons is decided, directly perceive and appreciate them. Only where love plays a part can justice, administration, and professionalism attain their highest potential as moral activities.

The ideal of *particularity*—so important in neighborly love and its institutional offspring, substantive justice—should not be equated with the ethos of *particularism*, explained above. If prosecutors, judges, and juries are to provide substantive justice, they must take account of concrete persons and circumstances. No continuing relationship is presumed, however, and none is formed. The officials do not have a personal tie to the defendants; nor, for the most part, are they responsible for them beyond the disposition of the case.

So, too, with the ideal of neighborly love. The individual human being, not the mass of humanity, is the preferred object of moral concern. But a particularist connection, on the model of family or friendship, is not necessarily contemplated. The ideal is to love every human as a neighbor, not to differentiate or discriminate among them. Therefore, the claims of particularism, though they overlap with those of particularity, must be examined on their merits.

### The Implicated Self

Consider the case of Mrs. Jellyby, a notorious character in Charles Dickens's novel *Bleak House*. Mrs. Jellyby practiced what Dickens called "telescopic philanthropy." She was indifferent to the chaos in her household and to the welfare of her husband and children. All her philanthropic energies were directed to furthering the prosperity of an African people who lived on the left bank of the Niger. Mrs. Jellyby is described as "a pretty, very diminutive, plump woman . . . with handsome eyes, though they had a curious habit of seeming to look a long way off. As if . . . they could see nothing nearer than Africa."[12]

Telescopic philanthropy is still philanthropy, which is much better than nothing from a moral point of view, and can often be justified. But charity begins at home. As a general rule we doubt the authenticity of sentiments that slight the interests of those in whom one's own life is directly involved. Mrs. Jellyby is a comic figure in the novel, an object of skepticism and scorn. That would not be the case if she were devoted to her family's health and comfort at the cost of neglecting her African friends. She seems to have her priorities wrong.

If there are special obligations, of the kind we might attribute to Mrs. Jellyby, what is their source and justification? According to David Hume, "We are naturally very limited in our kindness and affection."[13] "Now it appears, that in the original frame of our mind, our strongest attention is confin'd to ourselves; our next is extended to our relations and acquaintance; and 'tis only the weakest which reaches to strangers and indifferent persons. . . . From all which it follows, that our natural uncultivated ideas of morality, instead of providing a remedy for the partiality of our affections, do rather conform themselves to that partiality, and give it an additional force and influence."[14]

Our "natural uncultivated ideas of morality" are entitled to respect. But they are not self-justifying. For one thing it is clear, as Hume observed, that even our "common judgments" will "blame a person who either centers all his affections in his family, or is so regardless of them . . . as to give the preference to a stranger, or mere chance acquaintance."[15] Thus uncultivated, unreflective morality is itself a resource for restraining partiality and extending affection to strangers. In striking the balance we implicitly recognize that particularism's claim to represent natural virtue must be scrutinized and assessed.

Robert E. Goodin has argued "that the most coherent theory available to explain our special responsibilities to family, friends, and so on also implies that we must give far more consideration than particularists allow to at least certain classes of strangers."[16] In other words, revealing the true grounds of special obligation will lead to a more generous view of what they entail.

According to Goodin, special obligations are both explained and justified by the vulnerabilities and dependencies we create: "What is crucial, in my view, is that others are depending upon us. They are particularly vulnerable to our actions and choices. That, I argue, is the true source of all the standard special responsibilities that we so readily acknowledge. The same considerations of vulnerability that make our obligations to our families, friends, clients, and compatriots especially strong can also give rise to similar responsibilities toward a much larger group of people who stand in none of the standard special relationships to us."[17]

With the added assumption that reference to "our" actions and choices means reponsibility is collective as well as individual, a case can be made for the welfare state, foreign aid, and concern for future generations, as well as, perhaps, animals and natural environments. In sum, "we should protect *all* those who are particularly vulnerable to our actions and choices, rather than restricting our attention to the narrowly defined subset enshrined in conventional morality."[18]

The vulnerability and dependency of others accounts for many moral duties. These extend not only to our children and dependent relatives but also to people who have relied on our promises or whom we have injured as a result of intentional or negligent conduct. Thus, the realm of special obligation extends well beyond particularist bonds of affinity. Special obligations arise whenever the choices we make, as individuals or as group members, impinge on the lives of others in ways that cause them to rely on us for restraint or benevolence. The "others" are not all of humanity, but they need not be limited to relatives, spouses, or friends.

This line of reasoning is compelling, but it has important limitations. As a critique of particularism it is unsatisfactory because, in choosing among competing claims, "whom we should favor depends, according to this analysis, upon the relative vulnerability of each party to us."[19] This calculus is no help when vulnerabilities are roughly equal, as they are in many emergencies, or when they are indeterminate, as they are in many situations, and yet one must decide between helping a close relative or a stranger. Nor does the thesis adequately account for obligations that arise from relationships that encompass much more than vulnerability. The morality of the "significant other" extends beyond damage control; it looks to the flourishing of children, spouses, friends, and community; it is not mainly a morality of reparation.

The fundamental source of moral obligation is our own sense of identity and relatedness, not the vulnerability of others. To be sure, many specific obligations are triggered and defined by vulnerability and dependency. What children need—and to whom they must turn—tells us what parents must do if they are to fulfill their responsibilities. But the ground of these obligations lies in the parental role, not in the child's needs. It is their commitment to relevant roles that governs how people should respond to the dependencies they create or accept.[20]

Many marital obligations, such as caring for one another during illness, fidelity in times of trouble, and appropriate settlement in case of divorce, are triggered by vulnerability. But it is the institution of marriage that confirms and undergirds these obligations. It is the institution that transforms a discretionary act of benevolence into a binding duty.

As the examples of marriage, employment, and naturalized citizenship make clear, the obligations of a status contract may indeed be self-assumed. What is remarkable about such contracts, however, once the relationship is established, is the waning of prior consent as a governing principle. Negotiation and bargaining continue (in marriage and employment, though not in naturalization), but typically as responses to new problems that cannot be solved by reference to the initial agreement and must be dealt with within the framework of new circumstances and emergent obligations. In redefining the relationship, the changing parameters of a marriage (especially the claims of children) or the present needs of an enterprise play a central part.

Two meanings of *self-assumed* should be distinguished. In one meaning, self-assumed obligations are narrowly contractual acts of promising, whereby the promisors know definitely just what their commitments are. Here *commitment* connotes a deliberate exercise of will and choice. It is an explicit decision to be bound, often expressed in a form of words, as a speech act.

Another meaning of *self-assumed* looks to the construction of the self. Here the formation of identity, character, and conscience is what matters, not the making of specific engagements. Obligations are assumed, but not necessarily as a result of conscious deliberation, and always within a demanding social context. Out of the meshing of lives and activities there emerges an implicated self whose obligations are neither wholly voluntary nor wholly imposed.

Obligations based on affinity are self-assumed in this second sense. They arise from the continuities of socialization, selfhood, and shared experience. They are faithful to and nourished by the sustaining particularities of emotion, interaction, and interdependence. This accounts for the depth and salience of such obligations, as well as for the peculiar combination they exhibit of open-ended yet bounded altruism.

In the morality of the significant other, commitment is selective but not segmental in the sense discussed above. The bond is between one living unity and another, rather than a coordination of specialized activities or interests. Obligation runs to definite persons, groups, and situations, not to abstract ideals or defined utilities. Since needs and interests are notoriously subject to change and redefinition, such a commitment calls for fidelity despite new and unforeseen demands. An ethos of diffuse, open-ended obligation prevails.

This open-endedness points to the moral worth of particularism, and therefore to its justification. For only thus can we make good "a deep caring and identification with the good of the other from whom one knows oneself clearly to be other."[21] In other words, only open-ended commitment, made by an integral, self-constituted being, is thoroughly and genuinely other-regarding. We cannot be other-regarding when we are concerned only with selected attributes of the other, such as a child's achievements, or when we are willing to give only a part of ourselves to the relationship.

There is no denying, of course, that particularism often shows the darker as well as the brighter face of human association. Bounded altruism can be a source of moral blindness. We know well that parochial attitudes breed willful ignorance, intolerance, group egotism, and worse. These evils must be disciplined by a universalist ethic. Nevertheless, the virtues and obligations we associate with particularism are, in their pure form, the fullest expression of other-regarding conduct.

The conventional forms of particularism—bonds of family, friendship, ethnicity, and locality—need not be perceived as its only province. The same ethos may be applied, with due respect for context, to wider worlds of work, education, and government. Virtues of caring, fidelity, and reverence—for persons, not abstractions—may flourish in many settings. And these virtues bring to those settings their greatest moral competence and worth.

### Individuals as Persons

In Western philosophy, theology, and social theory *person* as a term of art has reappeared perennially since ancient times.[22] Although frustratingly vague and elusive, the idea persists because there is a core of meaning which seems indispensable to moral thought and judgment.

Many analysts of Western thought have found it helpful to distinguish between *individual* and *person*.[23] That is so because, in the doctrines of modernity, individuals tend to lose their distinctiveness. They become interchangeable, ahistorical units within a political, legal, or economic scheme of things. The driving ideals of liberal capitalism—nationalism, the rule of law, political democracy, free enterprise—all have the effect of identifying people by general categories rather than by the concreteness of selfhood, connection, and context. As the category is abstract, so, too, is the individual; hence the phrase "abstract individual." This abstraction is one of the more barren and dehumanizing legacies of modern rationalism.

Such an outcome was certainly not intended. The architects of the Enlightenment wanted to enhance and vindicate, not diminish, the moral worth of the individual person. They therefore stressed the importance of moral autonomy and freedom, including freedom from unchosen obligation and the fetters of the past. In this process it was natural to celebrate detached individuals, responsible for their own fates, authors of their own opinions, finding their own ways to association, prosperity, and God. Rationalists took for granted much in traditional society, especially the continuities of family and rural life. They did not foresee the moral and cultural attenuation that would stem from an ethos of individualism set loose in a world of industrial and urban expansion.

To many observers, conservative as well as progressive, *individual* and *individualism* have taken on connotations that are deeply offensive from a moral point of view. The image of a self-distancing individual is hardly a convincing or attractive picture of what participation in a moral order should entail. When the human being is abstracted from history and context, we lose purchase on what it means to be a multi-dimensional moral actor and a fully realized object of moral concern. In short, the texture of moral ordering is lost.

The concept of *person* is an effort to retrieve that texture. The individual as person is discovered, protected, and fulfilled only within a specific historical setting. This particularity resists and mitigates abstraction. Yet the point of the exercise is to vindicate a general idea: human dignity and worth. Although the value at stake is necessarily abstract, it is realized through concreteness. This union of the general and the particular distinguishes the person from the abstract individual.

In etymology and social theory *person* suggests particularity, coherence, and responsibility. The Latin and Greek terms (*persona* and *prosōpon*) refer to the masks used in classical drama and, by extension, the part or character represented by the actor. This identification of person with role takes on ethical meaning in the Stoic tradition. It is the duty of moral persons to "play well" the roles they are assigned: "The well-written part, furthermore, particularizes the universal in accordance with the nature peculiar to each individual and grounds it in a rational mean. In this way the aim of the Stoics is realized. . . . For everything is as it should be and the course of life is beautiful when the will of the universal disposer and the *daemon* of the individual are in harmony. Inasmuch as the role is subordinated to the drama as a whole, but has its being nevertheless in the particular part, it is an artistic way of stating the Stoic doctrine."[24]

The Stoic ideal presumes a moral order largely founded on assigned roles and fixed statuses. In such a society role and person are closely congruent; indeed, roles are constitutive of personal identities. To meet the expectations one's received identity generates is the main criterion of social reponsibility. Thus to be a person is to be defined by one's place in the moral order.

These overtones of hierarchy and discipline are reflected in what used to be called the law of persons. Historically this branch of Anglo-American law dealt with all those relations that could be said to create a legal identity: slave, serf, master, servant, ward, infant, husband, wife, cleric, king. All these were statuses recognized by law. Each clothed the individual with salient, identity-fixing privileges or disabilities. Thus, the law of persons was the law of status. It was rooted in a society where everyone was presumed to belong somewhere, and the great parameters of belonging were kinship, locality, religion, and social rank. In all spheres of life, including spiritual communion, subordination to legitimate authority was thought to be a natural, inevitable, and welcome avenue to moral grace and practical virtue.

By the middle of the nineteenth century it was clear that the law of persons would soon become an anachronism. The knell was tolled by Henry Sumner Maine in his famous "law of progress." "The movement of the progressive societies," he wrote, "has hitherto been a movement *from Status to Contract*."[25] Maine perceived that contract was the preferred form of legal relation in modern society. The effect of the change was to diminish the perceived reality of both persons and groups. Persons are reduced to individual units of investment, labor, or consumption. Their special identities are lost in the egalitarian, free-market imagery of "economic man." The group becomes an aggregate or, at best, a composite of freely chosen individual arrangements.

This transition brings home the fact that the historical reality of personhood is closely associated with status and subordination. With that in mind it is easy to appreciate how great was the appeal of the new individualism and the contract model. As it developed in the nineteenth century, the law of contract embodied values of freedom, equality, and self-government. Contract law was liberating and facilitative, a channel for the release of energies through economic cooperation, a powerful device for defining rights and enforcing accountability. All this weighed heavily against the received morality of role and status.

The lesson is that our understanding of personhood should give full weight to *self-affirming* participation in a moral order. Respect for individuals as persons requires "that we regard and act towards [them] in their concrete specificity, that we take full account of their specific aims and purposes and of their own definitions of their [social] situations."[26] In other words, the person as an object of moral concern can never be an abstraction, never wholly subordinated to social needs, never dissolved into a group or process. Here again the primacy of the particular is reaffirmed.

The moral unity of the person is a counterweight to demands for sacrifice to the common good. As Bernard Williams has argued, "there can come a point at which it is quite unreasonable for a man to give up, in the name of the impartial good ordering of the world of moral agents, something which is a condition of his having any interest in being around in that world at all."[27] This something is what Williams calls a "ground project," that is, a set of activities and commitments that, taken together, construct a moral identity and give meaning to a life. Such identities are ever-present sources of conflict among persons, including friends and relatives, and between the individual and society. The implicated self is also a particular self, with its own claims to individuality and autonomy.

But this is the autonomy of selfhood, not of unfettered or ungoverned choice. An unspoken condition of moral individuality is that "ground projects" must meet a threshold standard of moral justification. Each project or way of life is unique, but this does not mean all are acceptable. It is not moral autonomy to do as I please, heedless of outcomes for my own character and integrity. Rather, self-determination is the freedom to find one's proper place within a moral order, not outside it. In doing so one takes account of the qualities of that order—its legitimacy and the propriety of its demands, for example—as well as one's own nature and experience.

This argument takes seriously the idea that persons are at once socially constituted and self-determining. To be socially constituted is not, in itself, to be imprisoned or oppressed; it does not require that people be puppets or act out prescribed roles in excruciating detail. Nor is self-determination properly understood as gratification of impulse, compulsive dependency, or opportunistic decision. Insofar as it has moral import, the theory of the social self makes plain that a morally competent self must be a product of affirmative social participation and of responsible emotion, belief, and conduct.

# 7  *ALAN WOLFE*

## Human Nature and the
## Quest for Community

### Introduction

For the past ten years or so, social and political theorists have turned their attention to the question of community.[1] Concerned about a weakened sense of obligation in advanced industrial societies, these scholars argue that liberal political theory, as important and defensible as it may be, pays insufficient attention to the ties that hold individuals together. Often the lines that are drawn in these matters are fine, but communitarians generally do not believe, with Ronald Dworkin, that individual rights should trump community solidarity when the community may be worse off as a consequence.[2] Belonging neither to the left nor the right, communitarian ideas seek to refocus public attention on the fragility of social ties, as if merely leaving people alone to do whatever they want can no longer guarantee a stable environment.

At the same time advanced industrial societies have also witnessed an outburst of new ideas involving the relationship between people and the natural environment they inhabit.[3] From the standpoint of a defense of nature against human incursions, liberal theory is once again faulted, this time for its Faustian inclinations to control and dominate the natural world.[4] Liberalism's chief social institution, the market, is moreover found wanting, for rationally choosing individuals have no incentive to protect the commons, with the result that if they do not form social institutions, they will all be worse off.[5] Like communitarians, ecologists want to protect a system viewed as fragile. They are convinced that people need to be warned about the potentially tragic consequences of their unthinking actions. Right and left tend to be irrelevant categories for the environmentalists, just as they are for the communitarians. The goal is a social theory, and a political movement, that will inspire respect for things generally taken for granted.

Because communitarianism and environmentalism are so similar in their outlook, it seems obvious that the insights of one can be applied to the insights of the other. And to some degree they can, for there will always be similarities among complex systems, whether social or natural. But as these two intellectual movements continue to develop, we should keep in mind that this is not the first time that ideas about society and ideas about nature have been linked. Just about every major innovation in social theory—including liberalism, conservatism, and Marxism—has been accompanied by a set of ideas of what is natural and what is not. However much they may have disagreed with each other over the future of capitalism, Herbert Spencer and Friedrich Engels both believed that nature provided the ultimate justification for his point of view.[6]

Of all the ways by which theories of society and theories of nature overlap, none is more important than initial assumptions about human nature. Granted that it may be difficult to prove that any particular social order, such as capitalism, corresponds with nature, social theorists have not been reluctant to argue that the human self does. Especially when stripped to their bare psychological essentials—when imagined outside of society as Robinson Crusoe, the wild boy of Avignon, or any one of a number of idiots savants—humans could, it was believed, be understood as captives of the nature they otherwise would like to subdue.[7] Instincts and drives shared by other species were also assumed to be shared by us. Even when a distinct social order was acknowledged, it was often viewed as precarious at best, constantly about to be overtaken by a human nature it could barely socialize and contain.

No wonder that, ever since humans discovered themselves as an object of study, theorists have linked their social institutions to various conceptions of what humans are really like.[8] The two most prevalent of such institutions in the modern world are states and markets, and each has a theory of human nature to support it. Since the days of Adam Smith, economists, while believing that humans are naturally self-interested, have rarely thought of them as malevolent. To be sure, the market is necessary to ensure that the individual actions of many people will be coordinated, but the market has been viewed by its defenders as a "soft" form of coercion because human nature is itself soft. People need to be guided, but they do not need to be pushed around at gunpoint. Give them the right incentivves, and they will figure out what to do all by themselves.[9]

Defenders of the state usually have a darker view of human nature, at least since Hobbes. People are not necessarily going to do what is right, even when the market guides them. Their tendency to pursue their self-interest can be taken to the extreme of war, which, human nature being what it is, can only be controlled by the state's monopoly on the means of violence. Coercion is not pretty, but it is often necessary to protect order, which is why one generally finds pessimistic views of human nature among foreign policy "realists."[10] Clear thinking and the ability to take difficult and unpopular actions are usually emphasized by those who defend the state. Even advocates of the market have come to realize the need for strong forms of authority, if not always governmental authority. We cannot allow people themselves to determine what they want because, some argue, all too often they do not know what they want. They are by nature concerned with the short-term and the close-at-hand; organizations such as business firms can function effectively in the larger market if they are internally organized by strong authority that can counterbalance opportunism.[11]

Communitarians think of themselves as searching for solutions that go beyond both the market and the state. Should they therefore search for an understanding of human nature that is similarly different from both the optimistic-harmonious view associated with the market and the pessimistic-realistic view associated with the state? There is one way to answer this question which seems intuitively correct and commonsensical. This is to argue that human beings are neither selfish and in need of coordination nor shortsighted and in need of a firm hand. They are, rather, sociable by nature. They are born to relate to others, to live in groups, and, when given the right environment, to sacrifice for the sake of the common good. The human and the social are one and the same.

Support for this position in biology is relatively recent. It was not that long ago when the lessons of nature were held to support a more Hobbesian view of behavior; writers like Konrad Lorenz and Robert Ardrey suggested that animals were by their very natures aggressive, and human beings, simply another form of animal, could not help but share those characteristics.[12] But this view is now judged empirically incorrect by many animal ethologists. Chimpanzees, for example, our closest relatives, have been found to be "peacemaking" creatures, even capable of negotiating differences through diplomacy.[13] Animals, we have been told, can perceive the world, have culture, develop extensive divisions of labor, and communicate with others of their species.[14] According to those who seek support for the hypothesis of human sociability in nature, we need no longer be afraid of biology, for it teaches us not that we will destroy each other in a vicious Darwinian struggle for survival but that we are more likely to live together in harmony with others.

Because it is natural for human beings to form communities, advocates of this position argue, earlier theories of human nature can be turned on their head. Instead of arguing that individual selfishness is natural and community an accident, one can claim that community is the more genuine and typical expression and self-interest the exception. No wonder the idea that humans are by nature sociable appeals to writers strongly moved by moral beliefs and the need for social order.[15] If human communities are understood to be evolutionary mechanisms developed over the millennia to facilitate the successful reproduction of our species, we need never apologize for communitarian sympathies.

Yet as appealing as such an argument from nature may be, it is, as I argue in this chapter, fundamentally mistaken. I advance three reasons for this claim. First, it is difficult, if not impossible, to use nature as a metaphor for society; although there are similarities between natural and human ecologies, there are also significant differences. Second, I argue that we do not know as much about the natural world as we sometimes think. The biological and the social sciences are both interpretative sciences, so that one cannot serve as the foundation or grounding for the other. And third, arguing now normatively, I suggest that the notion of a sociable human nature serves communitarian goals badly and that we would be better off pursuing those goals through a more indeterminate understanding of what nature gives to human beings.

### Social and Natural Ecologies

It is obvious that human and natural ecologies share much in common. Both are interdependent, fragile, adaptable, and in need of cultivation. Yet in exploring some of these similarities, it also becomes clear why too close an analogy between nature and human society does not satisfy the goal of developing a theory which stresses the importance of human communities.

Contemporary ecological theory has demonstrated the degree to which organisms found in nature are interrelated.[16] If any single property of a natural system is altered, everything else changes as well, with consequences difficult to predict in advance. In similar ways interdependence and its resulting unpredictability are found in human life. We know, for example, that the loss of jobs in inner cities affects the crime rate, which in turn affects the social fabric of the neighborhood, which in its turn makes the environment less attractive to employers who might have jobs to offer, all of which, in turn, reacts once again on the crime rate. It is easy to imagine families, schools, neighborhoods, and factories as tied together in an ecological system in such a way that any change in one of the ingredients affects every other one as well.

Not all forms of interdependence are the same, however, and in thinking about the ways in which both nature and society link their parts together, we ought to keep in mind one difference. The interdependence found in nature has no particular purpose outside of the maintenance and reproducibility of the organisms that constitute the system. Although sociological theorists from Durkheim to Parsons have on occasion envisioned human society in similarly functional terms,[17] human social interaction is usually organized with a particular end in mind. We are concerned with unemployment not only because it will have negative consequences for family structure but because human beings who have the capacity to work but who cannot work are understood to be missing some larger purpose in their lives. Because human practices are organized and reproduced for some purpose beyond interaction itself, an ecological model stressing functional reproduction will always miss something crucial about the kinds of communities formed by human beings, communities that are different from the social groupings found among other animal species.

A second way in which natural and social communities are similar but also different involves their fragility. It is by now a cliché among the ecologically conscious that natural phenomena are in danger of extinction. The language of contemporary ecology is Cassandra-like in its insistence that features of the natural world as we know them— moderate climate, breathable air, landscapes, rain forests—may, if not treated properly, disappear. In some versions of these theories, human beings themselves will disappear, for their irresponsible treatment of nature will cause them to destroy aspects of the natural world that sustain human life. Indeed, it may not even be regrettable should this happen, for nature ought to be valued more highly than the human beings who (temporarily) inhabit it.[18]

In its own way this more extreme ecological position touches on the major difference between natural and social fragilities. Social institutions are actually more fragile than natural ones; they are more recent in historical time, they change more frequently, and there are social worlds which have disappeared while natural ones remain in place. Within one person's lifetime, the social world can undergo changes, sometimes destructive changes, that are far more rapid than anything which happens in nature; to consider just one example, think of the decline of once-thriving urban neighborhoods.[19] No wonder the Cassandra-like warnings about the destruction of nature have been accompanied by similar alarms about the decline of fragile social institutions such as families.[20]

Generally speaking it is liberals who suggest that the natural environment is in trouble and conservatives who argue that fears of incipient natural disasters are overdrawn.[21] On the other hand, conservatives worry about the future of social institutions, and liberals hold that fears of social destruction are exaggerated; the family, it has been suggested, is not in decline but is changing form, and may even be strengthening itself.[22]

Both sides in debates such as these tend to miss the point. It is not whether both natural and social ecologies are in danger but the different kinds of dangers they face that are important. Social institutions may be more fragile than natural ones, but they are also, ironically, more capable of renewal. Composed of individual human beings who can make sense out of the world around them, social institutions can weaken without necessarily weakening the individual capacities of their members. In their critique of the family decline literature, feminists argue that less authoritarian families are better for the people within them, especially women. Their critics charge that family decline hurts everyone, women included, by weakening the social fabric that makes society possible. It is beyond my scope here to suggest who is correct; the point I am trying to make instead is that to the degree that we focus on the health and well-being of particular people in the debate over the family, we are talking about a social institution's fragility in a very different way than when we talk about the fragility of a natural environment.

If things found in nature are fragile, they are also, paradoxically, adaptable. Species can survive challenges; indeed, one of the things that contributes to the reproductive fitness of natural organisms is their ability to adapt to new circumstances. It is clear why Social Darwinism was a theory of society based on an analogy with nature, for notions of adaptability and reproductive fitness were crucial to conservative ideas. Not only could defenders of the status quo argue that whatever survived did so because it was fated to survive, they could also add the notion that adaptability is unpredictable and complex. Nature should be allowed to run its course for a number of reasons, but most importantly because if it did so, it would find a mechanism of adaptability which worked more efficiently than any effort to adapt through planning and predicting the future.[23]

One can also find such ideas about adaptability applied to social institutions, but here—as I have already suggested—the evolutionary arguments come from the left, not the right. Family forms "evolve" constantly over time, historians tell us, so we ought not to be surprised that the ones we have now are different from those of a generation ago.[24] As with natural phenomenon, these changes are the results of adaptations to new environmental realities, especially women's entry into the labor force. To try and put a stop to the process—for example, by encouraging nuclear families in the way we think about social welfare policy—will fail, just as conservatives once insisted that governmental attempts to regulate monopolies would fail. We should learn to let social institutions be, however much we might want to regulate economic institutions instead.

The fact that left and right adopt the same form of rhetoric but on opposite sides of the nature/society divide may indicate that the question of adaptability is problematic in both accounts. Even defenders of the natural environment now recognize that in the name of protecting nature against society, we occasionally have to use society to intervene in nature. If we leave seashores, forests, and precious animal species to the whims of nature, we will lose them; the real question is not to leave nature alone but to find the right way to help it sustain itself.

Much the same is true of social institutions. We probably ought to respect the capacity of social institutions, and the people within them, to participate in the process by which new forms emerge. But it does not follow that because social institutions can adapt, we ought to leave them alone. Many writers who would like to see family forms evolve in ways that are compatible with greater freedom for women would not want to see them evolve in ways that encouraged rape within marriage, wife beating, and child abuse. Just as nineteenth-century theorists of laissez-faire would tolerate intervention into the economy in ways favorable to business, twentieth-century laissez-faire theorists of the family would tolerate intervention favorable to women. I am not accusing either of hypocrisy. I am rather suggesting that if adaptability in nature is taken, even if incorrectly, as an argument to leave nature alone, adaptability in society is not, and should not be, an argument to leave either economic or social institutions alone.

Both nature and society require that kind of constant attention we usually call *cultivation*; the term itself, after all, comes from culture.[25] Images of things running wild apply to both realms; one heard much, for example, of the phenomenon of urban "wilding": young boys, held to be without proper cultivation, who roam parks preying on the innocent and unprotected. Whether we are speaking of plants, babies, the moral senses, the virtues, or minds, we speak of the ways it is necessary to cultivate them so that they flourish.

As with some of the other points being discussed here, the question is not really the similarities between nature and society but the differences. Cultivation in nature is inherently paternalistic. The task is to protect the thing being cultivated from the forces that surround it. The cultivator is the active agent, the one who decides what has to be pruned and trimmed for the long-term survival of the objects in the garden. But can the virtues, sensibilities, and minds of human beings be cultivated in the same way? For Platonists the answer may be positive, but in a modern age we generally recognize that the cultivation of human capabilities requires participation of the thing being cultivated. It is unlikely that a project designed to weed out the "unfit"—say, through population control or behavioral retraining—is unlikely to have much appeal in a democratic age. We are better off thinking of human capacities in other than paternalistic metaphors. Human virtues and capacities do require cultivation, but we will not be able to accomplish our cultivating objectives without recognizing that we cannot prune and shear at will.

In short, the most fundamental difference between natural and human ecologies is that the latter contain individuals who are active agents in transforming and understanding the environment in which they exist. Even if the social orders developed by other animal species can be thought of as "communities," they are not human communities. They are passive forms of social organization that keep order, but they do so without the active participation of their members in determining the kind of community they want. One of the major problems in reasoning from human nature to a natural sociability for humans is that the kind of sociability produced by nature is not one that would allow human beings to live together as human beings. Nature gives human beings sociability, perhaps, but not community, at least not in any meaningful sense of the term appropriate to humans.

### The Biological and Social Sciences

The notion that human beings are by their very nature sociable can be understood as an effort to provide a scientific foundation for the human sciences. In this, it is no different from the economic and political views of human nature associated with markets and states. For the seventeenth- and eighteenth-century efforts to create a science of human behavior were very much linked to the development of the physical and natural sciences. Both Thomas Hobbes and Adam Smith assumed there was scientific support for their understanding of what humans are really like.

Yet of all the natural sciences, biology, while most certainly a science, is still evolving theoretically.[26] Animal ethology is a descriptive science still in its infancy; there remains an enormous amount that we do not know about such topics as whether animals cooperate, think, use language, or communicate through symbols. Sociobiology and various versions of evolutionary theory are even more interpretative, resembling history far more than physics in their attempts to reconstruct an account of what may have happened. It may well be the case that biological theories can only be valid for specific species and not across the full range of organisms possessing life.[27] But most importantly of all for present purposes, the line where biology merges into human psychology is blurred, and when theorists approach that line, they rarely do so with certainty. Despite two or more centuries of efforts to find a scientific grounding for human behavior, we still know remarkably little for certain about how and why we act as we do.

If we are therefore to base a theory of human sociability on biology, to what findings ought we to turn for support? A recent effort to establish a biological basis for human sociability indicates some of the difficulties involved in answering this question. According to James Q. Wilson, the biological grounds that establish that human beings are by nature social is the bonding that takes place between infants and their mothers.[28] This is held to be a natural fact, not unlike the way other species close to us also experience birth. (Of course there are numerous animal species that possess nothing even faintly resembling mother-infant bonding.) Infants who are secure and well attached to their mothers are more active and well-balanced as children; those who are insecure and unattached are more likely to experience behavioral problems. The whole argument seems to suggest that human beings need bonding in roughly the same way they need nutrition. If the one is not provided or provided in inadequate doses, irritability, antisocial behavior, and eventually death will result. The same is true for the other.

Whether or not one believes that mother-infant bonding is a good thing, however, there is far less scientific support for the notion than first appears. There is substantial criticism of the findings that place a great deal of importance on the infant's attachment to the mother.[29] As Diane Eyer has shown, the concept of mother-infant bonding shifted with every turn in the research, until the point where the mother was dropped from the bonding situation.[30] Even Wilson acknowledges that the scientific basis for the notion is weak. He notes that rats that were handled during infancy are different from those that were not, but then he quite properly points out that "we cannot be certain that this happens with human infants." Changes in weight and activity among infants that are correlated with handling "may well" have been accompanied by changes in brain structure or neural systems. The human brain cells that survive are "in all probability" those that are used. This is not the language of scientific certainty.

The same lack of certainly exists with respect to other efforts to find scientific grounding for aspects of human sociability. To be sure, humans and other animal species share the ability to communicate, but human language is capable of so much greater dexterity and subtlety than the signs and utterings of other animals that very little can be learned from the latter about the former.[31] As I have argued elsewhere, the same is true for other features of thought and behavior that humans share with some other animal species, including thought, the division of labor, reciprocal altruism, or self-reflection.[32] The reason why it remains so difficult to generalize from what science teaches us about other animal species to human beings is that the latter have the capacity not only to follow rules but also to make and interpret them. So long as that is the case, the foundations needed for a science of human behavior cannot be found in the study of nonhuman behavior.

Nor can we learn very much about human social behavior through the study of the biological, genetic, or neurological features of human themselves. Consider whether homosexuality has genetic roots or is learned behavior. The overriding answer to this question from science is that we do not yet know (although there have been suggestions of a genetic link). But this has not prevented from people from trying to link their moral positions to one or another scientific finding. Presumably the aim of such a linkage is to provide a trump card in moral argument, but the fact is that even the political positions associated with one side or the other of the scientific questions constantly shift. We would expect conservatives to be associated with the former position that biology is destiny, for conservatives usually argue this way with respect to gender. We would also expect gay activists themselves to hold that homosexuality is, in the jargon of the day, "socially constructed." But this is not the way these associations have unfolded. Because homosexuality is learned, some conservatives argue, it can be unlearned. Because homosexuality is determined, argue others, we should no more discriminate against gays than we should against racial minorities, who also inherited the characteristic that leads others to discriminate against them. It is not clear that biology or genetics will ever tell a community how it ought to handle discrimination against homosexuals.

Even if we do find a biological or genetic cause for certain human behaviors, what would we then know? Let us assume that after a long search, scientists are successful in demonstrating that a particular gene or chemical compound in the brain is the main cause of criminal conduct. We could then presumably control crime by controlling its biological origin. But would such a crime-free community necessarily serve communitarian objectives? It all depends on what those objectives are. It may be far more communitarian to have some crime, not so much as to destroy the social fabric but enough, as Durkheim reminds us, to serve as a warning about why we need laws. Or we might conclude that a society without criminals would also be a society without great literature, or at least that literature which uses crime to illuminate aspects of the human condition. Or, finally, we might be willing to tolerate some crime if the alternative, the complete regulation of human behavior, allowed for little freedom. There certainly would be reason to want to know whether human behaviors have biological roots, but that information by itself tells us little about the kind of communities in which we might want to live.

Because it is so difficult to establish a scientific foundation for arguments about human community, we gain a false sense of security when we think that biology has provided an answer to any question in political and social theory. This is as true of human nature as any other topic. To argue that humans are by nature sociable forecloses too many interesting questions. We would still want to know what people can learn, how their social institutions ought to be designed, which incentives would make them more sociable rather than less, why they are more sociable at some historical periods than they are at others, why they seem to get along with some people better than others, and which conditions lead their sociability to break down. Even those who believe that human beings are by nature sociable want to ask questions such as these, and when they do, they tend to argue, as Wilson does, that sociability is only a precondition for, not a determinant of, moral order. The quest for a biological understanding of human nature only displaces the important sociological questions involving community somewhere else; it never satisfactorily resolves them.

### The Normative Objection

One final reason to question the assumption that human beings are by nature sociable is that the normative positions that follow from such a position are questionable from a communitarian standpoint. This may sound odd, for surely communitarians want people to be able to get along better with others. But implicit throughout my entire discussion in this chapter is a normative point which ought to be made more explicit. Sociability can be obtained at too high a price. For if a human community is sociable, but such sociability is achieved without the active participation of its members, it is a community not worth having.

If human beings are understood to be instinctively or naturally sociable, they need never practice the skills of sociability. Because community is a given, there is little need to engage in community building. Such individuals would never have to struggle with balancing individual rights and collective obligations; the latter could simply be programmed to rule over the former. Socialization would be understood as less a process of education and more a problem of finding the right technology of behavior control. The attainment of citizenship would be a process roughly equivalent to physical maturation. Content with finding shortcuts to sociability, there would be less emphasis on the contingent, the situational, the unexpected, the ambiguous, the long-term. And, although this may not bother all that many people, there would be no need for a discipline called sociology, for it would be replaced by pharmacology or neuroscience.

There are dangers, then, of drawing discussions about the kind of community we want to have too short by resorting to arguments about human nature. Community is not an end in itself; the question of community for what must also be addressed. Of course this question in turn is also treacherous, for if we define the goals of a community too precisely, we identify those who do not happen to share those goals as enemies of the community. It is possible, however, to find some middle ground between ignoring the question of community objectives and defining them too strictly. We can insist that one of the objectives of community ought to be the enhancement of the human capacities of their members: that individuals should be encouraged to use their capacities for language, thought, and meaning in an active way which enables such capacities to flourish and grow. To do that requires that we not appeal to the inherent sociability of human beings, for then we will have presumed exactly what we want to encourage.

At the same time there are also positive normative advantages in keeping the question of human nature indeterminate. Ideas about fixed human nature are usually associated with traditionalism; the notion that human beings are really like this or that is usually a product of a community which is rooted in a specific place and characterized by a common heritage. More modern societies are characterized by extreme mobility, as people move from one place to another. They are composed of individuals of widely different religious, ethnic, and racial backgrounds. Traditional authority roles are challenged. A premium is placed on merit, which leads to an emphasis on education and training. Under these circumstances a more plastic understanding of human nature seems more appropriate. Leaving open the question of what humans are really like will be more compatible with a pluralistic understanding of community objectives, one that seeks to allow for difference even while emphasizing commonality. If a liberal understanding of the priority of rights runs the risk of paying insufficient attention to obligation, a communitarian understanding of duty always runs the risk of paying insufficient attention to minority concerns. At least some of that criticism can be met by avoiding any effort to foreclose options by appealing to human nature.

Keeping the question of human nature open or indeterminate has its limits, of course. In this essay I have suggested some of those limits: by insisting on moral pluralism, the possibility of human nature being monistic is ruled out; by suggesting that the goal of community is to enhance human capabilities, one forecloses a conception of human nature which would restrict human capabilities. There will, in short, always be some conception of human nature, even in an argument warning of the dangers of too closely drawn theories of human nature. Still, the major point remains: to what degree ought we to attribute what we do to the nature we have as human beings versus the social institutions we try to build. If we want a society which enables people to cultivate a sense of responsibility toward others, we ought to attribute far more to the latter than to the former.

Like the environmental and ecological movements with which it shares some similarities, communitarianism is an effort to break through some of the logjams of contemporary social and political thinking. What is appealing about it is not that it gives definitive answers to age-old questions, for it raises as many as it solves. Rather communitarianism seeks to shed new light on such issues by raising questions of obligation that often go unanswered—or are answered unsatisfactorily—by those ways of thinking that are tied to markets and states. If this novelty is one of the more attractive features of communitarianism, it is also one of the things that would have to be sacrificed if communitarianism were to associate itself with any specific theory of human nature. For then it would have a sure answer to any question that might emerge, even if its answers might well be misplaced or incorrect. An inclusive and open theory of society requires, at the very least, an inclusive and open theory of the nature of the human beings who will live in that society.

VIRTUE IN A

CONSTITUTIONAL

DEMOCRACY

*DAVID*
*HOLLENBACH, S.J.*

# Virtue, the Common
# Good, and Democracy

This essay argues that a recovery of the idea of the common good and a strong sense of the virtues of citizenship are vitally important in the present moment of American history.[1] It claims that sustaining a democratic form of life depends on the presence of citizens who understand themselves as responsible to and for the quality of their common life together. Thus, individualistic understandings of the human person common in American culture today need to be transformed by more communal and solidaristic sensibilities.

In order to make a plausible case for virtue and the common good, however, it is necessary to address legitimate fears that revival of these notions in practice will lead to a stifling of freedom. It is a historical fact that individualistic concepts of self-realization emerged out of the struggle against arbitrary power, both the political power of the monarchies of the ancien régime and the economic power of the aristocracy. The defense of individual rights and freedoms was without doubt a kind of liberation movement. Contemporary liberal theorists are rightly wary of forms of communal solidarity that threaten freedom through paternalistic or authoritarian political programs. They are also suspicious of the potential for conflict and even violence that strong religious, ethnic, and national solidarities have exhibited in the past and continue to show today in some settings.

These fears are founded on what John Rawls calls "the fact of pluralism." The stress on freedom and autonomy characteristic of modern liberal democracies developed historically as a way of responding to the diversity of conceptions of the meaning and purpose of life. This pluralism is most evident in the religious domain. But there is also a deep pluralism in philosophical conceptions of how to live a good life. Rawls says that this religious and philosophical pluralism "is not a mere historical condition that will soon pass away; it is, I believe, a permanent feature of the public culture of modern democracies. Under the political and social conditions secured by the basic rights and liberties historically associated with these regimes, the diversity of views will persist and may increase."[2] Thus, the "common sense political sociology of democratic societies" tells us that agreement on a single conception of the good life among all citizens is unattainable. Such agreement could be maintained "only by the oppressive use of state power."[3]

There is no doubt that Rawls is right about the deep disputes about the meaning of the good life that are present in our society. But for him there is no way to resolve these disputes. Therefore, he argues that in politics we must deal with disagreements about the comprehensive good of human life by what he calls "the method of avoidance." By this he means that in political life "we try, so far as we can, neither to assert nor to deny any religious, philosophical or moral views, or their associated philosophical accounts of truth and the status of values."[4] Only in this way will we have a chance of achieving that level of consensus that is necessary for social harmony to exist at all. His prescription, therefore, is that "we apply the principle of toleration to philosophy itself" when debating the basic political and economic institutions that will structure social life.[5] Each man or woman must be free to hold his or her view of what the full good really is. But these comprehensive views of the good life must remain the private convictions of individuals. "In applying the principle of toleration to philosophy itself it is left to citizens individually to resolve the questions of religion, philosophy and morals in accordance with the views they freely affirm."[6] Or as Richard Rorty puts it, religious and philosophical convictions should be exempt from coercion in a liberal society under one condition: that such convictions "be reserved for private life."

Argument about the common good is also to be avoided in debates about more specific public policies. Liberal democracy aims at "disengaging discussions of such questions from discussions of public policy."[7] This privatization of "thick" visions of the good is not only a sociologically given fact; it is a moral constraint on political activity.

As one contemplates the sad state of the former Yugoslavia and other places where communal conflict is rife, the dangers of exclusivist forms of solidarity and the virtues of liberal tolerance are evident. One can ask, however, whether the prescription that comprehensive visions of the good life should be reserved for the private sphere and that public life should be built solely around the value of tolerance is in fact the medicine needed to heal what ails the United States today. For example, in the United States citizenship has itself become a problematic concept in our time, and we are experiencing an "eclipse of citizenship."[8] The low percentage of Americans who exercise their right to vote is the most visible evidence for this. This is caused in part by a lack of confidence that individual people can have any meaningful influence in a political society as vast as ours. Many people, including many in the middle class, feel politically powerless.

In an insightful book titled *Why Americans Hate Politics*, E. J. Dionne argues that this alienation can be attributed to the fact that current political discourse fails to address the real needs of communities.[9] This failure is itself partly the result of the fact that interest-group politics is frequently incapable of even naming the social bonds that increasingly destine us to sharing either a common good or a "common bad." Politics is perceived as a contest among groups with little or no concern for the wider society and its problems. Rawls's recommendation that we avoid introducing conceptions of the full human good into political discourse is designed to neutralize potential conflicts and to promote democratic social harmony. But it may ironically have the effect of threatening democracy through alienation and anomie rather than conflict or violence. A principled commitment to avoiding sustained discourse about the common good can produce a downward spiral in which shared meaning, understanding, and community become even harder to achieve in practice.

This was the fear implicit in the United States Catholic bishops' 1986 pastoral letter, *Economic Justice for All*. Echoing numerous sociologists, the bishops noted that there are deep structural causes for the contemporary devaluation of citizenship. Modern societies are characterized by a division of labor into highly specialized jobs and professions. Individual lives are further fragmented by the way family life, the world of work, networks of friendship, and religious community are so often lived out in separate compartments.[10] In the words of Robert Bellah and his coauthors in the book *Habits of the Heart*, contemporary American culture is a "culture of separation." It is increasingly difficult to see how our chopped-up segments of experience fit together in anything like a meaningful whole. "The world comes to us in pieces, in fragments, lacking any overall pattern."[11] This fragmentation can undermine the sense of overall purpose in the lives of individual persons, leading to a seemingly endless quest for one's own identity. Because of the complexity and high degree of differentiation characteristic of modern social existence, individuals lack a readily intelligible map by which they can locate themselves and chart their course through life.

Thus, when modern society and culture are contrasted with the more organic and integrated world of the premodern era, a characteristic of great moral significance stands out. In Peter Berger's analysis this fragmentation of the social world means that "the individual's experience of himself becomes more real to him than his experience of the objective social world. Therefore, the individual seeks to find his 'foothold' in reality in himself rather than outside himself. One of the consequences of this is that the individual's subjective reality . . . becomes increasingly differentiated, complex—and 'interesting' to himself. Subjectivity acquires previously unconceived depths."[12] Such preoccupation with personal identity makes it very difficult to see how the kinds of lives we lead make a difference for the common good of the whole community. And lack of public discussion of the common good in turn generates a heightened sense that individuals are powerless over the larger social forces that shape their lives. It also helps explain the prevalence of single-issue styles of political action among many who do continue to see politics as a sphere open to at least some influence.

There is great irony here. For the same social conditions that encourage individualism and preoccupation with the private world of subjectivity on the level of consciousness are also the sources of a qualitatively new form of objective, structured interdependence among persons. Technology, bureaucracy, mobility, and mass communication make the public world seem alien and impersonal. At the same time these factors heighten the impact that the structures of the public world actually have on the dignity and meaning of individual lives. In such circumstances narrow focus on private goods and individual interests threatens to allow large domains of social existence to slip from the control of human freedom or to fall under the direction of powerful elites. Thus at the very time that it has become increasingly difficult to sustain a vision of the common good, it is also more urgently important to do so if we are to sustain democratic practices.

I would propose that achieving this desideratum depends on rethinking the sharp division between the private and public spheres of social existence. Thinkers like Rawls and Rorty fear the presence of comprehensive understandings of the good life in public because they identify public life with the domain governed by the coercive power of the state. Others with a more libertarian bent are worried that too much public presence of visions of the common good will restrict economic freedom by setting political constraints on the market. In both cases the discussion of the role of comprehensive understandings of the good in public life presupposes that the public sphere is identified with the state and/or the market. The relation of private and public spheres is one of isolated individuals confronting anonymous and impersonal "megastructures."[13] The defense of freedom thus becomes identified with the defense of a zone of privacy.

One can raise serious questions, however, about the adequacy of this bipolar disjunction of human activity into public and private spheres. For example, Alan Wolfe has argued that the increasingly dense and complex spheres of government and the marketplace threaten to overwhelm whatever remnants of private freedom still exist in advanced modern societies. The sphere of freedom is "increasingly squeezed from two directions": from the one side by the bureaucracy of the administrative state and from the other by powerful determinisms of markets linked together in a vast global network.[14] Wolfe argues that if the freedom promised by modernity is to survive under the conditions that prevail in advanced societies in the late twentieth century, we need a counterweight to this pressure from the state and the market. Solitary, private individuals cannot provide this counterweight. In his words, "We need civil society—families, communities, friendship networks, solidaristic workplace ties, voluntarism, spontaneous groups and movements—not to reject, but to complete the project of modernity."[15] The strong communal links found in the diverse groups of civil society must have greater public presence.

Wolfe's argument strikes a sympathetic chord in one like myself who has been shaped by the tradition of Roman Catholic social thought. For a variety of reasons, Catholicism had an adversarial relationship with the rising liberal democracies of western Europe through the modern period up to the middle of this century.[16] Through the influence of thinkers such as Jacques Maritain and John Courtney Murray, however, in recent decades this relationship has been transformed into a strong Catholic alliance with democratic principles. This alliance has been evident in the highly visible role played by the Catholic community in numerous recent democratic movements from Poland to the Philippines, from Chile to South Korea.[17] One of the central conceptual sources of this dramatic shift was Maritain and Murray's retrieval of the distinction between civil society and the state. Civil society is the more encompassing reality, composed of numerous communities of small or intermediate size such as families, neighborhoods, churches, labor unions, corporations, professional associations, credit unions, cooperatives, universities, and a host of other associations. Note that though these communities are not political in the sense of being part of the government, they are not private either. They are social realities and form the rich fabric of the body politic.

In a democratic society government does not rule but rather serves the social "body" animated by the activity of these intermediate communities. The bonds of communal solidarity formed in them enable persons to act together, empowering them to influence larger social institutions such as the state and the economy. Pope Pius XI formulated the matter in what came to be known as the principle of subsidiarity: government "should, by its very nature, provide help [*subsidium*] to members of the body social, it should never destroy or absorb them."[18]

According to this way of thinking, the basis of democracy is not atomistic individual autonomy. Participation in democratic life and the exercise of real freedom in society depend on the strength of the communal relationships that give persons a measure of real power to shape their environment, including their political environment. As John Coleman has argued, the Catholic commitment to democracy rests on "a presumptive rule about where real vitality exists in society."[19] The presumption here is that solitary individuals, especially solitary individuals motivated solely by self-interest and the protection of their rights to privacy, will be incapable of democratic self-government. Democracy requires more than this. It requires the virtues of mutual cooperation, mutual responsibility, and what Aristotle called friendship, concord, and amity.[20]

Of course Aristotle knew well that there were limits to how wide a circle of friends one might have, as he knew there were limits to the size of a city-state. Today we are acutely aware that a nation as vast and diverse as the United States cannot hope to achieve the kind of social unity that might have been possible in the Athenian polis. While it might be true that the virtues of mutual cooperation, responsibility, and friendship can exert positive influence in small communities governed by town meetings, in clubs, and in churches that share a common vision of the final good and meaning of life, we hardly expect this to occur on a national, much less the international, level.

But here the irony of modernity once again becomes vividly visible. As the scale and diversity of the world tempts us to conclude that community is achievable only in private enclaves of the like-minded, de facto technological, political, and economic interdependence calls out for a conscious acknowledgment of and commitment to our moral interdependence. The principle of subsidiarity, with its stress on the importance of the local, the small-scale, and the particular, must be complemented by a kind of solidarity that is more universal in scope. This wider solidarity is essential if communitarian values are to avoid becoming a source of increased conflict in a world already riven by narrowness of vision. Commitment to small-scale communities with particular traditions must be complemented by a sense of the national and the global common good and the need for a vision shaped not only by particularist traditions but by hospitable encounters with traditions and peoples that are different.

The tradition of Western liberalism deals with the problem of diversity of communities, traditions, and peoples by invoking the idea of toleration. In public at least, it proposes that these differences be dealt with by finding a way to avoid discussing them. In my view, however, what Rawls calls "the method of avoidance" is inadequate to the challenge we face today. The problems of a deeply interdependent world in which diverse communities not only rub shoulders but must rely on each other for their very survival demand more. They demand positive engagement with those who are other or different. Such positive engagement cannot be mandated by an administrative state, much less an authoritarian one. It can be dealt with only on the cultural level, the domain where people's values and imaginative vision of the good are operative in uncoerced, free interaction with each other. This larger solidarity, therefore, is a matter of the kind of virtue that members of the body politic or civil society are capable of attaining.

Solidarity does not appear among the cardinal virtues of prudence, justice, temperance, and fortitude that were central for the Greeks and Romans, nor among the theological virtues of faith, hope, and love enumerated by Christian thinkers like Augustine and Aquinas. Pope John Paul II, however, has recently proposed to add solidarity to these classic lists by calling solidarity a key virtue needed to address the problems of our world. He defined this virtue as "a firm and persevering determination to commit oneself to the common good."[21] It is a moral attitude and social awareness which transforms the de facto interdependence of persons and groups into a conscious bond of mutual responsibility.

Such solidarity has both intellectual and social dimensions. What I propose to call *intellectual solidarity* is a spirit of willingness to take other persons and groups seriously enough to engage them in conversation and debate about how the interdependent world we share should be shaped and structured. Thus, it calls for public discourse about diverse visions of the good life. Such discourse is quite different from the tolerance recommended by Rawls as the best we can do in responding to pluralism. Tolerance is a strategy of disengagement and avoidance of fundamental questions of value in public life. This disengagement is precisely what we cannot afford if we wish to shape our interdependent existence in humanly worthy ways. In contrast with this, intellectual solidarity calls for engagement with the other through both listening and speaking, in the hope that understanding might replace incomprehension and that perhaps even agreement could result.

The principal venues in which such intellectual solidarity can develop are the domains of civil society and culture. Though the achievement of such solidarity will ultimately have important political and economic implications, it is more a matter of imagination and the larger vision of what makes for good human lives than debate about specific public policies. And since intellectual solidarity demands mutual listening and speaking, it can only occur in an environment where all are genuinely free to set forward their vision of the common good and the reasons why they hold it. Aristotle maintained that the very existence of the polis is dependent on the human power of speech, the ability of citizens to set forth their understanding of "the expedient and the inexpedient, and therefore likewise the just and the unjust." And these understandings are rooted in a "sense of good and evil" which only human beings possess.[22] Thus, to avoid serious public speech about the good life and the good society is itself already to surrender a major dimension of the human good. It will also have the further effect of undermining the concrete conditions necessary for a life of freedom. As Benjamin Barber has warned, "Citizens so tame as to shrink from the consequences of what they take to be public justice and common interest are scarcely citizens at all and are unlikely to be capable of defending freedom in any form."[23] Put positively, because intellectual solidarity is mutual, the freedom it both presupposes and generates will not be the freedom of an atomistic self. Where conversation about the good life begins and develops in intellectual solidarity, a community of freedom begins to exist. And this is itself a major part of the common good. Indeed, it is this freedom in reciprocal dialogue that is one of the characteristics that distinguishes a community of solidarity from one marked by domination and repression.

Such conversation and argument about the common good will not occur, in the first instance, in the legislature or in the political sphere narrowly conceived as the domain in which conflict of interest and power are adjudicated. Rather, it will develop in genuine freedom in those components of civil society that are the primary bearers of cultural meaning and value. These include universities, religious communities, the world of the arts, the sphere of serious journalism. It can occur wherever thoughtful men and women bring their received historical traditions on the meaning of the good life into intelligent and critical encounter with understandings of this good held by other peoples with other traditions. It occurs, in short, wherever education about and serious inquiry into the meaning of the good life takes place.

Despite its seeming abstractness, this virtue of intellectual solidarity has significant concrete implications. For example, it means that universities should be places where real argument about the adequacy and, yes, the truth of diverse visions of the common good should be occurring. Rawls's effort to construct a political philosophy based on the conviction that such argument will almost certainly be fruitless unfortunately seems to me a counsel of despair which not only encourages political alienation but threatens the intellectual mission of the university as well. Religious communities are similarly challenged to real encounter and dialogue with those of other faiths as they seek some degree of common understanding of our life together on this planet. Much of discussion of the public role of religion in recent political thought presupposes that religion is more likely to fan the flames of discord than to contribute to social concord. This is certainly true of some forms of religious belief, but hardly of all. Many religious communities recognize that their traditions are dynamic and that their understandings of God are not identical with the reality of God. Such communities have in the past and can in the future engage in the religious equivalent of intellectual solidarity called ecumenical or inter-religious dialogue. And the "velvet revolution" in Czechoslovakia that began in Prague's Magic Lantern Theater provided vivid evidence of the role that the arts can play in encouraging both democracy and a vision of the social good.

In addition to these intellectual aspects, the virtue of solidarity also has a social dimension. A virtuous community of freedom must address not only heights to which human culture can rise but also the depths of suffering into which societies can descend. There are strong currents in American life today that insulate many of the privileged parts of civil society from experience of the suffering that exists in other parts of the body politic. Though it is obvious that individuals and groups can never share the experience of all others, nevertheless encouraging commitment to the common good calls for new ways of overcoming this insularity in at least incremental ways. Here again, universities, churches, the arts, and journalism can play important roles in opening up avenues to enhanced social solidarity.

The impact of the growth of these forms of solidarity in civil society and culture on the political sphere of government will be largely indirect. But its importance should not be underestimated. Rawls maintains that argument about both the basic structure of democratic societies and more specific policies that rely on the coercive power of government should be based on "public reason." This he defines as "the shared methods of, and the public knowledge available to, common sense, and the conclusions of science when these are not controversial."[24] As noted above, he also maintains that the "common sense political sociology of democratic societies" indicates that full agreement on the meaning of the good life is unattainable in a pluralistic society. On this latter point, I am in agreement: unanimous consensus on the full meaning of the common good is not historically achievable. But this most definitely does not mean that no consensus is possible at all (a view that Rawls himself rejects) or that variations in the degree and scope of consensus are negligible. I would argue that the conversation and argument that can occur in civil society when citizens act on the basis of the virtues of intellectual and social solidarity can broaden and deepen the level of consensus they attain. Similarly, failure to act in accord with these virtues will shrink the common ground they share. This means that the "common sense" that regulates what counts as "public reason" in arguments about basic institutions and public policies can have different meanings at different historical moments. The interaction that takes place in the community of freedom that is civil society thus determines what sort of arguments can legitimately be made about the use of political power.

For example, the abolition of slavery, the expansion of suffrage to include women, the development of legal protections for labor, the civil rights movement, and the growing efforts to secure adequate health care and environmental standards all occurred through challenging previously reigning standards of common sense. Churches, universities, and numerous voluntary associations mounted these challenges by raising arguments that were not at the time taken for granted in the culture but that subsequently became so. In so doing they helped form new standards of political rationality in the United States.

This process of expanding and deepening the consensus so far achieved must continue if we are to deal with the new forms of social interdependence that mark the late twentieth century. The virtues of solidarity and mutual responsibility among citizens are prerequisites for addressing this interdependence in a way which is both oriented to the common good and at the same time democratic.

# The Virtues of Democratic
# Self-Constraint

$\mathbf{M}$any people distrust democracy because of its potential for legitimating majority tyranny. Popular rule on all political matters is a recipe for majority tyranny, just as minority rule on all political matters is a recipe for minority tyranny, which is even worse because it promises greater tyranny and does not even attempt to honor the ideal of equal political liberty. Constitutional democracy in the United States is commonly identified with various constraints on popular rule—checks and balances, perhaps most prominently judicial review—but it also, and as importantly, depends upon self-constraint on the part of citizens and public officials. Both sorts of constraints are justified on democratic grounds, for the sake of securing basic freedoms and opportunities for all persons. Because so much more has been written about the rationale for judicial review and other external constraints on popular rule, I want to concentrate on the complementary reasons why it is important to foster democratic self-constraint and what such self-constraint requires of citizens and public officials. When we succeed in constraining ourselves for the sake of securing basic liberties and opportunities for everyone, we create the conditions of a political community that is just and democratic. This is the morally best political community to which we can aspire.

Some political philosophers have claimed that democratic self-constraint requires a life dominated by political participation. "In a well-ordered city every man flies to the assemblies," Rousseau argued in making his case against representative democracy. The private affairs of citizens are of relatively little importance in a well-ordered (direct) democracy, according to Rousseau, because political life furnishes such a great proportion of the happiness of each person, or at least of each man, "that there is less for him to seek in particular cares."[1] Even Rousseau's model of a female citizen, the Spartan mother in *Emile*, cares more about whether her city was victorious than about whether her five sons were slain in battle. This is politics with a vengeance against all other values.

Constitutional democracy does not demand such political devotion of ordinary citizens, nor even of most public officials. Public officials consent to giving up only those pursuits that conflict with their duties of office. They need not give up the satisfaction of family, friendship, and other private associations. However, they must exercise self-constraint with regard to ends that conflict with their public duties, or else be constrained by others to fulfill their public duties.

Democratic citizens, other theorists suggest, ought to devote themselves to a life of politics because political life is the highest form of human existence. People owe it not so much to their society as to themselves, to their own self-perfection, to restrain their private pleasures for political pursuits. Democratic governments therefore should be designed to inculcate universal commitment to a life of political participation. Constitutional democracy, although committed to an inclusive citizenry, does not claim that people perfect themselves, or live what some philosophers have argued is the noblest life, through political participation. The political ideal that captures the best in the American tradition of constitutional democracy does not take a position on whether political life is a life of self-perfection. I have serious doubts about this claim, but my doubts are beside the point of constitutional democracy.

Constitutional democracy does not advise endless participation among citizens, but it does advise eternal vigilance.[2] Politics is not a universal profession, but it should be part, even if a relatively small part, of the life of every citizen for the sake of doing our fair share in pursuing justice for our fellow citizens. In conditions of social inter-dependence, politics is an inescapable part of every person's life. An advisory of eternal political vigilance is a far cry from being forced, or even encouraged, to live a life dominated by political participation. But eternal vigilance does presuppose political interest, knowledge, and understanding among (almost) all citizens, at least to the extent neces-sary to combat tyranny and to ensure political accountability for the sake of "liberty and justice for all."

Liberty and justice for all is a vague standard, some critics would say a vacuous one. The distrust of democracy cannot be fully mitigated unless democrats can provide more content to the idea that all political authority, including popular political authorities, must be constrained by the protection of individual freedoms and the pursuit of social justice in order to be legitimate. Democrats need to say more about how popular political authority is best constrained and by what principles.

### Protecting Individuals

Let's begin with the how. Constitutional democracies typically protect individuals, to the extent possible, by institutional bulwarks against the abuse of political power by both majorities and minorities. Democ-racies may rely upon institutional checks and balances, including judicial review, to prevent, as far as is practically possible, the denial of basic freedoms and opportunities to any individual.

A distinctive feature of a deliberative constitutional democracy is its striving for a situation in which citizens and their political representa-tives deliberatively consent, either prospectively or retrospectively, to those constraints, such as judicial protection of free speech and due process, that are necessary to prevent political authorities from violat-ing democratic principles.[3] Deliberation is both a practical and an intellectual political activity: it is the give-and-take of argument among decision makers for the sake of reaching a justifiable action-guiding decision. Democratic self-constraint follows the model of Ulysses, who had the foresight to consider his likely reaction to the Sirens' songs and had himself tied to the mast beforehand so as to resist them.

Deliberative democracy converts self-constraint into a collective virtue. Citizens and public officials deliberate among themselves be-fore facing situations in which they would otherwise be likely to act

unjustly, against the constitutive principles of democracy. With deliberative foresight, they agree to tie themselves to the mast of judicial
review so as to prevent popularly elected legislatures, for example,
from punishing unpopular political speech such as flag burning even
though they find flag burning morally offensive.

Because the democratic model of self-constraint refers to a col-
lectivity, not an individual, deliberative democracies cannot rely on
unanimous consent. Ongoing deliberation about the justification of
judicial review, its advantages and disadvantages from a democratic
perspective, is likely to lead to more widespread approval by citizens
of constitutional constraints provided they are educated to deliberate
about politically relevant issues, their social institutions are conducive to deliberation, and the institution of judicial review turns out
to be justifiable, after due deliberation. A well-ordered democracy
strives for unanimous consent to justifiable constitutional constraints
but settles for a widespread consensus based on deliberation, not
indoctrination.[4]

Deliberation also aims to minimize the need for external constraints
on popular authority by encouraging citizens and public officials to
constrain themselves, as individuals who deliberate and agree upon a
(noncomprehensive) set of democratic principles. Popularly elected
officials, for example, need not be subject to judicial review so long as
they restrain themselves by mutual acceptance of constitutional principles. These principles do not subsume everything important in politics, and therefore deliberative democracy leaves a lot of room for
political disagreements, which are part of everyday democratic politics. But deliberation also supports a justifiable democratic consensus
on constitutional principles.

Representative democracies work best when citizens and public
officials restrain their own political decision making by constitutional
principles that they freely accept by virtue of their reasonableness.
Deliberation is a central feature of a well-ordered constitutional democracy because agreement upon constitutional principles cannot be taken
for granted, and achieving agreement through indoctrination violates
freedom of thought while using deceptive means undermines democratic accountability. The most justifiable political means of encouraging self-constraint on the part of citizens, public officials, and politically
powerful institutions is to encourage the give-and-take of reasoned
argument about constitutional principles in as many public forums as

possible. If constitutional democracy is justified, then the constitutional principles that constrain the exercise of political power should be rationally justifiable to the people who are bound by those powers. By making schools, legislatures, and other public institutions more deliberative, democracies hold out the promise of arriving at a broad public consensus on the reasonableness of constitutional principles.

There are other important virtues, such as self-control and a sense of duty, that are conducive to democratic self-constraint. Although this essay focuses on deliberation, because it is a relatively neglected democratic virtue that political institutions can do a lot more to cultivate, the perspective of deliberative democracy is consistent with virtues such as self-control and a sense of social duty playing a key role, necessary but not sufficient, in cultivating democratic self-constraint. For democratic self-constraint to take hold in a society, most citizens must be disposed to nonviolence, honesty, and toleration, for example. These virtues, not coincidentally, are also necessary conditions for deliberation. The give-and-take of respectful argument among a diverse people is impossible in the absence of a disposition to nonviolence, honesty, toleration, and other basic (political and personal) virtues.

Why place so much emphasis on self-constraint, rather than rely upon more external constraints that require only a small subsection of citizenry to worry about constitutional principles? Because it is hard to imagine a well-ordered representative democracy which relies primarily on judges for interpreting and upholding all constitutional principles while leaving legislators and citizens free to make policy without themselves worrying first and foremost about constitutional principles. Constitutional principles protect the basic liberties and opportunities of individuals, but the Constitution of the United States does not explicitly protect all constitutional principles, especially those that require a lot of social resources to secure.

Consider access to adequate health care, without which most Americans cannot live a good life, let alone have the opportunity of choosing among good lives. The Constitution does not explicitly support access to adequate health care for all Americans, and it is not easy for judges to read this right into the Constitution. Nor is it impossible, as the constitutional theorist Frank Michelman's effort indicates.[5] But even constitutional theorists who read welfare rights into the Constitution do not count upon the Supreme Court to follow their lead. It surely would be preferable to secure these rights through popularly supported legislation that simultaneously funds health care for all Americans, a power which courts conspicuously lack.

There are other good reasons for not wanting judges single-handedly to rule upon welfare rights. Giving judges great freedom in interpreting the Constitution when there is little explicit constitutional language to guide them has served at times as a recipe for judicial tyranny. Consider the principle regulating property as stated in the Fifth Amendment: "nor shall any person . . . be deprived of . . . property, without due process of law; nor shall private property be taken for public use, without just compensation." Had judges been the primary interpreters of this right, with legislators and citizens deferring to their supposedly greater understanding and expertise, the United States would be even further from a just society than we are now. This is not an argument against either judicial review or what is often indiscriminately called "judicial activism." On the contrary, this argument maintains the role of the courts in protecting constitutional principles but expands the role of citizens and other public officials. Given the injustices remaining in our society today, basic liberties and opportunities need all the help they can get.

There is no way of preventing judges from reading the wrong private property rights into the Constitution without also preventing them from reading the right ones in. This argument for expanding rather than contracting the political arenas that centrally concern themselves with constitutional principle extends to courts as well as legislatures. For example, the right of children to an adequate and appropriate education, included in many state constitutions, has been interpreted very broadly by some state courts. The concern of state judges for specifying constitutional principles has brought us closer to protecting disadvantaged children against neglect by legislative majorities. Judicial activism in this arena has not eroded either legislative energy or the political interest of local communities in their children's education. And yet constitutional democracy would surely have been better off had state legislators and local school boards secured an adequate and appropriate education for disadvantaged children before state judges constrained them to do so.

The judiciary best serves as one of the last recourses, not the first for securing basic individual freedoms and opportunities. The judicial branch ultimately relies upon democratic assent to its authority. It cannot effectively uphold constitutional principles when most citizens and elected public officials refuse to guide their own political decisions by respect for those principles.

Concern among citizens and public officials for upholding constitutional principles is all the more important because courts are less reliable and effective protectors of rights in some areas than in others. We do not need to settle the question of whether courts are in general better protectors of constitutional principles than legislatures to recognize the need for citizens and public officials to concern themselves with upholding constitutional principles quite independently of the results of judicial review, which at its best is an imperfect and uncertain constraint on the abuse of political power.

### Influencing Decision Making

What constitutional principles should guide citizens and public officials in their political decision making? One reason that we cannot settle the question of whether courts are better protectors of constitutional principles than legislatures is that we reasonably disagree over the content of constitutional principles and will continue to disagree as long as we are a free society. A deliberative democracy makes a virtue out of the necessity of our moral disagreement over constitutional principles. The virtue, simply stated, is that public deliberation about constitutional principles is the best way of provisionally justifying a (necessarily) controversial set of constitutional principles. The constitutional principles that result from public deliberations will not always be the right ones (no political procedure can promise this result), but they will be more enlightened by the moral understandings of the diverse members of a constitutional democracy than principles that would result from the nondeliberative decision making of unaccountable "experts." Deliberation also increases public understanding and acceptance of provisionally justifiable constitutional principles.

A deliberative democracy authorizes all its members to deliberate as political equals over their collective future. Not everyone deliberates equally (or at all) on every issue, but everyone has an effective political opportunity to do so whenever necessary or desirable. In this sense, democratic citizens are political equals and must have the constitutional rights of political equals.[6] Deliberative democracy affords all citizens an effective opportunity to participate in the political processes that shape their collective future. It is committed to what I call *conscious social reproduction.*

In a deliberative democracy public officials, whether elected or appointed, are ultimately accountable to citizens who are willing and able to deliberate about their rights and responsibilities. Deliberation is a basic constitutional principle because democracy has no more justifiable means than the give-and-take of reasoned argument among citizens and public officials for provisionally justifying its controversial understandings of constitutional principles. The principle of deliberation is itself subject to deliberative justification. Public deliberation is the democratic means of conscious social reproduction.

A society committed to conscious social reproduction must honor two other basic constitutional principles that complement deliberative decision making and make it fully democratic. For a democratic society to reproduce itself consciously, it must be nonrepressive. It must not restrict political understanding, including consideration of controversial issues that inform citizens' perspectives on politics. For a society, rather than some segment of it, to reproduce itself, it must be nondiscriminatory. Every adult must be treated as a free and equal citizen, and every child must therefore be educated for democratic citizenship. A democratic society must not deprive people of basic social goods, such as freedom of speech, association, education, health care, and opportunities for social office, on grounds that are irrelevant to the legitimate social purpose of these goods. Nondiscrimination extends the logic of nonrepression, since governments are often selectively repressive by excluding disadvantaged minorities and women from the full benefits of citizenship (and sometimes also its honored burdens, such as military service). Nondiscrimination is the distributional complement to nonrepression.

A democracy that is nonrepressive and nondiscriminatory respects those freedoms and provides those opportunities that are necessary for the fair functioning of deliberative democratic politics over time. And it does so even if freely and fairly elected majorities decide to the contrary. As Michael Walzer aptly puts it, "They can rightly say: because we argued and organized, persuaded the assembly or carried the election, we shall rule over you. But it would be tyrannical to say: we shall rule over you forever. Political rights are permanent guarantees; they underpin a process that has no endpoint, an argument that has no definite conclusion. In democratic politics, all destinations are temporary. No citizen can ever claim to have persuaded his fellows once and for all."[7] When majorities are committed to ruling over others forever, there is little courts can do to stop them. But if the argument about democratic self-constraint is correct, citizens in a well-ordered democracy generally constrain themselves by the principles of non-repression and nondiscrimination.

Nonrepression and nondiscrimination commit democracies to protecting a wide range of rights that are often identified with liberalism, although the democratic rationale for these rights may be distinct.[8] Nonrepression and nondiscrimination protect individual freedoms and opportunities for the sake of democratic citizenship. But many, indeed most, liberties and opportunities that can be credibly defended on the liberal grounds of individual autonomy are also preconditions of being a free and equal citizen of a deliberative democracy. This is not a coincidence but rather indicates that deliberative democracy incorporates a significant part of the liberal ideal of autonomy into its understanding of citizenship.

The democratic principle of nonrepression diverges dramatically only from a liberalism of purely negative liberties, a liberalism committed to protecting only freedom from interference. No democratic version of liberalism is so restricted. Most versions of liberalism are democratic. Although nonrepression is not a principle of purely negative freedom, it secures many negative freedoms, including freedom of speech, conscience, press, and association, all of which are necessary elements of deliberative democratic citizenship. The principle of nonrepression also secures a host of so-called positive rights, including the protections of individual dignity afforded by the rule of law, due process, the right to a fair trial, and, perhaps most fundamentally of all, the entitlement of every child to a nonrepressive education. Nonrepression requires democratic governments to cultivate the capacity for political deliberation among all future citizens.[9]

The principles of nonrepression and nondiscrimination are not neutral among all conceptions of the good life, either in their justification or their effects. A deliberative democracy can flourish only with a citizenry whose minds are open to respecting reasonable points of view with which they disagree. Respect entails a reciprocal positive regard among people who advocate morally reasonable but opposing positions in politics.[10] When citizens perceive their political opposition as unreasonable, their commitment to democratic decision making is weakened unless they are confident of political victory. Sometimes this perception of unreasonableness is correct, but citizens who are educated to assume that their political position is uniquely reasonable erode legitimate support for democratic government. Liberal democracy can try to persuade closed-minded citizens to respect reasonable opposition, but the realm of public schooling is its single most powerful and legitimate means of teaching open-mindedness and respect for reasonable political disagreement.

Schools should teach these virtues not by indoctrination but by exposing children to different points of view on politically relevant issues, asking them to take these points of view seriously enough to respond with well-reasoned argument. Diane Ravitch offers an excellent example of the way schools can teach deliberation. The scene is an American history class in a public high school in Brooklyn. The teacher, Mr. Bruckner, has asked his students to discuss whether it was moral for the United States to drop the atomic bomb on Japan: "The lesson was taught in a Socratic manner. Bruckner did not lecture. He asked questions and kept up a rapid-fire dialogue among the students. 'Why?' 'How do you know?' 'What does this mean?' . . . By the time the class was finished, the students had covered a great deal of material about American foreign and domestic politics during World War II; they had argued heatedly; most of them had tried out different points of view, seeing the problem from different angles."[11] Thinking about what makes a class like this possible also alerts us to the fact that the success of deliberation depends on the cultivation of other virtues presupposed by deliberation, virtues as basic as veracity, tolerance, rationality, and a disposition to nonviolence, which enable students to learn and engage in respectful dialogue with each other.

In teaching all children to be open-minded with regard to the reasonableness of different political perspectives, public schools need not (and should not) be teaching skepticism. They should be teaching children a democratic virtue, which is also a form of self-discipline: the willingness to distinguish between reasonable and unreasonable points of view and to evaluate different political perspectives. The aim is certainly not to make children doubt the value of their parents' way of life, although only a thoroughgoing indoctrination can ever preclude this possibility. The aim is the nonrepressive teaching of the deliberative virtues that are conducive to a flourishing democracy.

William Galston thoughtfully criticizes this aim in the light of parental opposition based on deep religious convictions, convictions that devalue deliberation among different political perspectives. Galston does not claim that parents have the right to indoctrinate their children or to pass on their own religious beliefs if that entails exempting their children from an education for liberal democratic citizenship. My authority as a parent is limited by the fact, Galston writes, that my "child is at once a future adult and a future citizen."[12] Parents may not "impede the acquisition of civic competence and loyalty" or interfere with "basic civic education."[13] So far, Galston is laying the groundwork for a robust defense of teaching deliberation. But Galston then suggests that public schools should not engage children in democratic deliberation if it conflicts with the religious convictions of parents. Exercises in democratic deliberation, like the one in which Mr. Bruckner engages his American history class, ask all students to take seriously a range of reasonable political points of view. Some parents object on religious grounds to some of these points of view, and therefore to teaching democratic deliberation.[14] Why should their religious freedom not take precedence over teaching children to argue about controversial issues in democratic politics?

If a basic civic education includes trying to teach children to deliberate about politics, then Galston should agree that religious freedom does not take precedence here or in any case in which parents are claiming a right to exclude their children from lessons in civic competence. Teaching civic competence includes lessons in reasoning about politics and not just rote learning of the basic facts about American history and government. Rote learning of civics is not only ineffectual but also an incomplete understanding of what counts as civic competence. The ability to deliberate about political issues with other people is as central a virtue of democratic citizenship as are the virtues of honesty, nonviolence, and industriousness. The religious convictions of parents therefore cannot consistently take precedence over the responsibility of schools to teach children to deliberate. To give religious convictions precedence in the realm of public schooling is to give up on the principle that all children should be educated as future democratic citizens, people who responsibly share in shaping the laws of their society.

At issue, then, is not mere exposure to different ways of life but rather teaching future citizens to evaluate different political perspectives, which are often associated with different ways of life.[15] Galston wants the liberal state to encourage parents to foster strong convictions because the greatest threat to children in contemporary liberal societies is that they will believe in nothing very deeply. But the liberal state does not have an interest in fostering strong convictions regardless of whether their content is compatible with the legitimate aims of civic education. Parental convictions that conflict with teaching children the virtues of democratic self-government must still be tolerated, but they should not be encouraged or subsidized by public schools. A public commitment to teaching deliberative virtues does not prevent parents from fostering deep religious beliefs in their children. It only sets principled limits on the authority parents can claim over their children's public education, even in the name of religious freedom. Most parents accept the limits of nonrepression and nondiscrimination as self-constraints. The religious convictions of most American citizens are consistent with teaching democratic deliberation. Only a small minority are not.

The widely publicized case of *Mozert v. Hawkins* presents a good illustration of religious convictions that conflict with a public commitment to teaching children the principles of democratic self-constraint.[16] In the mid-1980s a group of parents whose children were enrolled in the public schools of Hawkins County, Tennessee, protested the use of a Holt, Rinehart and Winston reading series. The series had been unanimously adopted by the Hawkins County Board of Education upon the recommendation of a textbook selection committee appointed in accordance with state regulations. Tennessee state law requires schools to include "character education" for democracy in all aspects of the curriculum.

The dissenting parents argued that the content of the Holt series conflicted with their religious beliefs. They therefore demanded that their children be exempted from regular reading classes and be assigned nonoffensive texts. Their objection was to their children reading the texts, not to their professing beliefs contrary to their religion. The reading classes did not require profession of belief. But the parents sincerely believed that their children would be corrupted by exposure to conflicting beliefs. They said that they could not condone such exposure without a statement that their religious beliefs were correct and the others incorrect. The parents' objections to the texts were far-ranging, indicating a fairly thoroughgoing rejection of the deliberative ideal of democratic education. They objected to, among other things; a story describing an Catholic Indian settlement in New Mexico (on grounds that it teaches Catholicism), a story depicting a boy having fun while cooking (on grounds that "it denigrates the differences between the sexes" that the Bible endorses), an excerpt from Anne Frank's *Diary of a Young Girl* (because Anne Frank writes in a letter to a friend that nonorthodox belief in God may be better than no belief at all), a story entitled "A Visit to Mars" (because it encourages children to use their imaginations in ways incompatible with their faith), and a text that describes a central idea of the Renaissance as being "a belief in the dignity and worth of human beings" (because that belief is incompatible with their faith). The school board refused to exempt the dissenting parents' children from their regular reading classes.[17] The parents took the school district to court.

The United States Court of Appeals for the Sixth Circuit decided against the parents' claims that they had a constitutional right, based on their First Amendment freedom of religion, to demand a public school curriculum for their children which was compatible with their religious beliefs. A public school, the Court of Appeals concluded in overturning the federal district court ruling, has a right to require children to read and think about ways of life that conflict with their parents' religious perspectives without attaching a warning to the readings that the views represented (but not advocated) in the texts are wrong and their parents' beliefs are right. Learning to think about different ways of life is a reasonable part, although only part, of "character education" for democracy.

This decision was defensible from a liberal democratic perspective. If we give up on the duty of public schools to teach children the virtues of democratic deliberation, we are left without a principled defense of public schooling. A society that gives parents the constitutional right to tailor a public school education to their own religious beliefs is giving up on this duty.[18] To base any such right on the First Amendment guarantee of religious freedom would be to extend the religious freedom of parents to a tyrannical authority over their children's education. Parents would be exempted from the democratic requirement of self-constraint when it comes to exercising authority over their children, and children would be exempted from the legitimate requirements (and benefits) of an education for citizenship, designed to foster democratic self-constraint in the future.

If the liberal state may properly foster those beliefs that are "needed to bolster the institutions that secure liberal rights," and political liberty is among those rights, then a liberal state may teach all children the intellectual skills of deliberation. Absent the capacity for deliberation, citizens cannot be expected to use reasoned judgment in evaluating political alternatives that public officials set before them. Nor can public officials, who are accountable to the people and chosen from their ranks, be expected to demonstrate respect toward different ways of life. "The need for public evaluation of leaders and policies," according to Galston, "means that the state has an interest in developing citizens with at least the minimal conditions of reasonable public judgment."[19]

A liberal democratic government has an interest in, and a responsibility for, fostering more than the minimal conditions of reasonable public judgment. But even such minimal conditions include the willingness and ability to evaluate competing political views. Publicly subsidized schooling is the primary realm in which a democratic government can foster reasonable public judgment. Families are the primary realm for fostering parental values in children. Both realms are central to a flourishing, free society. What happens when the claims of the two realms conflict? Does a democratic government include the teaching of racial nondiscrimination as an essential part of public education even if some parents object on religious grounds to such teaching within the public educational realm?

A liberal who does not include nondiscrimination in the minimal conditions of reasonable public judgment resembles Robert Frost's characterization of a liberal as someone who cannot take his own side in an argument.[20] Public education that defers to deeply held religious beliefs in racial discrimination, for example, sacrifices liberalism's morally best means of living up to the constitutional principle of nondiscrimination. And it makes this sacrifice not merely by tolerating deeply held religious beliefs that are antithetical to liberalism but by (unnecessarily) fostering those beliefs. If the minimal conditions of public reasonableness in the United States today include a well-reasoned appreciation of the constitutional principles of nonrepression and nondiscrimination, then democratic government may teach children respect for different ways of life even against the deeply held religious beliefs of parents. Indeed, democratic governments have a public duty to do so.

But democratic governments should be careful not to confuse teaching children the virtues of democratic deliberation with teaching them either moral skepticism or "skeptical reflection on ways of life inherited from parents or local communities."[21] Liberal democratic virtues cannot be well taught without asking children to reflect on competing political perspectives, which are often associated with different ways of life, but such reflection does not entail either moral or metaphysical skepticism. Reflection on the reasonableness of democratic principles is an antidote to moral skepticism, and reflection on competing political perspectives is an antidote to dogmatism. In neither case does democratic education require giving up deeply held personal commitments, except for the unreflective commitment not to reflect on matters relevant to social justice. A democratic education has no better alternative than to take its own side in an argument about the public reasonableness of politically relevant reflection.

Deliberative democracy recognizes that the popularity of political authority is an insufficient grounds for its justification, but it goes one important step further than liberal democracy in finding more effective ways of constraining political authority by constitutional principles. Deliberative democracy defends publicly accountable deliberation as an essential means to democratic self-constraint. Decision makers must justify their decisions to the people who are governed by them.

Deliberation is also a good way of arriving at publicly defensible understandings of the demands of justice in the many situations where these demands are in reasonable dispute. There is no consensus among reasonable people who have thought long and hard about the just distribution of health care in the United States on precisely what justice demands. There may be a consensus that all Americans are entitled to "basic" health care, the care necessary for normal functioning or the opportunity to pursue a good life, but these standards are far from self-elucidating, and any complete elucidation is bound to be open to reasonable disagreement.[22] The choice between high-cost lifesaving technologies and low-cost opportunity-enhancing (but not lifesaving or life-preserving) health care is a hard one, about which people reasonably disagree. Deliberation among public officials who must offer an account of their decision and the reasons behind it to the citizens bound by it is both a means of arriving at provisionally justified decisions and also a component of justice, since justice entails offering acceptable reasons to the people who are bound by decisions.[23]

Democracies are therefore well advised to support deliberative institutions. Fostering publicly accountable deliberation is the most consistently democratic means of self-constraint available to political institutions. Collective self-constraint is the ideal democratic way of realizing constitutional principles. External constraints on popular authority still may be justified in the name of democracy when popular authority fails to constrain itself.

The idea that popular authority should constrain itself or be constrained by constitutional principles is less controversial among political philosophers than the idea that these constraints may be justified in the name of democracy itself. I have also defended this more controversial idea. It is this idea that I think best accounts for the widespread view of democracy as a political ideal, and not merely as an instrumental means to the realization of other political ideals. To say that democracy is more than merely instrumental is not, however, to say that it is an end-in-itself. Deliberative democracy, as I understand it, is valuable neither as an end-in-itself nor merely as an instrument for realizing values external to itself. Its full value cannot be divorced from in its own internal commitments to deliberation, nonrepression, and nondiscrimination.

I do not rule out instrumental reasons for valuing deliberative democracy, nor do I want to deny that there are other, nondemocratic ways of defending nonrepression, nondiscrimination, and perhaps even democratic deliberation. But it is important to recognize that a deliberative ideal of democracy itself contains a commitment to fulfilling these principles. Because deliberative democracy contains these commitments, it is misleading to say that democracy is merely an instrumental value and troubling to treat democratic institutions as such. In valuing deliberative democracy, we are valuing a representative government that is committed to treating all its adult members as free and equal citizens and all its minors as future citizens who are expected to deliberate about the future of their society. This self-understanding and the institutions appropriate to it support democratic self-constraint.

# 10 *WILLIAM M. SULLIVAN*

# Institutions as the

# Infrastructure of Democracy

### Limitations of the Instrumental View

American thinking has long been famous for its technical and instrumental bent. Americans have enjoyed their self-image as a people who excel at getting things done. This emphasis on effective technique has resonated with another national characteristic, the wish to invent one's life as much as possible on one's own terms. American individualism, that is, has long cohabited happily with a certain instrumental cast of mind. Working together, instrumentalism and individualism have rendered social life as a field of opportunities and constraints, structured by procedural rules. In this construction individual or collective actors are thought to be guided by preferences or values, but these are assumed to be reducible to some common coin of self-interest.

From this perspective institutions have appeared as instruments for the efficient pursuit of individual and collective satisfaction. From the family to the law, institutions have been reduced to an instrumental status, as little more than arrangements for the mutual convenience of the parties involved. The values or preferences of actors have been analytically separated from the contexts in which their values have been formed. In American intellectual culture as in popular opinion, the dominant theme has been to free individuals from social constraint, to enhance agency. This tendency has been buttressed by currents within philosophical liberalism, a body of theories in many ways congenial to instrumentalist as well as individualistic sentiments.[1] While foregrounding agency, this approach has often minimized the significance of institutions as the necessary contexts for the development of individuals, as enabling and not only as constraining forms of life.

During the postwar era the cultural, if not the strictly conceptual, deck has been stacked in favor of individualist instrumentalism, whether the vogue was economic rationality, strategic rationality, or rational choice theory. Today, however, phenomena such as a fragmenting social fabric increasingly polarized between rich and poor and the very weakness of the national capacity for organizing to meet new challenges seem to be propelling a willingness to entertain a more complex understanding of social life.

New questions are now being asked about the adequacy of the received instrumental and individualistic approaches to social reality. Notions such as character, virtue, culture, and community, though still ridiculed as confused and moralistic concepts, are receiving serious attention. The growing interest in communitarian themes is itself an indicator of the new climate of opinion. While these developments have appeared simultaneously in disparate areas of thinking and research, their common themes point toward an expanded and enriched understanding of institutions as essential for grasping the challenge of democracy in contemporary society.

### Institutions as the Missing Dimension

Faced with simultaneous threats to its traditional values of inclusion, equality, and economic opportunity, to say nothing of individual security, the contemporary American polity appears to be in a genuine quandary about how to understand its problems and go about seeking reform. The 1980s produced only a temporary and selective escape from the sense of economic decline and social fragmentation. Today there is a broad consensus that a significant part of what is wrong derives from public confusion about the common values that are worth preserving and lethargy in advancing them, a condition manifest in what is seen as excesses of personal license at the expense of responsibility for the common welfare. The accepted need is to learn better how to increase the social trust needed for working together toward common ends by enlisting rather than crushing individual initiative or stifling dissent. The difficulties appear once the issue is posed as to how to address this task, which is nothing less than revitalizing democratic life.

In a society which has long celebrated individual freedom as a high end, it is perhaps not surprising that the first response to the challenges of economic change and social disarray would focus mostly on individual consciousness and will. Repeatedly in American history major social dislocations have given rise to calls for moral reform. Whole social movements have sprung up to spur such moral reform, as in the movements for abolition and temperance. Today there is a good deal of sentiment about for moral crusades and reforms, which often frightens liberals, recalling the viciousness of the McCarthy era. While it would be absurd to imagine that significant social reform could be effected without the kind of moral effervescence that social movements manifest—think of the movement for civil rights in the 1960s—it is also clear that aroused moral sentiment by itself does not directly lead to a more active or effective democratic polity. The problem lies in developing a more adequate understanding of what might be called the social basis of moral life.

It has long been understood that individual welfare and freedom depend upon an antecedent security and reliability of social relationships. Led by faith in individualism on the one hand and instrumentalism on the other, however, many Americans have wished to believe that these conditions could be secured either by spontaneous goodwill among individuals or through the automatic functioning of well-designed social instruments. For instance, the provisions of the Federal Constitution have been regarded as machinery that could be counted upon to channel self-interest in benign directions without need for much concern among parties about the effects of their aims upon the whole. Or, the free market has been hailed as in principle the perfect regulator of social relationships if only it could be organized in pure form.

When these hopes have failed, the response has been to look toward expert steering and guidance, only to lead to further disillusionment with the quality of the steering and the limitations of the guardians. This cycle of reliance upon the unfettered market or the bureaucratic regulatory state has dominated national politics in the United States for most of this century.

Sensing that these old arguments have declining purchase on today's problems, recent thinkers have stressed the need to attend to the whole realm of organizations and associations that are neither simply parts of the market nor agencies of the state. This is the much-invoked idea of civil society.[2] While this conception adds a social depth often lacking in the conventional debate, it also fails by one-sidedness. It fails to note that the realm of civil society is itself deeply interconnected with market and state, both through the market processes that sustain the lives of families, organizations, and associations of all kinds and by the state in the form of law, regulation, and direct subsidy. While it is certainly true that significant social reform will have to rely on the moral energies of people in the myriad associations to which they have many of their deepest attachments, those associations must be seen as interwoven with the larger social processes we call market and state.

The missing dimension in the civil society discussion had already been seen by Alexis de Tocqueville. As is well-known, Tocqueville noted that small-scale associational life, such as the family, the school, and the religious congregation, provided the social bases of public-spiritedness and political skills. These were the schools of civic virtue that produced a civic culture of responsible citizenship and ordered liberty. What especially interested Tocqueville, however, was the normative aspect of these activities. The American constitutional order, the laws, but especially the customs of everyday life, worked together to produce an ensemble effect which made certain civic virtues—public engagement, reciprocity, mutual trust, tolerance within a general agreement about purposes—reliable features of American life.

As Tocqueville saw it, it was the institutional order, the patterns of normative, sanctioned interaction themselves, which worked through daily life to shape the imagination and character of the citizens. That is, institutionalized mores linked market, state, and civil society into the mutually reinforcing whole Tocqueville identified as American democracy. Besides individual consciousness and social interaction, human life also entails shared, socially sanctioned patterns of purpose. These are the institutional forms of family, school, religious congregation, business firm, and club, which structure the patterns of everyday life. Individual agency and moral responsibility depend upon the cultivation of certain kinds of social relationships that can be sustained over time only if institutionalized in customary and legal forms.

The nature as well as the importance of such a noninstrumental understanding of institutions becomes clearer as we inquire further into the practical conditions necessary for the civic culture of democracy. That is, what kind of person, with what kinds of dispositions, is necessary for the continued health of a civic culture characterized by public engagement in common causes, generalized reciprocity among citizens, and mutual trust and tolerance? How are such dispositions to be cultivated and transmitted? These questions invoke an old theme in political philosophy: that the quality of a political regime is interdependent with the character of its citizens. The most plausible account of how to sustain the character and customs necessary for a civic regime must give a central place to a noninstrumental conception of institutions.

## Institutions and Democracy

The need for a richer conception of institution to fill out the account of civic culture is perhaps most readily seen when approached from the side of character. This theme has been illuminated by recent work in the philosophy of agency and identity. In order to act human beings must have some understanding of the world and their place in it, an understanding most often implicit in their inherited attitudes and assumptions. Personal identity is thus not a given but an achievement, a process of self-development worked out with others within inherited cultural repertoires. Originality itself becomes intelligible and possible only against the backdrop of complex repertoires of action in which orientation and meaning inhere.

Alasdair MacIntyre has described these repertoires as centered on "practices," or shared, purposive activities that are not instruments toward other goals but whose ends lie principally within their own performance. In MacIntyre's account the typical social roles of parent, teacher, athlete, or citizen derive their significance and value from the goods realized in the practices constitutive of playing these roles well.[3] Persons who master these roles become virtuous in the sense that they perform well important functions of their lives. Concentration upon the intrinsic goods of practices can coexist with the use of such capacities for instrumental purposes. But when such roles are turned into nothing more than means to other ends, something essential to the identity of parent, citizen and so forth is lost. That something is the focus on goods intrinsic to the practices themselves.

The engaged, self-disciplined, and cooperative citizens invoked by theorists of democracy fall under this understanding of identity as achieved in the performance of valued practices. It is important to note that individuals in civic contexts are able to be virtuous largely because of the authoritative obligations and expectations that inhere in the customs and practices of public life. These form the borders, as it were, within which individuals conceive and pursue their purposes. In societies that lack such customs and practices, recent empirical research has shown that the civic virtues are much rarer.[4] In other words, individual freedom, the ability to realize a particular life plan or identity, turns out to be heavily conditioned by the kinds of practices and moral understandings available to persons in a particular life context.[5] The available normative patterns of expectation and significance set the limits for both public activity and individual motivation. Such patterns, otherwise described, are institutions.

Institutions, as we have seen, are normative patterns that define purposes and practices, patterns embedded in and sanctioned by customs and law.[6] They are patterns of social relationship that structure experience and shape character by assigning responsibility, demanding accountability, and providing the standards in terms of which each individual takes stock of his or her own life. Institutions are complex wholes that guide individual activity and sustain identity. For example, the institution of the family gives sense and purpose to the lives of its members, in part by providing the role identities of spouses, parents, children, siblings. Families also give their members better or worse possibilities for realizing themselves as spouses, parents, and children.

The "better or worse" is important since it calls to mind the important distinction between institution as a kind of substantial form and concrete organizations, such as a specific family or corporation. A given organization may realize institutional purposes more or less well. Much intrafamilial and organizational dispute is precisely about whether theirs is a "good" or a "real" family or corporation. But institutional patterns themselves may be judged praiseworthy or blamable according to how well they realize the goods that participants believe they should realize. So, for example, critics of marriage and family laws have argued that their present instantiation inhibits the development of women or fails to provide adequately for the needs of children.

Living in institutions is thus always in part centered in language. It is a conversation, sometimes an argument about who and what we and our shared form of life are. This process is a moral and, implicitly, a political one, since institutional life is always making some forms of activity possible and others impossible, some kinds of life legitimate and others illegitimate. It is noteworthy that even critics of institutions frequently find themselves unable to criticize the present form without using language, metaphors, and themes derived from the history of the institution itself. Institutions provide the socially enacted metaphors of family, team, school, army, court, church, and state through which individuals inescapably interpret situations and actions. This suggests the profound influence that institutional patterns as such exert on the thinking and aspiration as well as the behavior of individuals.

As they are embodied in organizations, institutions are the chief source of individual and collective identity and meaning. But the effects do not proceed in only one direction. As individuals seek their ends within organizations, organizational activity subtly or sometimes dramatically modifies the institutional order. There thus exists a reciprocity between individuals and particular organizations, on the one hand, and the normative structure of institutions, on the other.[7] This connection has been missing from conventional instrumentalist theories that have placed individual agency and institutional structures in opposition to each other. By contrast, effective democratic statesmanship always demands a practical understanding of the reciprocity and mutual interaction between the two.

It is not hyperbole, then, to say that human beings necessarily live in and through institutions. The opportunities open to each individual depend upon the possibilities made available in the institutional contexts within which that person participates. As Americans recognize in sports but often seem to forget in the rest of life, there could be no individual home runs without the collective effort, including not only the competitive antagonism of the teams on the field but also the whole supporting edifice of baseball: umpires, leagues, fans, finances. However, while institutions thus shape our lives and identities in intimate as well as collective dimensions, individuals are also continually engaged in creating and re-creating the very institutions that make their life and identity possible. Concretely, this takes place through organizations, as when groups succeed or fail to take effective responsibility for their aims or come to modify their ends or organization as the result of their experience. This is the reciprocity between individual and institution, the mutual implication of personal agency and social form.

This symbiosis—though never conflation—between the most intimate aspects of personality and forms of institutional life appears most strikingly in the realm of moral responsibility. While it is common to think of moral responsibility as a very private and lonely weighing of choices, it is also the case that typically the most important moral decisions an individual makes are made within and on behalf of institutions. As the mention of the roles suggests, the moral choices of spouses, parents, educators, and judges but also of business persons, pilots, clerks, and physicians are almost always exercised in their capacity, we might say their identity, as participants in institutions. That is, we always take responsibility as individuals, but we do so almost always within and on behalf of the goods and purposes defined by the forms of social life through which we live. Another important role of institutions is thus to provide the dramatic setting, and often the subject matter, of the moral dramas of individual life.

## Strengthening Institutions by Improving Organizations

These reflections suggest that the failure to comprehend the importance of institutions, and not simply individual malfeasance, is at the root of much of the moral confusion that threatens us. The achievements of democratic life rest in large measure upon the maintenance of strong institutions that support civic attitudes. But institutional forms live and grow through particular organizations and associations, individual families and schools, specific unions and business firms. Without substantial investment of human energy and commitment in developing organizations that can act as schools of civic virtue, a culture of individual responsibility would have to be an accidental or a miraculous outcome. If we fail to "endow" our organizations with our attention and resources, psychic as well as material, the larger institutional purposes will grow faint and confused, with attendant ills of individual demoralization and social waste.

The opposite of institutional cultivation through organizational development might be imagined on the analogy of reckless exploitation of natural resources: to take out more than one puts in, to use a complex interactive system sheerly as a means to goals extrinsic to its welfare. Destroying forests for fuel without thought of replenishing the source is a tragically self-defeating strategy. The same is also true of the single-minded exploitation of human resources. For millennia societies have done this to those they could coerce by enslavement, forced tribute, or mass conscription. However, one of the most important positive contributions of modern economics, if not always an intended one, is to reveal that the law of diminishing returns applies to the use of human resources as well. One might say that the secret to successful civic cultures is that they have replaced unilateral exploitation with self-restraint and reciprocal benefaction. The result is literally better conditions for all, and continuing incentives to continue in the course of mutual solidarity.

The analogy to the natural environment is fortunately imperfect. In human affairs the way persons think about their world and themselves importantly affects their future conduct. When in times of major social change such as the present short-term results reward those who regard institutions only as means toward extrinsic goals, as instruments to be used and discarded, then the hegemony of individualist and instrumental understandings can generate a self-fulfilling prophecy. On the other hand, there are plentiful examples of the opposite, positive direction.

By general agreement one of the fundamental goods of any society, and the first object of government, is to secure the safety of its citizens. Such security is the prerequisite for the success of almost all other institutional ends of a democratic society. By all accounts, this fundamental aim is seriously at risk in American society, particularly in the areas inhabited by its poorest and most vulnerable members. One response to this has been the effort by all with the means to protect their security by removing themselves as far as possible from sources of danger. This has been coupled by the strategy of enhancing police forces to "fight crime." Faced with the failure of these efforts to stem the increase of fear, as well as the growing numbers of incarcerated citizens, a number of cities have begun to experiment with "community policing." It is an approach which illustrates in a microcontext the strategy of strengthening institutions through developing organizations and association.

"The central premise of community policing is that the public should play a more active and coordinated part in enhancing safety," states an influential work on the subject.[8] But this shift from a passive to an active role for the public requires two simultaneous changes. The police force must significantly reform its normal procedures, shifting from centrally dispatched patrol cars to foot patrols, from distant surveillance to close involvement in the life of the community. These changes pose new challenges to police morale and efficiency. At the same time the public in high-crime areas is frequently fragmentary at best. Thus, community policing, as it gradually shifts the police organization from crime fighting to crime control, must also succeed in stimulating new citizens' associations. The aim is to increase the level of individual participation in the area while also strenghening the density of organizational life.

Where successful, the outcome is a slow upward spiral of more social cohesion, with mutual accountability between police and community and among citizens. By itself, community policing is rarely enough to stop social decay, but when well supported in both material and human terms, its trajectory illustrates the way intensified organizational life enhances individual well-being by strengthening institutional norms and purposes across an interacting network of associations. The "endowing" of organizations and associations, through the investment of time and energy, when held accountable for public ends can strengthen institutions by making their purposes better understood and more widely shared. This in turn makes civic virtue and democratic accountability more likely to be the accepted norms of everyday life.

Hopes for a democratic society rest upon the willingness to act on the belief that there is a synergy in human affairs such that concerted investment of effort and intelligence in places, societies, and organizations does, over time, result in strengthened institutions. The result is a continuing upward spiral in which civic "endowment" generates more civic virtue among citizens who in turn further develop their stock of trust, shared goals, and mutual respect.

The key contrast is between societies that are able to sustain over time a well-integrated infrastructure of civic institutions and those which fail or refuse to do so. The key variable is the willingness and capacities of citizens to cooperate actively in the strengthening of their associational life.[9] This need not threaten individual liberty or initiative. On the contrary, prudent efforts to stimulate organization and cultivate linkages among associations generate a kind of civic enrichment with palpably positive effects upon the social fabric and individual well-being, as the example of community policing illustrates.

Such a conclusion should not be construed as blindly optimistic, however. Gloomy tendencies toward social entropy are all too visible in wide areas of American life today. As this chapter has tried to argue, they have been aided by the simplistic and misleading view that institutions are simply neutral mechanisms for enhancing individual and social utility. But fortunately, in human affairs the recognition of problems need not entail fatalism. Recognizing that a weakening of civic bonds stems from mistaken social choices opens the possibility of changing the situation for the better by working to enhance the strength of civic culture. Taking responsibility for the well-being of our institutional structure importantly aids the renewal of democratic life. Public discussion of the nature and civic role of institutions can itself be a step in that direction.

# THE INSTITUTIONAL
# REQUIREMENTS OF
# CONSTITUTIONAL DEMOCRACY

# 11 *CHARLES TAYLOR*

# Liberal Politics and the

# Public Sphere

## Defining a Liberal Society

What exactly is a liberal society? What makes it possible? And what are the dangers it faces? These are the questions I'd like to explore in this chapter.

The problem is that all of these questions permit of answers of indefinite length. The dangers, for instance, of liberal society are not denumerable. Threats can come from an uncountable number of directions. So I'm going to be selective. There are problems and difficulties that seem to me widespread in our age, and I'm going to put them in the foreground. In doing that, I'm aware that I'll be speaking out of a parochial experience. Societies of a liberal type are now aspired to almost everywhere in the globe, in radically different conditions. No finite discussions can do justice to all these situations.

But surely, if the dangers are infinite, the first question, which calls for a definition of liberal society, permits of a clear and finite answer? So one might think, and a number of thinkers have tried to proffer clear definitions. But I think that here, too, the complexity of the reality and the multiplicity of its facets defeats us. Indeed, I think there is a danger in trying to make clear definitions, because this may narrow the scope of our attention in ways that may be damaging or fatal.

But don't we have to know what we're talking about? I will grudgingly admit this and am willing to offer a rough delineation of what I mean by liberal society at the outset. But as the discussion proceeds, the slippery and multifaceted nature of this description should become evident.

We can delineate *liberal society* in terms of its characteristic forms, for instance, representative government, the rule of law, a regime of entrenched rights, the guarantees of certain freedoms. But I'd prefer to start off on another footing and think of a liberal society as one which is trying to realize in the highest possible degree certain goods or principles of right. We might think of it as trying to maximize the goods of freedom and collective self-rule, in conformity with a rule of right founded on equality. The unsatisfactory nature of this as a definition springs to our attention as soon as we ponder what *freedom* means here. It's clear that this is much contested. For some, it might just mean negative freedom, being able to do what you want without interference from others, and particularly from authority. But for others, the meaningful freedom here involves real self-determination, an excellence of moral development. Someone who was merely negatively free, doing what he or she wanted, might be largely governed by unreflective convention or timidly conforming to norms that were not at all inwardly accepted, that he or she might even inwardly chafe at. This wouldn't be the more robust freedom of self-responsible life choice, which John Stuart Mill makes his standard in *On Liberty*, as when he praises "a person whose desires and impulses are his own—are the expression of his own nature, as it has been developed and modified by his own culture."[1]

But with all its fuzziness and uncertainties, this description will be good enough to be getting along with. It will enable us to begin examining some of the bases and dangers of a society dedicated to these ends.

I want to start the discussion by looking at Western liberal societies, the original models. Among the bulwarks of freedom here have been, for instance, the emphasis on the rule of law, on entrenched rights, recoverable by judicial action, and various modes of dividing power. I mean not only the division of powers as it exists in the United States Constitution but other ways of distributing power in different hands, for instance, through federal structures or autonomous local governments, and the like.

But in part freedom has been based in Western liberal societies on the development of social forms in which society as a whole can function outside the ambit of the state. These forms have often been referred to under the general description "civil society," taking the term in its post-Hegelian meaning as designating something distinct from the state.[2] The notion of civil society comprises the host of free associations, existing outside of any official sponsorship, and often dedicated to ends which we generally consider nonpolitical. No society can be called free in which these are not able to function, and the pulse of freedom will beat very slowly where they are not being spontaneously formed.

But civil society in a strong sense exists where beyond these multiple associations, or through their combination, society can operate as a whole outside the ambit of the state. I mean by this ways in which society can be said to act, or to generate or sustain a certain condition, without the agency of government. The very idea of their being such modes of extrapolitical action or pattern maintenance by the whole society is foreign to a great many historical civilizations; for instance, traditional Chinese society, or—to take an example very far removed from this—the ancient polis. And if we take other civilizations, like the Indian or the medieval European, where the society also has extrapolitical authorities, the striking difference in the modern West lies in the fact that the forms of civil society are purely secular.

Two major forms of civil society that have played a big role in Western freedom (or at any rate have been thought to play such a role) are the public sphere and the market economy. To put some flesh on this rather abstract discussion of extrapolitical and secular action of the whole, I shall talk in a little more detail of the rise of the public sphere.

### Exploring the Public Sphere

What do I mean by a *public sphere*? I want to describe it as a common space in which the members of society are deemed to meet through a variety of media: print, electronic, and also face-to-face encounters; to discuss matters of common interest; and thus to be able to form a common mind about these. I say "a common space," because although the media are multiple, as well as the exchanges that take place in them, these are deemed to be in principle intercommunicating. The discussion we're watching on television now takes account of what was said in the newspaper this morning, which in turn reports on the radio debate yesterday, and so on. That's why we usually speak of the public sphere, in the singular.

The public sphere is a central feature of modern society. So much so, that even where it is in fact suppressed or manipulated, it has to be faked. Modern despotic societies have generally felt compelled to go through the motions. Editorials appear in the party newspapers, purporting to express the opinions of the writers, offered for the consideration of their fellow citizens; mass demonstrations are organized, purporting to give vent to the felt indignation of large numbers of people. All this takes place as though a genuine process were in train of forming a common mind through exchange, even though the result is carefully controlled from the beginning.

Why this semblance? Because the public sphere is not only a ubiquitous feature of any modern society; it also plays a crucial role in its self-justification as a free self-governing society, that is, as a society in which (a) people form their opinions freely, both as individuals and in coming to a common mind, and (b) these common opinions matter: they in some way take effect on or control government. Just because it has this central role, the public sphere is the object of concern and criticism in liberal societies as well. One question is whether the debate is not being controlled and manipulated here as well, in a fashion less obvious than within despotic regimes but all the more insidiously, by money, or government, or some collusive combination of the two. Another is whether the nature of certain modern media permits the truly open, multilateral exchange that is supposed to issue in a truly common opinion on public matters.

There is a tendency to consider something which is so important and central to our lives almost as a fact of nature, as though something of the sort had always been there. Modern liberal society would then have innovated in allowing the public sphere its freedom and in making government in a sense responsible to it instead of the other way around. But something like public opinion would always have existed. This, however, would be an anachronistic error, which obscures what is new and as yet not fully understood in this kind of common space. I want to try to cast a little more light on this and in the process get clearer on the transformations in background understanding and social imagery that produced modern civilization.

In this discussion I draw in particular on two very interesting books, one published almost thirty years ago but recently translated into English, Jurgen Habermas's *The Structural Transformation of the Public Sphere*,[3] which deals with the development of public opinion in eighteenth-century western Europe; the other a very recent publication by Michael Warner, *The Letters of the Republic*,[4] which describes the analogous phenomenon in the British-American colonies.

A central theme of Habermas's book is the emergence in western Europe in the eighteenth century of a new concept of public opinion. Getting clear what was new in this will help to define what is special about the modern public sphere. Following the anachronistic reading we might think that what was new in the eighteenth-century appeals to public opinion was the demand that government be responsive to it, but that which government was called on to heed could be deemed to have already been in existence for an indefinite period. But this would be a mistake.

People had, of course, always recognized something like a general opinion, which held in a particular society, or perhaps among mankind as a whole. This might be looked down on, as a source of error, following Plato's low estimation of *doxa*. Or it might be seen in other contexts as setting standards for right conduct.[5] But in either case it is different from the new public opinion in three important respects: "the opinion of mankind" is seen as (i) unreflected, (ii) unmediated by discussion and critique, and (iii) passively inculcated in each successive generation. Public opinion, by contrast, is meant (i) to be the product of reflection, (ii) to emerge from discussion, and (iii) to reflect an actively produced consensus.

The difference lies in more than the evaluation, there passive acceptance, here critical thinking. It was not just that the eighteenth century decided to pin Cartesian medals onto the opinion of mankind. The crucial change is that the underlying process is different. Where the opinion of mankind was supposed to have passed down in each case from parents and elders, in a myriad of unlinked, local acts of transmission, public opinion was deemed to have been elaborated by a discussion among those who held it, wherein their different views were somehow confronted, and they were able to come to a common mind. The opinion of mankind is probably held in identical form by you and me, because we are formed by the same socializing process. We share in a common public opinion, if we do, because we have worked it out together. We don't just happen to have identical views; we have elaborated our common convictions in a common act of definition.

But now in each case, whether as opinion of mankind or public opinion, the same views will be held by people who have never met. That's why the two can be confused. But in the latter case, something else is supposed: it is understood that the two widely separated people sharing the same view have been linked in a kind of space of discussion, wherein they have been able to exchange ideas together with others and reach this common end point.

What is this common space? It's a rather strange thing, when one comes to think of it. The two people I'm invoking here have by hypothesis never met. But they are seen as linked in a common space of discussion through media: in the eighteenth-century print media. Books, pamphlets, newspapers circulated among the educated public, vehicling analyses, arguments, counterarguments, referring to and refuting each other. These were widely read and often discussed in face-to-face gatherings, in drawing rooms, coffeehouses, salons, and/ or in more (authoritatively) "public" places, like Parliament. The sensed general view that resulted from all this, if any, counted as public opinion in this new sense.

I say "counted as" public opinion. And here we get to the heart of the strangeness. Because an essential part of the difference is made by what the process is deemed to amount to. The opinion of mankind spreads through myriad unlinked acts of transmission, while public opinion is formed by the participants together. But if one made an exhaustive list of all the face-to-face encounters that occur in each case, the two processes wouldn't look all that different. In both cases, masses of people sharing the same views never meet, but everyone is linked with everyone through some chain of personal or written transmission. Crucial to the difference is that in the formation of public opinion, each of these linked physical or print-mediated encounters is understood by the participants as forming part of a single discussion proceeding toward a common resolution. This can't be all, of course; that is, the encounters couldn't be the same in all other respects and just differ in how they were understood by the participants. For instance, it is crucial to these linked encounters that they are constantly interreferring: I attempt to refute in my conversation with you today the *Times* editorial of last week, which took some public figure to task for a speech she made the week before, etc. It is also crucial that they be carried on as arguments. If in each case someone just passively accepted what another told him—as in the ideal-typical case, of authoritative transmission of tradition from parents to children—these events couldn't be plausibly construed as forming part of a society-wide discussion. But without this common understanding of their linkage on the part of the participants, no one even from the outside could take them as constituting a common discussion with a potentially single outcome. A general understanding of what things count as is constitutive of the reality here which we call the public sphere.

In a similar fashion there are clearly infrastructural conditions to the rise of the public sphere. There had to be printed materials, circulating from a plurality of independent sources, for there to be the bases of what could be seen as a common discussion. As is often said, the modern public sphere relied on "print capitalism" to get going. But as Warner shows, printing itself, and even print capitalism, didn't provide a sufficient condition. They had to be taken up in the right cultural context, where the essential common understandings could arise.[6]

We are now in a slightly better position to understand what kind of thing a public sphere is, and why it was new in the eighteenth century. It's a kind of common space, in which people who never meet understand themselves to be engaged in discussion and capable to reaching a common mind. Let me introduce some new terminology. We can speak of *common space* when people come together in a common act of focus for whatever purpose, be it ritual, the enjoyment of a play, conversation, the celebration of a major event, or whatever. Their focus is common, as against merely convergent, because it is part of what is commonly understood that they are attending to the common object, or purpose, together, as against each person just happening, on his or her own, to be concerned with the same thing. In this sense, the "opinion of mankind" offers a merely convergent unity, while public opinion is supposedly generated out of a series of common actions.

Now an intuitively understandable kind of common space is set up when people are assembled for some purpose, be it on an intimate level for conversation or on a larger, more public scale for a deliberative assembly, a ritual, a celebration, or the enjoyment of a football match or an opera, and the like. Common space arising from assembly in some locale, I want to call *topical common space*.

But the public sphere, as we have been defining it, is something different. It transcends such topical spaces. We might say that it knits together a plurality of such spaces into one larger space of nonassembly. The same public discussion is deemed to pass through our debate today, and someone else's earnest conversation tomorrow, and the newspaper interview Thursday, and so on. I want to call this larger kind of nonlocal common space *metatopical*. The public sphere that emerges in the eighteenth century is a *metatopical common space*.

What we have been discovering about such spaces is that they are partly constituted by common understandings; that is, they are not reducible to, but cannot exist without, such understandings. New, unprecedented kinds of spaces require new and unprecedented understandings. Such is the case for the public sphere.

What is new is not metatopicality. The church, the state were already existing metatopical spaces. But getting clear about the novelty brings us to the essential features of modernity. We can articulate the new on two levels: what the public sphere does, and what it is.

First, what it does; or rather, what is done in it. The public sphere is the locus of a discussion potentially engaging everyone (although in the eighteenth century the claim was only to involve the educated or "enlightened" minority) in which the society can come to a common mind about important matters. This common mind is a reflective view, emerging from critical debate, and not just a summation of whatever views happen to be held in the population.[7] As a consequence it has a normative status: government ought to listen to it. There were two reasons for this, of which one tended to gain ground and ultimately swallow up the other. The first is, that this opinion is likely to be enlightened, and hence, government would be well-advised to follow it. This statement by Louis Sebastien Mercier, quoted by Habermas, give clear expression to this idea: "Les bons livres dépendent des lumières dans toutes les classes du peuple; ils ornent la vérité. Ce sont eux qui déjà gouvernent l'Europe; ils éclairent le gouvernement sur ses devoirs, sur sa faute, sur son veritable intérêt, sur l'opinion publique qu'il doit écouter et suivre: ces bons livres sont des maîtres patients que attendent le réveil des administrateurs des états et le calme de leurs passions."[8] Kant famously had a similar view.

The second reason emerges with the view that the people is sovereign. Government is then not only wise to follow opinion; it is morally bound to do so. Governments ought to legislate and rule in the midst of a reasoning public. Parliament, or the court, in taking its decisions ought to be concentrating together and enacting what has already been emerging out of enlightened debate among the people. From this arises what Warner, following Habermas, calls the "principle of supervision," which insists that the proceedings of governing bodies be public, open to the scrutiny of the discerning public.[9] By going public, legislative deliberation informs public opinion and allows it to be maximally rational, while at the same time exposing itself to its pressure and thus acknowledging that legislation should ultimately bow to the clear mandates of this opinion.[10]

The public sphere is, then, a locus in which rational views are elaborated which should guide government. This comes to be seen as an essential feature of a free society. As Burke put it, "In a free country, every man thinks he has a concern in all public matters."[11] There is, of course, something very new about this in the eighteenth century, compared to the immediate past of Europe. But one might ask, is this new in history? Isn't this a feature of all free societies?

No; there is a subtle but important difference. Let's compare the modern society with a public sphere with an ancient republic or polis. In this latter we can imagine that debate on public affairs may be carried on in a host of settings: among friends at a symposium, between those who meet in the agora, and then of course in the *ekklēsia* where the thing is finally decided. The debate swirls around and ultimately reaches its conclusion in the competent decision-making body. Now the difference is that the discussions outside this body prepare for the action ultimately taken by the same people within it. The "unofficial" discussions are not separated off, given a status of their own, and seen to constitute a kind of metatopical space.

But that is what happens with the modern public sphere. It is a space of discussion which is self-consciously seen as being outside power. It is supposed to be listened to by power, but it is not itself an exercise of power. Its in this sense extrapolitical status is crucial. It links the public sphere with other facets of modern society which also are seen as essentially extrapolitical. The extrapolitical status is not just defined negatively, as a lack of power. It is also seen positively: just because public opinion is not an exercise of power, it can be ideally disengaged from partisan spirit and rational.

In other words, with the modern public sphere comes the idea that political power must be supervised and checked by something outside. What was new, of course, was not that there was an outside check but rather the nature of this instance. It is not defined as the will of God or the Law of Nature (although it could be thought to articulate these) but as a kind of discourse, emanating from reason and not from power or traditional authority. As Habermas puts it, power was to be tamed by reason. The notion was that "veritas non auctoritas facit legem."[12]

In this way the public sphere was different from everything preceding it. An "unofficial" discussion, which nevertheless can come to a verdict of great importance, it is defined outside the sphere of power. It borrows some of the images from ancient assemblies, as we saw above from the American case, to project the whole public as one space of discussion. But as Warner shows, it innovates in relation to this model. Those who intervene are, as it were, like speakers before an assembly. But unlike their models in real ancient assemblies, they strive for a certain impersonality, a certain impartiality, an eschewing of party spirit. They strive to negate their own particularity and thus to rise above "any private or partial view." This is what Warner calls "the principle of negativity." And we can see it not only as suiting with the print, as against spoken, medium but also as giving expression to this crucial feature of the new public sphere as extrapolitical, as a discourse of reason on and to power, rather than by power.[13]

As Warner points out, the rise of the public sphere involves a breach in the old ideal of a social order undivided by conflict and difference. On the contrary, it means that debate breaks out, and continues, involving in principle everybody, and this is perfectly legitimate. The old unity will be gone forever. But a new unity is to be substituted. For the ever-continuing controversy is not meant to be an exercise in power, a quasi-civil war carried on by dialectical means. Its potentially divisive and destructive consequences are offset by the fact that it is a debate outside of power, a rational debate, striving without parti pris to define the common good. "The language of resistance to controversy articulates a norm for controversy. It silently transforms the ideal of a social order free from conflictual debate into an ideal of debate free from social conflict."[14]

So what the public sphere does, is enable the society to come to a common mind, without the mediation of the political sphere, in a discourse of reason outside power, which nevertheless is normative for power. Now let's try to see what, in order to do this, it has to be.

We can perhaps best do this by trying to define what is new and unprecedented in it. And I want to get to this in two steps, as it were. First, there is the aspect of its novelty, which has already been touched on. When we compare the public sphere with one of the important sources of its constitutive images, viz., the ancient republic, what springs to our notice is its extrapolitical locus. The "Republic of Letters" was a common term which the members of the international society of savants in interchange gave themselves toward the end of the seventeenth century. This was a precursor phenomenon to the public sphere; indeed, the interchange contributed to shaping it. Here was a "republic" constituted outside of the political. Both the analogy and the difference gave its force and point to this image: it was a republic as a unified association, grouping all enlightened participants across political boundaries; but it was all a republic in being free from subjection; its "citizens" owed no allegiance to it so long as they went about the business of Letters.

Something of this is inherited by the eighteenth-century public sphere. Within it, the members of society come together and pursue a common end; they form and understand themselves to form an association, which is nevertheless not constituted by its political structure. This was not true of the ancient polis or republic. Athens was a society, a koinonia, only as constituted politically. And the same was true of Rome. The ancient society was given its identity by its laws. On the banners of the legions, "SPQR" stood for "Senatus populusque Romanus," but the *populus* here was the ensemble of Roman citizens, that is, those defined as such by the laws. The people didn't have an identity, didn't constitute a unity prior to and outside of these laws.

By contrast, in projecting a public sphere, our eighteenth-century forebears were placing themselves in an association, this common space of discussion, which owed nothing to political structures but was seen as existing independently of them.

This extrapolitical status is one aspect of the newness: that all the members of a political society (or at least, all the competent and "enlightened" members) should be seen as also forming a society outside the state. Indeed, this society was wider than any one state; it extended for some purposes to all of civilized Europe. This is an extremely important aspect and corresponds to a crucial feature of our contemporary civilization, which emerges at this time, and which is visible in more than the public sphere. I want to take this up in a minute, but first we have to take the second step.

For it is obvious that an extrapolitical, international society is by itself not new. It is preceded by the Stoic cosmopolis and, more immediately, by the Christian Church. Europeans were used to living in a dual society, one organized by two mutually irreducible principles. So the second facet of the newness of the public sphere has to be defined as its radical secularity.

This is not easy to define, and I am taking a risk in using a term which already is thrown around very loosely in attempts to describe modern civilization. If I nevertheless adopt it, it's because I think an awareness of its etymology may help us to understand what is at stake here, which has something to do with the way human society inhabits time. But this way of describing the difference can only be brought in later, after some preliminary exploration.

The notion of secularity I'm using here is radical, because it stands not only in contrast with a divine foundation for society but with any idea of society as constituted in something which transcends contemporary common action. For instance, some hierarchical societies conceive themselves as bodying forth some part of the Chain of Being. Behind the empirical fillers of the slots of kingship, aristocracy, and so on, lie the Ideas, or the persisting metaphysical Realities that these people are momentarily embodying. The king has two bodies, only one being the particular, perishable one, which is now being fed and clothed and will later be buried.[15] Within this outlook, what constitutes a society as such is the metaphysical order it embodies.[16] People act within a framework which is there prior to and independent of their action.

But secularity contrasts not only with divinely established churches or Great Chains. It is also different from an understanding of our society as constituted by a law which has been ours since time out of mind. Because this, too, places our action within a framework, one which binds us together and makes us a society and which transcends our common action.

In contradistinction to all this, the public sphere is an association which is constituted by nothing outside of the common action we carry out in it: coming to a common mind, where possible, through the exchange of ideas. Its existence as an association is just our acting together in this way. This common action is not made possible by a framework which needs to be established in some action-transcendent dimension: either by an act of God, or in a Great Chain, or by a law which comes down to us since time out of mind. This is what makes it radically secular. And this, I want to claim, gets us to the heart of what is new and unprecedented in it.

This is baldly stated. Obviously, this notion of secularity still needs to be made clearer. Perhaps the contrast is obvious enough with Mystical Bodies and Great Chains. But I am claiming a difference from traditional tribal society as well, the kind of thing the German peoples had who founded our modern North Atlantic polities, or in another form what constituted the ancient republics and poleis. And this might be challenged.

These societies were defined by a law. But is that all that different from the public sphere? After all, whenever we want to act in this sphere, we meet a number of structures already in place: there are certain newspapers, television networks, publishing houses, and the rest. We act within the channels that these provide. Is this not rather analogous to any member of a tribe, who also has to act within established structures, of chieftainships, councils, annual meetings, and the rest? Of course, the institutions of the public sphere change; newspapers go broke, television networks merge, and the like. But no tribe remains absolutely fixed in its forms; these, too, evolve over time. If one wanted to claim that this preexisting structure is valid for ongoing action but not for the founding acts that set up the public sphere, the answer might be that these are impossible to identify in the stream of time, any more than they are for the tribe. And if we want to insist that there must be such a moment, then we should remark that many tribes as well hand down legends of a founding act, when a Lycurgus, for instance, laid down their laws. Surely he acted outside of existing structures.

Talking of actions within structures brings out the similarities. But there is an important difference which resides in the respective common understandings. It is true that in a functioning public sphere, action at any time is carried out within structures laid down earlier. There is a de facto arrangement of things. But this arrangement doesn't enjoy any privilege over the action carried out within it. The structures were set up during previous acts of communication in common space, on all fours with those we are carrying out now. Our present action may modify these structures, and that is perfectly legitimate, because these are seen as nothing more than precipitates and facilitators of such communicative action.

But the traditional law of a tribe usually enjoys a different status. We may, of course, alter it over time, following the prescription it itself provides. But it is not seen just as precipitate and facilitator of action. The abolition of the law would mean the abolition of the subject of common action, because the law defines the tribe as an entity. Whereas a public sphere could start up again, even where all media has been abolished, simply by founding new ones, a tribe can only resume its life on the understanding that the law, although perhaps interrupted in its efficacy by foreign conquest, is still in force.

That's what I mean when I say that what constitutes the society, what makes the common agency possible and transcends the structures we need for today's common action, arose as a consequence of yesterday's, which however was no different in nature from today's. Rather, the traditional law is a precondition of any common action, at whatever time, because this common agency couldn't exist without it. It is in this sense transcendent. By contrast, in a purely secular association (in my sense), common agency arises simply in and as a precipitate of common action.

The crucial distinction underlying the concept of secularity I'm trying to define here can thus be related to this issue: what constitutes the association? Or otherwise put, what makes this group of people as they continue over time a common agent? Where this is something which transcends the realm of those common actions this agency engages in, the association is nonsecular. Where the constituting factor is nothing other than such common action—whether the founding acts have already occurred in the past or are now coming about is immaterial—we have secularity.

Now the claim I want to make is that this kind of secularity is modern; that it comes about very recently in the history of mankind. Of course, there have been all sorts of momentary and topical common agents which have arisen just from common action. A crowd gathers, people shout protests, and then the governor's house is stoned, or the chateau is burned down. But prior to the modern day, enduring, metatopical common agency was inconceivable on a purely secular basis. People could only see themselves as constituted into such by something action-transcendent, be it a foundation by God, or a Chain of Being which society bodied forth, or some traditional law which defined our people. The eighteenth-century public sphere thus represents an instance of a new kind: a metatopical common space and common agency without an action-transcendent constitution, an agency grounded purely in its own common actions.

But how about the founding moments that traditional societies often "remembered"? What about Lycurgus's action in giving Sparta its laws? Surely these show us examples of the constituting factor (here law) issuing from common action: Lycurgus proposes, the Spartans accept. But it is in the nature of such founding moments that they are not put on the same plane as contemporary common action. The foundation acts are displaced onto a higher plane, into a heroic time, an *illud tempus* which is not seen as qualitatively on a level with what we do today. The founding action is not just like our action, not just an earlier similar act whose precipitate structures ours. It is not just earlier, but in another kind of time, an exemplary time.

And this is why I am tempted to use the term *secular*, in spite of all the misunderstandings that may arise. Because it's clear that I don't only mean "not tied to religion."[17] The exclusion is much broader. But the original sense of *secular* was "of the age," that is, pertaining to profane time. It was close to the sense of *temporal* in the opposition temporal/spiritual. The understanding was that this profane time existed in relation to (surrounded by, penetrated by: it is hard to find the right words here) another time, that of God. This could also be conceived as eternity, which was not just endless profane time but a kind of gathering of time into a unity; hence the expression "hoi aiones ton aionon," or "saecula saeculorum."

The crucial point is things and events had to be situated in relation to more than one kind of time. This is why events that were far apart in profane time could nevertheless be closely linked. Benedict Anderson in a penetrating discussion of the same transition I am trying to describe here quotes Auerbach on the relation prefiguring-fulfilling in which events of the Old Testament were held to stand to those in the New, for instance the sacrifice of Isaac and the Crucifixion of Christ.[18] These two events were linked through their immediate contiguous places in the divine plan. They are drawn close to identity in eternity, even though they are centuries (that is, eons or *saecula*) apart. In God's time there is a sort of simultaneity of sacrifice and Crucifixion.

Modern *secularization* can be seen from one angle as the rejection of divine time and the positing of time as purely profane. Events now exist only in this one dimension, in which they stand at greater and lesser temporal distance and in relations of causality with other events of the same kind. The modern notion of simultaneity comes to be, in which events utterly unrelated in cause or meaning are held together simply by their co-occurrence at the same point in this single profane time line. Modern literature, as well as news media, seconded by social science, has accustomed us to think of society in terms of vertical time slices, holding together myriad happenings, related and unrelated. I think Anderson is right that this is a typically modern mode of social imagination, which our medieval forebears would have found difficult to understand, for where events in profane time are very differently related to higher time, it seems unnatural just to group them side by side in the modern relation of simultaneity. This carries a presumption of homogeneity which is essentially negated by the dominant time consciousness.[18]

Now the move to what I am calling *secularity* is obviously related to this radically purged time consciousness. Premodern understandings of time seem to have always been multidimensional. The Christian relating of time and eternity was not the only game in town, even in Christendom. There was also the much more widespread sense of a foundation time, a "time of origins" as Eliade used to call it,[19] which was complexly related to the present moment in ordinary time, in that it frequently could be ritually approached and its force partly reappropriated at certain privileged moments. That's why it could not simply be unambiguously placed in the past (in ordinary time). The Christian liturgical year draws on this kind of time consciousness, widely shared by other religious outlooks, in reenacting the "founding" events of Christ's life.

It also seems to have been the universal norm to see the important metatopical spaces and agencies as constituted in some mode of higher time. States and churches were seen to exist almost necessarily in more than one time dimension, as though it was inconceivable that they have their being purely in the profane or ordinary time. A state which bodied forth the Great Chain was connected to the eternal realm of the Ideas; a people defined by its law communicated with the founding time where this was laid down; and so on.

The move to what I am calling *secularity* comes when associations are placed firmly and wholly in homogeneous, profane time, whether or not the higher time is negated altogether, or other associations are still admitted to exist in it. Such I want to argue is the case with the public sphere, and therein lies its new and unprecedented nature.

I can now perhaps draw this discussion together and try to state what the public sphere was. It was a new metatopical space, in which members of society could exchange ideas and come to a common mind. As such it constituted a metatopical agency, but one which was understood to exist independent of the political constitution of society and completely in profane time.

### Genuine Democratic Decision

An extrapolitical, secular, metatopical space, this is what the public sphere was and is. And the importance of understanding this lies partly in the fact that it was not the only such, that it was part of a development which transformed our whole understanding of time and society, so that we have trouble recalling what it was like before.

I have already mentioned the market economy as another supposed extrapolitical bulwark of freedom. This is, indeed, not a common space, that is, it is not considered the locus of a common action. Rather, the notion that descends from Smith is that it is a field of interaction, in which a myriad of small-scale, bilateral common actions generate an overall pattern, behind the backs of the agents, by an "invisible hand." But the economy is similar to the public sphere in this, that it is an extrapolitical field of purely secular action, in which society is thought to be capable of generating an overall pattern outside the political domain. I haven't got the space to go into it here, but that the two have common origins in the cultural changes of early modern Europe seems to me quite evident. Habermas makes a similar point.

I have described both public sphere and market economy in their ideal-typical forms, as existing quite outside the political domain. Neither was ever integrally realized in this form, although in the age of absolutism, the new public sphere was in a sense excluded from power in a way that it most emphatically is not and cannot be in a modern democratic society. Of course, the market is always to some extent steered, controlled, limited by state action. In fact, a totally uncontrolled market economy would rapidly self-destruct. Of course, the public sphere is inhabited by all sorts of agents, including those with large political axes to grind, and not least those who are linked to established government. But although encroached on in practice to some degree, the fact that these domains operate and are seen to operate by their own dynamic has been of crucial importance to the limitation of power and hence the maintenance of freedom in the modern West. This seems to me beyond contest.

The differences arise when one tries to define just what this importance is. And here two camps form within Western democracies. There are those who hold that their main significance is as limits on potentially all-invasive state power; and that consequently they operate best the more they approach their ideal type of total independence. Let the market economy be as free of state interference as it is possible to make it. Let the public sphere be as clearly demarcated from the political as can be, constituted at the limit exclusively by media that claim total political neutrality. The camp is deeply imbued with the idea that the extrapolitical is the main bulwark of freedom.

Against them is ranged another camp, which holds that the attempt to limit power cannot be our exclusive concern. Liberalism must also be concerned with self-rule, that is, it must strive to make power and in general whatever shapes the conditions of our lives responsive to collective decisions. The exclusive focus on limiting power can hamper this goal. In one obvious way the concern above all to free the market can foster conditions that adversely affect a great many people but that they will be unable to change if the limits of interference are very narrowly drawn.

The concern of this second tendency is also with the health of democracy as a system of collective self-government. From this standpoint the public sphere plays not only a limiting, whistle-blowing role. It also can serve or disserve, raise or lower, facilitate or hamper the common debate and exchange that is an intrinsic part of conscious, informed collective decision.

What divides these two views is partly the different priority they place on the two main goods sought by liberal society, individual freedom and self-rule. Plainly those who strive above all to limit power place a greater importance on the first goal relative to the second. The two camps are also frequently divided in their understandings of the requirements of equality. But there also are important differences in their assessment of the conditions of stability and legitimacy in liberal societies.

Following Tocqueville, many would want to argue that self-rule has become one of the dominant ideals of modern liberal society. Indeed, this could hardly have been otherwise. The same cultural and political changes that brought about the public sphere as a space of extrapolitical common action, to which power was obligated to listen, needed only to be carried a little further to the proposition that the people should rule, that sovereignty belongs to the people. If this ideal really is widely and deeply felt in modern society, then an atrophy of self-rule poses a danger to the stability of liberal society, and hence also to the freedoms it protects. The fate of negative liberty would thus be connected to that of what Tocqueville called "political liberty." This farsighted thinker constantly argued that atrophy of the latter puts the former in danger. If you hold this view, then you have an additional reason to adhere to the second camp and to concern yourself with the quality of our collective decisions.

But this is a source of great puzzlement to us in modern democratic society. What exactly are we assessing when we concern ourselves with the quality of our collective decisions? It's easy to express the democratic aspirations. The rules and decisions that govern us ought to be determined by the people. That means that (1) the mass of the people ought to have some say in what they are going to be, and not just be told what they are; (2) this say should be genuinely theirs, and not manipulated by propaganda, misinformation, or irrational fears; and (3) it ought to some extent to reflect their considered opinions and aspirations, as against ill-informed and knee-jerk prejudice.

Once spelled out like this, truly democratic decision making has seemed a utopia to many observers. It has been argued that the third condition is virtually never met in mass democracies, that the average voter is too little informed, and too marginally interested, to cast an enlightened ballot. Reflections of this order led to the school of democratic "revisionists" after the Second World War, who argued that democracy was sufficiently served if the mass of the population could decide the competition between potential governing elites. However irrational the choice, their dependence on the people would force the elites to pay attention to their interests.[20]

Criticism of decision making in mass democracies also comes from another direction, from those who wonder whether the second condition is really met. The suspicion is that powerful interests are manipulating the public, through their control of media, major political parties, and the means of propaganda, and in fact are steering the public debate into narrow channels that serve their goals.[21]

Trying to assess these claims can be difficult. Just what standard of rationality ought one to adopt in assessing whether the third condition is met? When are the media leading or controlling the public, and when are they responding to mass prejudice? But underlying all this is a major difficulty, which arises from the very nature of such mass decisions, as well as from deeply embedded philosophical prejudices that make it hard to conceptualize this nature adequately.

I'm referring here to a feature I mentioned above in connection with the public sphere, that it is partly constituted by the common understanding of the participants. The public sphere generated a "public opinion" which was held to arise out of a common discussion, even though the participants never met in a single place and moment. The dispersed exchanges of small face-to-face groups, among whom printed materials circulated, were held to amount to a discussion from which a common sense emerged. An essential condition for this phenomenon of dispersed "public opinion" is that the participants understand what they are doing in this light.

A similar point holds for democratic decision making in modern polities. There isn't and cannot be a meeting of the whole population in an *ekklesia*, outside the celebrated cases of some Swiss cantons. What in fact happens is a dispersed process of public discussion through media, the casting of ballots to elect representative assemblies and executive officeholders, and decisions rendered by these latter that then have the value of common decisions. It is crucial to this political reality that the outcome of this dispersed process is understood to count as a decision of the nation or society. A common understanding of a certain kind is a necessary condition of this.

Necessary, but not of course sufficient. Things can go wrong. The debate can be manipulated; alternatives can be artificially narrowed through misinformation or control of the channels of decision. But we have difficulty grasping exactly how things can go wrong, because we haven't got too firm a grip on what it is for them to go right. A claim is being made: something is supposed to be a genuine, unforced common decision. This claim can be bogus. We normally understand what is involved in adjudicating this kind of thing: we compare the claim with an independent reality, and see if the two match. But here the reality is not entirely independent. Part of the successful reality consists of people understanding it to be so, and yet this understanding is exactly what we would like to challenge when we fear manipulation or sense that the process has been vitiated by a lack of real information or comprehension.

Here the temptation arises to refashion our model of democratic decision in order to avoid these perplexities. We simplify the phenomenon, thus altering the criteria of success. One way, common on the Left, is to follow Rousseau and see genuine democratic decision as the effecting of a general will, that is, some unanimous purpose. There are moments when a whole population feels strongly and at one on some question, often matters of foreign policy: Great Britain in 1940, the United States at the height of the Gulf War. We know what such moments are like, and we know that they seem to admit of little doubt. So we make this the benchmark of democratic decision and devalue all our ambivalent majority decisions as the result of manipulation and false consciousness.

Of course, philosophical doubt arising from the paradoxes of a social reality partly constituted by self-understanding is not the only motive here. There is the independent force of the Jacobin-Bolshevik tradition, which holds that the true people's will must be through class rule, or the work of factions. But the drive for unanimity is partly a drive for transparency, and this is given additional force by the philosophical doubts that center on collective decision in a diverse society.

Another way of refashioning the model to make the issue more tractable starts from the fact of diversity and purports to assess democratic decision objectively. People have interests that can be identified prior to decisions being taken, and the decisions favor some interests and frustrate others. Is the majority favored? Then democracy is served. If not, then there has been illegitimate elite control.

But each of these views offers criteria for valid democratic decision suitable for a social reality which is not the one we live. The Jacobin view can't accommodate real diversity of opinion, aspirations, agenda. The objective interest view can't accommodate all those decisions, often reflecting our moral views, where there are no clearly identifiable *ex ante* interests. More seriously, it can't take account of the fact that people's views can be altered by the interchange, that consensus sometimes emerges, that citizens frequently understand themselves as part of a community and therefore do not vote out of individual interest alone. We might say that, while the Jacobin view can't accommodate diversity, the interest view can't accommodate anything else; in particular, it can't account for the degree to which a political society functions as a community.

The conditions for a genuine democratic decision can't be defined in abstraction from self-understanding. They include (*a*) that the people concerned understand themselves as belonging to a community which shares some common purposes and recognizes its members as sharing in these purposes, and (*b*) that the various groups, types, and classes of citizens have been given a genuine hearing and have been able to have an impact on the debate, and (*c*) that the decision that emerges from this is really the majority preference.

In a society of mutually disinterested agents, intent only on their own individual life plans, conditions *b* and *c* (perhaps even condition *c* alone) would be all that one could ask. In such a society the objective interest criterion would indeed be adequate. But this is not what modern democracies are like. The idea underlying popular sovereignty is that the people who are sovereign form some kind of unit. They are not a scratch team picked by history, without anything more in common than the passenger list of some international flight. And this is hardly an accident. It is difficult to conceive of a widespread acceptance to abide by the rules and outcomes of democratic decision among people who had no bond whatever to each other. Only those with a supermuscular Kantian conscience would be willing to knuckle under to a majority with which they felt no links.

It is this dimension (condition *a*) of modern democratic society which makes self-understanding relevant, because there cannot be a community in any meaningful sense that doesn't understand itself to be such. But this fact also impacts on what we will want to count as fulfilling condition *b*. In our imagined aggregation of mutually disinterested agents, condition *b* could be measured in some purely objective terms, like the number of column inches devoted to a given position in the papers or the number of minutes of television exposure. But if one wanted to go beyond this and ask whether a given point of view was really heard, or whether it wasn't screened out and discounted in advance through prejudice or the nonrecognition of its protagonists, it's not clear how this could be assessed. Indeed, one might doubt whether agents who were truly mutually disinterested, and each involved in their own life plan, could give much sense to the idea of hearing another's point of view. In such a world there would be nothing between having your point of view ignored by your compatriots and having it endorsed. Agreement would be the only available criterion of genuine hearing.

Things can be very different in a community. Here the sense that one has been given a hearing depends not just on the particular interchange but on the state of the whole relationship. One could say that people can have a sense that they are heard because they know themselves to be valued in a certain way, even when some particular demands are not met. Their sense of being heard or not will also depend on the relation of their goal to common purposes and to the goals of other groups with whom they feel some solidarity in the light of these purposes. In this context a refusal of one of their proposals may be consistent in their view with their having been heard. For instance, in the light of common understandings, it is possible to see that certain demands represent a tall order for other groups, whereas others are relatively easy to grant. Blocking the second may indeed appear indistinguishable from a rejection of those who make the demands, whereas a demurral on the first may be easy to accept.

I've just slid here into putting it in terms of the sense of being heard. But the point is that we cannot drive a sharp wedge here between perception and reality. It is not that perceptions can't be mistaken, but that the reality, because it is connected with the whole state of the relationship, cannot be entirely divorced from participants' understanding. It is not just a perception-transcendent state of affairs which can be independently assessed. Whether some group is heard on some matter is, indeed, a matter of a number of things, including the bonds of common understanding and respect that link it with the majority or fail to do so, as well as common understandings of how hard or easy the demands are to accommodate.

Democratic decision making in large-scale societies is therefore something like the public sphere; whether and how it comes off has something to do with the self-understandings involved. But democracy is not just like the public sphere. It is plain that the operation of a public sphere is involved centrally in the process. Once we leave behind the Jacobin and objective interest criteria of democracy, which allow us simply to compare the outcome with some preexisting standard—the general will or individuals' interests—we have to take account not just the outcome but the process. That is the significance of requirement *b*, that various types, groups, and classes of citizens have been given a genuine hearing in the debate. But then it becomes clear that in a modern society the political system narrowly defined (say, parties, legislatures, and governments) cannot carry an adequate debate on its own. A debate within these channels alone would leave a large number of citizens and groups uninvolved. The issues also have to be thrashed out in what we are calling the public sphere, the public space of dispersed discussion circulating through media that are not directly part of the political system or that have taken a stance of political neutrality in relation to it.

A flourishing public sphere is essential to democracy. This is universally felt, and that is why contemporary despotisms feel impelled to fake one. But now we can see that this is not just because free media can play a watchdog role, carefully surveying power and sounding the alarm when it oversteps its limits. This function is important, but it doesn't exhaust their relevance. The quality and functioning of media in the public sphere can also do a lot to determine the quality and outreach of the public debate. The dramatic significance of whistle-blowing gives it an aura which it is hard to match in any other function. The saga of Watergate has entered into the imagination of generations of younger American reporters. But the tireless attempt to empty the last skeleton from the closet may actually impede the opening of a healthy debate on crucial issues, as the course of recent American presidential campaigning illustrates.

These remarks about genuine democratic decision suggest the different ways in which it can fail. Condition *b* can fail to be met; various groups or classes may be excluded, or their voices very feebly heard, their concerns barely impinging on the national agenda. Or else, condition *a* may be in danger, because various groups or classes or subcommunities feel excluded or perhaps on other grounds no longer understand themselves as linked with their compatriots in a single unit of decision based on common understandings. A democratic society—a "sovereign people"—may find that its capacity to render genuine democratic decisions is enfeebled either through a narrowing of participation or through a rift in the political community. These two modes of failure obviously can be closely interwoven, in that each helps to exacerbate the other. But they are notionally distinct, and in some cases one or other may be dominant.

### Failures of the Democratic Process

I would now like to look by way of illustration at some familiar types of failure of the democratic process, and at their possible remedies.

1. The first is the familiar sense of citizen alienation in large, centralized, bureaucratic societies. The average citizen feels power to be at a great distance and frequently unresponsive to him or her. There is a sense of powerlessness in the face of a governing machine which continues on its way without regard to the interests of ordinary people, who seem to have little recourse to make their needs felt. There seems to be no way that the ordinary citizen can have an impact on this process, either to determine its general direction or to fine-tune its application to his or her own case. This effect is the greater the more matters are concentrated in the hands of a remote central government and the more bureaucratized the procedures of government are.

Centralized bureaucratic power does not mean, of course, that the government has things all its own way. Powerful lobbies intervene and affect its course. But these, too, are remote from the ordinary citizen and generally equally impervious to his or her input.

This is the situation Tocqueville warned about, and he discussed one of the remedies at length. It consists of decentralized power, of having certain functions of government exercised at a more local level, where citizen mobilization to make an impact is a less daunting task.

But hypercentralization is not only a danger of the political system. It also affects the public sphere. Just as in politics, local concerns may impinge only with difficulty on the center, so the national debate may become concentrated in a small number of large-scale media that are impervious to local input. The sense becomes widespread that the debate on the major television networks, for instance, is shaped by relatively narrow groups or interests, and that its animators operate within a charmed circle which it is very difficult to penetrate. Other views, other ways of posing the questions, other agendas cannot get a hearing.

Tocquevillian decentralization is necessary in the public sphere as well. And indeed, each can support the other. The fact that important issues are decided locally enhances the importance of local media, which in turn focus the debate on these issues by those affected.

But it is not just a matter of bringing certain issues down to the local level where the local debate can affect them. The national debate can be changed as well by effective local public spheres. The model that seems to work here is one in which smaller public spheres are nested within larger ones, in the sense that what goes on in the smaller ones feeds into and has an impact on the agenda of the national sphere. The public sphere of a regional society can have that kind of impact, provided the political life of this society itself has some significance for the whole, a good example of how political decentralization also facilitates the enlarging of the public sphere.

But there are other kinds of smaller spheres as well. An example of a type which has been significant for some Western societies is provided by certain political parties and social movements. These can function as nested public spheres to the extent that their internal debate is open to the larger public. Then, depending on the significance of the party or movement politically, their inner debate can spill over and help to determine the national agenda. Some parties have had this function. But the most striking examples in recent decades are found in some of the "new social movements": for instance, the feminist movement (to the extent that one can speak of it in the singular) and ecological campaigns. These movements have not impacted on the political process the way lobbies usually do, mobilizing their efforts behind some agreed public stance and keeping their internal discussion to themselves. On the contrary, their internal debates have been out there for all to see, and it is as much through these as through their global impact that they have helped reshape the public agenda. That is why I want to speak of them as nested public spheres.

To some extent the drift toward centralization and bureaucratization is unavoidable in contemporary society. This is bad for democracy. It makes it hard to meet condition *b*. The nightmare scenario is a hypercentralized government, existing in a space of powerful elite-run lobbies and national television networks, each as impervious as the others to input from local sources. But this drift can be offset by a double decentralization, toward regional societies and nested public spheres, which can mediate the input from masses of ordinary citizens, who otherwise feel excluded from everything but the periodic national elections.

The model of public sphere that is emerging in this discussion is clearly different from the original eighteenth-century paradigm, and that in at least two respects. That original model seemed to posit a unitary space, and I'm suggesting here a multiplicity of public spheres nested within each other. There is a central arena of debate on national policy, but it is not the public sphere analogue of a unitary state but rather of a central government in a federation. Second, the clear boundary between the political system and the public sphere has to be relaxed. Some of the most effective nested public spheres are in fact political parties and advocacy movements, which operate in the gray zone between the two. In a modern democratic polity, the boundary between political system and public sphere has to be maximally porous.

That is, if we want this sphere to play its role in widening and expanding the public debate. If we think of it as a watchdog, limiting power, then the old model seems right. It is obviously easier for national networks or prestigious papers with a national reputation to take on the power holders. For the purposes of this function, a sphere dominated by large and powerful units, maintaining political neutrality, can seem ideal. But it can be disastrous for a genuine national debate.

2. Democratic decision making can also be impeded, even stymied altogether, by rifts within the political community. These can arise in a number of ways. One is a modality of class war, in which the least-favored citizens sense that their interests are systematically neglected or denied. In this regard it is clear that the kind of solidarity expressed in most Western democracies in the various measures of the welfare state, apart from their intrinsic justification, may also be crucial to the maintenance of a functioning democratic society.

Another kind of rift may arise when a group or cultural community feels itself to be unrecognized by the larger society and becomes less willing in consequence to function on a basis of common understanding with the majority. This may give rise to a demand for secession, but even short of this it creates a sense of injury and exclusion, in which requirement *b*, that all groups be adequately heard, seems impossible of fulfillment. In the climate of presumed exclusion, nothing can count as being heard in the eyes of the group in question short of total compliance with its demands. There is no simple way to deal with this kind of rift once it arises, but one of the major objectives of democratic politics ought to be to prevent them arising. This is another reason why ensuring that all groups have a bearing is of the utmost importance. This is not easy to achieve in our present era of multiculturalism.[22]

3. The effects of centralization and divisions can be exacerbated if they produce what I want to call *political fragmentation*. That is, if they impact on the political process and change its form. People can respond to a sense of exclusion by practicing a mode of politics which seems predicated on the belief that society is at best composed of mutually disinterested citizens, and perhaps for the most part even citizens who are malevolent to the group in question. To the extent that the people concerned have already come to accept an atomistic outlook, which sees society as an aggregation of individuals with their life plans and denies the reality of political community, this reaction is all the more readily available. Or, the response may be powered by a philosophic vision of exclusion, say, a Marxist view of bourgeois society as irretrievably divided by class war or certain feminist views of liberal society as irremediably vitiated by patriarchy, such that any invocation of political community is made to appear a sham and a delusion.

The kind of politics that tends to emerge out of this sense of exclusion, whether grounded in reality or philosophically projected (and it is often a mixture of both), is one which eschews the building of coalitions on a broad range of policies around some conception of the general good. Its attempt is rather to mobilize behind the group's demands on a narrow agenda, regardless of the overall picture and the impact on the community at large. Any invocation of the community good as grounds for restraint in this politics tends to be viewed with suspicion.

This is what I want to call *political fragmentation*, the breaking up of the potential constituencies for majority coalitions behind multifaceted programs designed to address the major problems of the society as a whole, into a congeries of campaigns around narrow objectives, each mobilizing a constituency determined to defend its turf at all costs.

The picture I am offering here is somewhat Tocquevillian, and yet it is significantly different from Tocqueville's. He apprehended a kind of vicious circle, in which citizen apathy would facilitate the growth of irresponsible government power, which would increase the sense of helplessness, which would in turn entrench apathy. But at the end of the spiral citizens would be governed by an "immense tutelary power."

Now Tocqueville's portrait of a "soft despotism," much as he means to distinguish it from traditional tyranny, still sounds too despotic in the traditional sense. Modern democratic societies seem far from this, because they are full of protest, free initiatives, and irreverent challenges to authority, and governments do in fact tremble before the anger and contempt of the governed, as these are revealed in the polls that rulers never cease taking.

But if we conceive Tocqueville's fear a little differently, then it does seem real enough. The danger is not actual despotic control but what I am calling *fragmentation*, that is, a people less and less capable of forming a common purpose and carrying it out. Fragmentation arises when people come to see themselves more and more atomistically or, otherwise put, as less and less bound to their fellow citizens in common projects and allegiances. They may indeed feel linked in common projects with some others, but these come more and more to be partial groupings rather than the whole society: for instance, a local community, an ethnic minority, the adherents of some religion or ideology, the promoters of some special interest.

This fragmentation comes about partly through a weakening of the bonds of sympathy, through a rift of one of the kinds described above, and partly also in a self-feeding way, through the failure of democratic initiative itself. The more fragmented a democratic electorate in this sense, the more they transfer their political energies to the promotion of their partial groupings, and the less possible it is to mobilize democratic majorities around commonly understood programs and policies. A sense grows that the electorate as a whole is defenseless against the leviathan state; a well-organized and integrated partial grouping may indeed be able to make a dent, but the idea that the majority of the people might frame and carry through a common project comes to seem utopian and naive. And so people give up. Already failing sympathy with others is further weakened by the lack of a common experience of action, and a sense of hopelessness makes it seem a waste of time to try. But that, of course, makes it hopeless, and a vicious circle is joined.

Now a society which goes this route can still be in one sense highly democratic, that is, egalitarian, and full of activity and challenge to authority, as is evident if we look at the contemporary United States. Politics begins to take on a different mold, in the way I indicated above. One common purpose which remains strongly shared, even as the others atrophy, is that society is organized in the defense of rights. The rule of law and the upholding of rights are seen as very much the "American way," that is, as the objects of a strong common allegiance. The extraordinary reaction to the Watergate scandals, which ended up unseating a president, are a testimony to this.

In keeping with this, two facets of political life take on greater and greater saliency. First, more and more turns on judicial battles. The Americans were the first to have an entrenched bill of rights, augmented since by provisions against discrimination, and important changes have been made in American society through court challenges to legislation or private arrangements allegedly in breach of these entrenched provisions. The famous case of *Brown v. Board of Education*, which desegregated the schools in 1954, is a case in point. In recent decades more and more energy in the American political process is turning toward this process of judicial review. Matters that in other societies are determined by legislation, after debate and sometimes compromise between different opinions, are seen as proper subjects for judicial decisions in the light of the Constitution. Abortion is a case in point. Since *Roe v. Wade* in 1973 greatly liberalized the abortion law in the country, the effort of conservatives, now gradually coming to fruition, has been to stack the Court in order to get a reversal. The result has been an astonishing intellectual effort, channeled into politics-as-judicial review, which has made law schools the dynamic centers of social and political thought on American campuses, and also a series of titanic battles over what used to be the relatively routine—or at least nonpartisan—matter of senatorial confirmation of presidential appointments to the Supreme Court.

Alongside judicial review, and woven into it, American energy is channeled into interest or advocacy politics. People throw themselves into single-issue campaigns and work fiercely for their favored cause. Both sides in the abortion debate are good examples. This facet overlaps the previous one, because part of the battle is judicial, but it also involves lobbying, mobilizing mass opinion, and selective intervention in election campaigns for or against targeted individual candidates.

All this makes for a lot of activity. A society in which this goes on is hardly a despotism. But the growth of these two facets is connected, part effect and part cause, with the atrophy of a third, which is the formation of democratic majorities around meaningful programs that can then be carried to completion. In this regard, the American political scene is abysmal. The debate between the major candidates becomes ever more disjointed, their statements ever more blatantly self-serving, their communication consisting more and more of the now famous sound bites, their promises risibly unbelievable ("Read my lips") and cynically unkept, while their attacks on their opponents sink to ever more dishonorable levels, seemingly with impunity. At the same time, in a complementary movement, voter participation in national elections declines and has recently hit 50 percent of the eligible population, way below that of other democratic societies.

Something can be said for, and perhaps a lot can be said against, this lopsided system. One might worry about its long-term stability, worry, that is, whether the citizen alienation caused by its less and less functional representative system can be compensated for by the greater energy of its special-interest politics. The point has also been made that this style of politics makes issues harder to resolve. Judicial decisions are usually winner take all; either you win or you lose. In particular, judicial decisions about rights tend to be conceived as all-or-nothing matters. The very concept of a right seems to call for integral satisfaction, if it's a right at all; and if not, then nothing. Abortion once more can serve as an example. Once you see it as the right of the fetus versus the right of the mother, there are few stopping places between the unlimited immunity of the one and the untrammeled freedom of the other. The penchant to settle things judicially, further polarized by rival special-interest campaigns, effectively cuts down the possibilities of compromise.[23]

We might also argue that it makes certain issues harder to address, those which require a wide democratic consensus around measures that will also involve some sacrifice and difficulty. Perhaps this is part of the continuing American problem in coming to terms with its declining economic situation through some form of intelligent industrial policy. And perhaps this has something to do with the underdeveloped nature of the welfare state in the United States, in particular, the lack of a public universal health scheme.[24] These kinds of common projects become more difficult to enact where this style of politics is dominant. For they cannot be carried through by mobilizing a clearly defined constituency around a single, narrowly focused front. They require rather the building of a wider alliance which can sustain a broader range of interlinked policies over time, the kind of politics practiced by social democratic parties in a number of Western democracies. (Or for that matter, by their opponents: see the Thatcher counterrevolution for an example.)

This unbalanced system both reflects and entrenches fragmentation. Its spirit is an adversarial one in which citizen efficacy consists in being able to get your rights, whatever the consequences for the whole. Both judicial retrieval and single-issue politics operate from this stance and further strengthen it. A fragmented society is one whose members find it harder and harder to identify with their political society as a community. And this is where a vicious circle can engage. The lack of identification may reflect an atomistic outlook, in which people come to see society purely instrumentally. But it also helps to entrench atomism, because the absence of effective common action on a more broadly based agenda through majority coalitions throws people back on themselves. Fragmentation is certainly intensified by the sense that government is impervious and the citizen powerless, acting through the normal electoral channels, to affect things significantly. But the politics of fragmentation further contributes to the inefficacy of these electoral channels, and a self-feeding spiral is joined. (This is perhaps why one of the most widely held social philosophies in the contemporary United States is the procedural liberalism of neutrality, which combines quite smoothly with an atomist outlook.)

How do you fight fragmentation? It's not easy, and there are no universal prescriptions. It depends very much on the particular situation. But we have seen that fragmentation grows to the extent that people no longer identify with their political community, that their sense of corporate belonging is transferred elsewhere or atrophies altogether. And it is fed, too, by the experience of political powerlessness. And these two developments mutually reinforce each other. A fading political identity makes it harder to mobilize effectively, and a sense of helplessness breeds alienation. Now we can see how in principle the potential vicious circle here could be turned into a virtuous circle. Successful common action can bring a sense of empowerment and also strengthen identification with the political community. Indeed, the debate around certain kinds of issues that foregrounds certain common goals, even though there are radical disagreements about the means, can help to make the sense of political community more vivid and thus to some extent offset the tendency of deep political divisions to paint the adversary as the devotee of utterly alien values. The contrast is striking with, say, the abortion debate, where both sides readily can come to believe that their opponents are enemies of morality and civilization.

This sounds like saying that the way to succeed here is to succeed, which is true if perhaps unhelpful. But we can say a little more. One of the important sources of the sense of powerlessness is that we are governed by large-scale, centralized, bureaucratic states. What can help mitigate this sense is decentralization of power, as Tocqueville saw. And so in general, devolution, or a division of power, as in a federal system, particularly one based on the principle of subsidiarity, can be good for democratic empowerment. And this is the more so, if the units to which power is devolved already figure as communities in the lives of their members.

We are back to the theme of Tocquevillian decentralization, which I have indicated should englobe not only the political system but the public sphere as well.

What this points to is a kind of equilibrium which a liberal political system should seek. It is a balance between the party electoral system, on one hand, and the proliferation of advocacy movements, on the other, that are not directly related, if related at all, to the partisan struggle. The first is the channel through which broad coalitions on connected issues can be built and can effect their purposes. When this atrophies or functions badly, effective citizen action on a large number of issues becomes difficult if not impossible. But if the party electoral system were be there alone, if the wide range of movements engaged in extraparliamentary politics were to disappear, then the society would be badly blocked in another way. It would lack that network of nested public spheres which alone keeps its agenda open and provides a way into political efficacy for large numbers of people who would never make the same impact through the established parties.

In a sense, there needs to be not only a balance between these two but a kind of symbiosis; or at least open frontiers, through which persons and ideas can pass from social movements to parties and back again. This is the kind of politics that liberal societies need.

### A Visible Liberal Society

I started with a discussion of liberal society, and I have ended up talking about the nature of liberal politics. I am aware that I have only tabled some of the more important issues, that much more needs to be said on these, and that there is an indefinite number of other ways in which the political system of a liberal society can go awry that I have not even touched on here.

All this underlines the lesson of how difficult and potentially unfruitful it can be to try to define the nature of liberalism in a few terse sentences. The temptation is highly understandable, because the rise of liberal society in the West has been inseparable from the promulgation of striking and unprecedented ideas and social forms. One of these has been the public sphere, which both illustrates and gives concrete shape to one of the principal foundations of Western liberalism, captured in the expression "civil society": the understanding that the society can function as a whole also outside the political realm, that society is not constituted by the state but limits it. Another such foundational idea has consisted in making the rule of right a central unifying principle of political society, in, for example, the conception of a political order founded on natural rights (or universal human rights; the variation in terms is much less significant than is usually supposed).

The temptation consists in taking one of these ideas and forms and making it the exclusive defining feature of liberalism. The (largely implicit) argument of this chapter is that this is an intellectual mistake, with possibly damaging practical consequences. The goals of liberalism have been generally plural, including at least the three factors I mentioned at the outset: freedom, self-government, and a rule of right founded on equality. Each of these is complex and many-faceted. A viable liberal society has to take account of all of them or risk the disaffection of significant numbers of its citizens. This means that liberal politics has to be concerned with the conditions of genuinely democratic common decisions, and that the public sphere cannot be seen only as a social form limiting the political but as a medium of democratic politics itself.

When we try to understand and assess the development of liberal regimes outside the Western heartland, we have even more reason not to be too centered on its specifically Western foundations. Our central concern should be to see how a political life fostering freedom and self-government under conditions of equality can be developed and promoted. This will certainly require some species of public sphere. But these spheres, existing in rather different cultural contexts, will in all likelihood be even more distant from our paradigm eighteenth-century model than the contemporary Western ones are. Some will certainly surprise us. We will have to be alert to potential new forms that can open channels for democratic decision. And "we" here includes not only Westerners but political actors in these new societies who might be tempted to imitate the supposedly successful paradigm models of the North Atlantic world.

It will help in discerning these new forms if we have some better idea what genuine democratic decision amounts to; and that is the issue I have been struggling with in the preceding pages, I hope not entirely in vain.

# Free Speech and Free Press

## A Communitarian Perspective

A central issue in current debates over free speech and free press in the United States is whether government may intervene in the "marketplace of ideas" to promote access for ideas or views that otherwise might not be heard. These debates over access capture the enduring tension between two competing understandings of the First Amendment.

One school of thought, typified by libertarian politics, insists that government must maintain a hands-off, laissez-faire approach to speaking and publishing, leaving the market free to determine who speaks and how loudly. In this view individuals have a right to choose for themselves what ideas are worth saying or hearing. Likewise, libertarians maintain, candidates for public office have a free speech right to buy as much speech as the market will bear. So too, in this view, does the First Amendment guarantee the press the right to make independent editorial decisions, free from imposed legal requirements about how to report the news.

The second school of thought, basic to communitarian politics, insists that the crucial democratic value is not an unregulated press but an accessible one. Of course, the public interest means that the press must be guaranteed the independence from government it takes to be an adversary and critic of government. But the public interest also requires that the crucial channels of mass communications be open to the citizenry at large, that political debate over the media be open to as wide an array of views and voices as is practically possible. If it takes legal regulations to achieve these access goals, then so be it. "Such regulation frees speech even as it restricts press prerogatives."[1] In an age of media giants such as Time Warner or Capital Cities/ABC, the metaphor of a free market in ideas is no longer persuasive in the way it might once have been when Holmes and Brandeis set out to protect fringe groups and radical publications from being censored by a government posted as cop at the entrance to the market.[2] Given the shift in media power, the end First Amendment value of a rich and robust public debate may require the government on occasion to play an active role in legislating public access to the media or creating alternative public access channels of communication for democracy's conversations.

Over the past generation the prevailing interpretation of the First Amendment, both in the courts and in administrative agencies such as the Federal Communications Commission (FCC), has moved dramatically in the direction of the libertarian school. There are a number of signs of this shift. In regard to free speech, the Supreme Court has increasingly insisted, since the early 1960s, that the core purposes of the First Amendment are individual rather than social. That is to say, the prime goal of the First Amendment is often said today to be promotion of "personal growth and self-realization."[3] "Assuring self-fulfillment," remarks one leading constitutional scholar, is a "good in itself," needing no further justification in terms of service to the common good.[4] To protect the individual's right of self-expression, the Supreme Court has fashioned a jurisprudence which virtually strips government of any power to make moral judgments about irresponsible or socially harmful exercises of expression. "Above all else, the First Amendment means that government has no power to restrict expression because of its message, its ideas, its subject matter, or its content."[5] Rather, government must remain neutral as to how individuals express themselves, a moral bystander, imposing no legal judgments about what are good or bad ideas to express. Obscenity remains one exception to this ban on moral judgment, where states still may punish *distribution* of hard-core pornography.[6] But since 1969 the Court has granted individuals the right to *possess* pornographic materials in the home, since the constitutional "right to receive information and ideas, regardless of their social worth [is] fundamental to our free society."[7]

In regard to free press, the clearest sign of the shift is the move during the 1980s to deregulate the broadcast media from their traditional responsibilities, dating back to the Communications Act of 1934, to act as "public trustees," licensed to broadcast over the public airwaves not merely for private gain but also to promote debate and deliberation on vital civic issues.[8] Public trustee status for broadcasters rested on the clear notion that the airwaves were public, not private, property; consequently those licensed to use the public's property had a responsibility to make radio and television stations accessible to speech by citizens at large, rather than claiming some putative First Amendment right to monopolize the assigned broadcast frequency for themselves. The FCC's repeal of the fairness doctrine in 1987, which once required broadcasters to devote airtime to issues of public importance and to cover these issues in a balanced way, was one recent sign among many of the triumph of the identification of the First Amendment with the political theory of deregulating the media and trusting market competition to serve all of democracy's needs.[9]

These highly private-market, individualistic interpretations of the First Amendment, however familiar today, in fact represent a break with the classical defenses of free speech as an instrument of democracy. These defenses did not focus on the isolated contribution that speech makes to individual self-development; they justified free speech as a crucial means of fostering the social virtues of citizenship and the practices of self-government. Such self-government defenses harked back to Madison's admonition that "a popular Government, without popular information, or the means of acquiring it, is but a Prologue to a Farce or a Tragedy; or, perhaps both."[10] The self-government rationale for protecting free speech was hardly neutral about the social value of speech. Alexander Meiklejohn noted that the democratic justification for protecting free speech grants priority of protection to public debate on issues of civic importance. These discussions must be absolutely protected in a democracy because "the primary purpose of the First Amendment is . . . that all the citizens shall, so far as possible, understand the issues which bear upon our common life." By contrast, "the private freedom of this or that individual" to express himself or herself on nonpolitical matters was of far less social value.[11]

Of course, there is considerable room for debating what is properly the subject of public speech in a self-governing community. Meiklejohn and his successors have had trouble in particular with artistic expression: should it be fully protected because art always if indirectly enriches the public's capacity for governance, or may the state regulate works of art ostensibly expressing only the artist's view of nonpolitical matters? The self-government rationale does indeed leave us with difficult problems in drawing the line between the political and non-political. Still, its merit is to peg First Amendment protection to a determination of whether common, rather than purely personal, interests are at stake.

Self-government, not self-expression, remained the key justifier of free speech into the 1960s. In 1966 constitutional scholar Harry Kalven, Jr. sharply distinguished between the importance of protecting criticism of government and protecting, say, obscenity. "A society can . . . either treat obscenity as a crime or not a crime without thereby altering its basic nature as a society," Kalven wrote. But any society that uses the concept of "seditious libel" to criminalize criticism of government is by definition "not a free society."[12]

Since the 1960s the self-expression theory of the First Amendment has clearly been in the ascendancy. Consider, for instance, a 1971 decision striking down a state law prohibiting the use of offensive language in public.[13] The Court faulted the law for imposing a moral judgment on how individuals choose to express themselves. The fact of the matter, for the Court, was that such legalized moral judgments lack any objective or rational basis; "one man's vulgarity is another's lyric." In the face of this moral relativism, law should free individuals to choose how to express themselves. The only alternative would be to grant government a "boundless" authority to pick and choose which words were too offensive for civil public discourse. Such moral policing of public discourse does not "comport with the premise of individual dignity and choice upon which our political system rests."[14]

The importance of granting individuals wide rights to express themselves should be given its due. Such rights do generally rule out government censorship of public debate and prohibit government from standing gatekeeper to the marketplace of ideas, possessed of authority to impose orthodox legal judgments on what are good or bad ideas to be debated. Compared to the state of free speech from the 1920s through the 1950s, when states and the federal government legally outlawed advocacy of socialism and communism,[15] the current principle requiring government to be "content neutral" when it comes to regulation of speech is of vital importance. Still, in a number of areas, American law seems to have lost sight of the need to consider the social as well as private purposes of free speech and free press in a democracy. In what follows, we concentrate on two such troubling areas. The first area is the Court's persistent hostility to campaign finance reforms that would lessen the influence of money on elections. The second area has to do with guaranteeing some level of public access to the media. Although different, both areas raise central questions about whether government may restrict pure individual rights of expression to further social values of equalizing speech or affording as many citizens as possible with effective opportunities for speaking over the most influential channels of communication in modern society.

### Access and Elections

The Supreme Court has noted, to its credit, that "virtually every means of communicating ideas in today's mass society requires the expenditure of money."[16] But the Court has put this realization to perverse uses. In *Buckley v. Valeo*,[17] the Court considered a series of challenges to the Federal Election Campaign Act of 1971 and as amended in 1974. The challenged provisions provided that:

> individual political contributions were limited to $1,000 to any single candidate per election;
>
> independent expenditures "relative to a clearly identified candidate" were limited to $1,000 a year;
>
> campaign spending by candidates for various federal offices were subject to prescribed limits;
>
> a system for public funding of presidential campaign activities was to be established.

The majority of the Court sustained the individual *contribution* limits, as well as the public financing scheme. But the Court declared unconstitutional the act's various ceilings on *expenditures*.[18] In 1985 the Court applied *Buckley* to strike down a $1,000 ceiling on expenditures by independent political action committees on behalf of a candidate.[19]

In *Buckley* defenders of the campaign expenditure limits argued to the Court that the limits served rather than hindered core First

Amendment procedural values. The purpose of the reforms was to enhance the effectiveness of the citizen's political voice, to minimize money's way of amplifying the views of some while drowning out the concerns of others. But the *Buckley* Court rejected the legitimacy of state action to "equalize" speech: "The concept that government may restrict the speech of some elements of our society in order to enhance the relative voice of others is wholly foreign to the First Amendment."[20] The reason such an "equality" concept is foreign, the Court went on, is because "the First Amendment . . . was designed to secure the widest possible dissemination of information from diverse and antagonistic sources."[21] But the Court seems guilty of a non sequitur here. When money determines the effectiveness of speech, there is no reason to presume citizens will debate "information from diverse and antagonistic sources." Rather, as one scholar argues, "community deliberation on public issues may be biased, and rational self-governance may therefore be impeded, if certain points of view are made much more prominent than others due to superior economic resources."[22]

Some scholars defend the *Buckley* decision by pointing out that expenditure limits tend to favor incumbents. This is because incumbents enjoy the advantages of name recognition and free publicity generated by their public duties. Other things being equal, challengers depend on spending during the campaign to offset the natural advantages of incumbency. Therefore, these scholars conclude, congressional incumbents were acting only in a suspiciously self-serving way when they passed the contribution and expenditure limits at issue in *Buckley*. There is some merit in this view. "Regulations to assure the equal availability of all legitimate viewpoints *are* difficult to construct fairly and they raise the dangers of a chilling effect and partisan abuse." But "in principle, at least, such restrictions could be designed to serve as a type of time, place, and quantity regulation which, like limits on noise levels, would be tailored to achieve on balance the maximum liberty for all."[23]

*Buckley* elevates the interests of individuals and interest groups in buying as much political speech (and influence) as they can over any competing public interest in the nature of a fair democratic process which grants effective access to ideas irrespective of the wealth that backs them. As one political philosopher puts it, *Buckley* views democracy as but the "regulated rivalry between economic classes and interest groups in which the outcome should properly depend on the ability and willingness of each to use its financial resources and skills, admittedly very unequal, to make its desires felt."[24]

A fuller vision of democracy goes beyond this thin sense of a deregulated marketplace of ideas properly producing winners and losers. Ultimately, we aspire to be a democracy which creates genuine opportunities for self-government by a citizen body jointly feeling moral responsibility for pursuing the common good and not just private interests. *Buckley* makes it more difficult to create the participatory conditions necessary to self-government by placing a constitutional choke hold on legislative reforms aimed at equalizing effective access to community deliberation on public issues.

The Court's mistake on access issues is neither trivial nor a sideshow. At stake is the repetition of the mistakes that earned the so-called Lochner era in American constitutional law its universally negative reputation.[25] In *Lochner v. New York* (1905)[26] and its progeny, the Court found in the Fourteenth Amendment due process clause a novel doctrine of individual liberty of contract which prevented the state from passing maximum hours or minimum wage laws. Ultimately, at the crest of the New Deal, the Court abandoned *Lochner*, and the consensus ever since has been that the Constitution contains no theory of individual liberty that prohibits the state from regulating contracts in the interest of improving the status of the less well-off.

In *Buckley v. Valeo* and its progeny, the current Supreme Court finds in the First Amendment a novel doctrine of individual liberty which prevents the state from regulating campaign expenditures by individuals or groups or candidates, in the interest of making certain that those with financial resources do not skew or semimonopolize the marketplace of ideas. This approach stands the noble purposes of the First Amendment on its head. After all, even by the Court's own philosophy of scrutinizing procedural flaws in democracy, the Court should have given Congress more elbowroom to experiment with ways to close the gap between the speech available to the haves and the have-nots. But the Burger and Rehnquist Courts have interpreted the First Amendment as ruling out any "egalitarian" attempts to regulate how much speech money can buy in elections. As in *Lochner*, the Court has fashioned a false understanding of liberty where the individual's interest in expressing his or her views is protected, no matter what the consequences for public debate or fair representation or genuine opportunity to run for office. Such an interpretation of the First Amendment cannot and should not long stand, since it essentially enshrines the individual interest in self-expression as an end in itself, the highest value in our culture, divorced from any need to consider how one person's exercise of liberty affects the ability of other persons to exercise equal and like liberties.

### Access and the Press

A generation ago the Supreme Court commendably noted that freedom of the press is not just the right of individual reporters and editors; it is the people's "collective right . . . to receive suitable access to social, political, esthetic, moral and other ideas and experiences."[27] This remark came in a landmark decision upholding an FCC requirement, elaborating on the fairness doctrine, that broadcasters provide rights of access, or free reply time, to individuals who are personally attacked on the air or to candidates who are disfavored by a political editorial. In upholding the FCC's authority to mandate access to the airwaves in such situations, the Court noted that "it is the right of the viewers and listeners, not the right of the broadcasters, which is paramount."[28]

In more recent years both the courts and the FCC have unfortunately whittled away the public service responsibilities and public access requirements that once came with the right to broadcast over the public airwaves. In 1987 the FCC formally repealed the fairness doctrine, following President Reagan's veto of a congressional bill which would have expressly enacted the doctrine into law.[29] In justifying the move to deregulate broadcasters, the FCC stated: "What we have come to realize is that the First Amendment was . . . founded on a belief that 'fairness' was far too fragile to be left for a Government bureaucracy to accomplish. . . . If we must choose whether the editorial decisions are to be made in the free judgment of individual broadcasters, or imposed by bureaucratic fiat, the choice must be for freedom."[30]

The repeal of the fairness doctrine, together with the personal attack and political editorial rules, served to harmonize the legal status of the print and broadcast media when it came to access requirements. In 1974 the Supreme Court invalidated a Florida law which would have granted free rights of reply to any political candidate or officeholder whose character or record was attacked in a newspaper editorial. Such rights of reply might be constitutional in the broadcast world due to scarcity of space on the airwaves, the Court reasoned. But the Court rejected arguments that economic concentration in the newspaper industry created similarly compelling conditions of scarcity. Instead, the Court found that right-of-reply laws would likely have a chilling effect on the editorial decision to criticize a candidate in the first place. Insulating the print press from government regulation was deemed the best way to encourage investigation and criticism of government.[31]

Since the 1987 repeal of the fairness doctrine, battles have continued to rage over how to reconcile the tradition of protecting press autonomy, exemplified in the print area, with the tradition of promoting public access to the media, once typified by the public trustee status of broadcasters under the Communications Act. As new media technologies emerge, ranging from cable television to videotex to electronic publishing over computers to satellite video transmission, the debate over regulation of, and access to, the media moves into new territory. Proponents of continued deregulation argue that technology has ended the scarcity of television frequencies that once justified the government in mandating access to the airwaves. We now live in an age of video abundance and video competition, with cable alone providing hundreds of channels into the home and with new broadband information technologies potentially providing superhighways into the home for voice, data, and video transmission. With the switch from scarcity to plenty, market competition allegedly can now be permitted to do its work, and government should abide by the principle of noninterference with the press, developed in regard to the print press.

The problem with deregulation of the media is that it ignores the phenomenon of media conglomeration that progressively characterizes ownership of the new and old media alike. The top ten cable systems, for instance, account for 41 percent of all cable subscribers.[32] Moreover, many of these multisystem cable operators are owned in whole or part by established media giants such as Time Warner, Viacom, or Storer Communications. Capital Cites/ABC and General Electric/NBC are heavily invested in cable as well as broadcasting. The power of these entrenched media giants means that leaving the media wholly unregulated by government may work against rich and robust public debate. At the consuming end of the video pipeline, consumers may now be able to flip among a great number of channels or to buy or rent an increasing supply of videocassettes. But at the supplier end, a small number of conglomerates still controls the bulk of what programs are produced, purchased, and distributed. In the face of such concentrated private power, the case for legal regulation and mandated public access requirements remains.[33]

As of this writing, the debate over public access to the media centers on how to define the First Amendment rights of cable system operators. Not surprisingly, industry representatives press the argument that local governments violate the First Amendment when they require cable operators to set aside a certain number of channels on their system for public, governmental, or educational access programming. "If a government required a newspaper to publish 10 pages of letters to the editor, you could be sure the publisher would have objections," a lawyer for the National Cable Television Association quipped.[34] But in response, one wonders whether the public interest in public affairs programming on cable would be served adequately by permitting one company, typically the only company franchised to wire a municipality for cable, the right to control the programming content of each and every channel on the system. Even in market terms, this seems an odd argument, since cable companies enjoy a local monopoly and do not face competition within their own medium. To accept the cable industry's free press claims, therefore, is to allow one private entity to control how an entire medium of communication is used in a locale. Not even the strongest free-market advocates should endorse such a claim. The public interest would seem far better served by continuing the practice of permitting cities and towns to negotiate for dedicated public access channels on cable. These channels, unfortunately, are used today only by a few. But at their best they promise to provide citizens wishing to "attend" a school board meeting or city council hearing with ways of participating electronically but actively in these meetings. Beyond passive attendance, technology has advanced to a point where genuine interactive conversation could flow over public access channels, with citizens in conversation with each other as well as with officeholders. Use of cable television and other emerging interactive technologies in this way would be a boon to the deliberations that are the hallmark of democracy. Public access television could foster not only a more informed citizen body but also a more engaged and participatory one. No interpretation of the First Amendment should handcuff government from promoting such public access uses of the media, uses that increase opportunities for citizens to engage in the political speech and debates that alone equip us for the responsibilities of self-government.

In the 1994 case *Turner Broadcasting* v. *FCC*, the Supreme Court breathed life back into access requirements under the First Amendment. In 1992 Congress enacted "must carry" rules that require most cable systems to devote a portion of their channels to the transmission of local broadcast television stations. Cable operators challenged the rules on free speech grounds. But the Court noted that, in the 60 percent of U.S. homes now wired for cable, the physical connection gives cable operators "bottleneck, or gatekeeper control over most (if not all) television programming that is channeled into the subscriber's home." The Court characterized "must carry" rules as a permissible way of avoiding the bottleneck, but it remanded the case for testimony as to whether a substantial bottleneck in fact existed.

## Free Speech and Community

Let us describe more fully the sharply contrasting political theories underlying the libertarian and communitarian views of the First Amendment. Whereas the libertarian defines liberty as the absence of government restrictions on individual value choices, the communitarian defines it as participation in self-government. The libertarian endows the individual with rights that trump communal judgments, but the communitarian believes that "civic commitments and common action . . . furnish both content and guidance to the exercise of rights."[35] While the libertarian assumes that individuals have exclusive access to their "preferences," the communitarian believes that citizens will be forever deprived of knowledge, even self-knowledge, unless they participate with others in communal judgment "about what is most desirable [for the community] to pursue within a given context of possibilities."[36] Since citizens live within the bounds and responsibilities of a community, they do not have full rein to express themselves without regard to the potentially harmful consequences for others.

Democracy, at its best, engages citizens in a way which enables them to participate in the pursuit of the common good. By contrast, to value democracy only for the opportunities it provides individuals to pursue their own interests, unfettered by communal responsibilities, is to permit public space to be used unabashedly for private ends. As Sheldon Wolin observes of this rather pale notion of political participation: "Interest politics dissolves the idea of the citizen as one for whom it is natural to join together with other citizens to act for purposes related to a general community and substitutes the idea of individuals who are grouped according to conflicting interests."[37]

Recent interpretations of the First Amendment elevate the individual's right to self-expression at the cost of promoting equal and effective citizen participation in the debates and deliberations over the common good. In *Buckley* the Court sadly dismissed the compelling public interest in lessening the influence of money on who and what gets heard during political campaigns; the Court made the individual's interest in speaking dominant over even the most elementary notions of preserving some rough equality in the ability of the democratic process to represent fairly the full range of political views. In the area of free press, the ongoing attack on mandatory public access requirements to the media betrays the same overly individualistic interpretation of the First Amendment. Both the Supreme Court and the FCC in recent years have stood ready to free the broadcast media in particular from the responsibilities of public service and accessibility to divergent views on issues of civic importance, responsibilities that once inhered in the notion that widespread public participation in the debates of the day was the ultimate purpose of the First Amendment.

In closing, it is important to note that a full communitarian interpretation of the First Amendment ultimately must balk at the reigning notion that communities are virtually powerless to make moral judgments about what individuals wish to say. This principle of "content neutrality" rests again on a highly individualistic political theory which exempts persons from the obligation to exercise self-restraint and to bear some responsibility for the common good. If democracy is not reducible to self-expression, then citizens must learn and exhibit certain character traits that dispose them toward a common good. A First Amendment jurisprudence which compels communities to stand by while some of its members suffer degradation through speech strains the loyalties and shared principles that make it possible in the first place for persons to form a community devoted to pursuing the common good.

CITIZENSHIP

IN AMERICA:

TWO VIEWS

# 13 *ROGERS M. SMITH*

# American Conceptions

# of Citizenship and

# National Service

$D$ebates over national service programs have been rekindled by Bill Clinton's warm support for the idea. As always, advocates and critics alike invoke ideals of American citizenship to defend or deny the obligation to serve and to define the qualities national service might foster. But too often both sides refer only to a narrow, sanitized subset of the conceptions of citizenship that have actually shaped civic institutions through most of United States history. The truth is that up until the 1960s the nation constructed both voluntary and obligatory service programs in ways that expressed and reinforced racial, ethnic, religious, and gender hierarchies as central constituents of American citizenship. If we do not see that this has been so, and why it has been so, we risk misunderstanding the role of national service programs in the nation's past; and, more importantly, we may not grasp the challenges and the opportunities new kinds of national service programs offer to America's future.

## The Conventional Debate

Most discussions of national service rely on a familiar narrative about American citizenship, one endorsed in much popular rhetoric and in the writings of prestigious authors ever since the nation was a glimmer in a few colonists' angry eyes. The American Creed holds, we are told, that to be an American citizen, one does not have to be of any particular race, gender, religion, ethnicity or original nationality, culture, or language. A person only has to support the American constitutional system and be law-abiding, though aliens must also give some minimal evidence that they are willing and able to work hard and be self-supporting. Unlike most other nationalities, then, American citizenship is said to rest on consent to the political principles valorizing personal liberties and democratic self-governance that are enshrined in America's Constitution and laws. American civic duties are centered on preserving those principles. To do so, some may be called to military service. But most citizens will be required only to gain in their youth the training needed to participate in democratic processes and in the commercial market economy that economic liberties generate; then, in adulthood they will have to pay taxes, do occasional jury duty, obey the laws, and little more.

Attentive readers will observe that this standard account includes (at least) two overlapping, often jointly held, but nonetheless analytically distinguishable conceptions of citizenship, with one largely submerged beneath the other. The more dominant "liberal" or "thin democratic" notion of citizenship presents the American citizen as essentially a bearer and enjoyer of individual rights, of economic, spiritual, intellectual, procedural, and only rather secondarily political liberties. She or he is likely to be most absorbed in pursuing happiness in forms of "private" life, work, church, and family and to act in national affairs, even to the modest extent of voting, only sporadically. Those brief interventions are likely to be aimed at protecting personal interests and making sure the government does not trample rights.

In contrast, a "strong democratic," "participatory democratic," or "civic republican" reading of American citizenship emphasizes not individual rights but participation in the forms of democratic self-governance and public service that the nation provides. In this view, involvement in American public life is not a nuisance, the price of preserving personal liberties. It is our prime civic duty, part of a shared commitment to help shape our lives in common and serve our common interests. It is also a vital fulfillment of our potential for both freedom and moral dignity, as we bring the social constituents of our lives under more conscious collective control.

The tendency of Americans to downplay this second, more "strong democratic" conception of citizenship matters. "Liberal" and "strong democratic" conceptions of American citizenship point to different positions in many regards, including national service. Liberal views stress development of the cognitive and economic skills that enable individuals to flourish in planning their own lives and in the marketplace. Their thrust is to present public service simply as an option which people may voluntarily choose to pursue, and as something which ordinarily should be compensated, not treated as obligatory. Liberal theorists have thus had notorious difficulties in justifying mandatory military service, requiring citizens to risk deaths for which there arguably cannot be an adequate recompense. Liberals have often favored voluntary professional armies organized at the national level, or at most mandatory national service that can be supplied in a variety of ways, including cash payments to a substitute or the government. That position has been of a piece with liberals' general advocacy of government that is efficient, open, and accountable but as little intrusive as possible on the day-to-day lives of citizens.

In contrast, "strong democratic" or "civic republican" theorists stress fostering the sense of civic responsibility and the skills of democratic participation that produce citizens who are more concerned about public life and vigorously active in politics, at least at some levels. The idiom of civic duty has come more naturally to these advocates, and so requirements of military service to help preserve the republic seem much less morally controversial. Many also have insisted that obligations to serve the common good apply to all citizens, that none should be able to evade direct personal service because of their wealth. But American civic republicans also have tended to favor extensive governance at local levels, because those levels are more accessible to democratic participation and control. Thus, civic republicans have always been wary of national standing armies that might be vehicles for domination by central governmental elites, preferring instead to make local civil militia the basic units of national defense. (Even so, American advocates of democratic civic conceptions accept much national governance, while insisting that it be as democratic as possible.)

Aspects of current discussions of national service are indeed instances of this long-running debate over whether more liberal or more democratic conceptions should guide American policies. Opponents

of national service proposals often see them at best as creating un-
productive, costly make-work jobs that burden taxpayers and divert
young citizens from their preferred personal pursuits and at worse as
supplying the central government with potentially totalitarian instruments of indoctrination and control. Supporters of national service
plans often promise they will provide concrete public benefits, such
as improved schools, health and sanitation systems, enhanced law
enforcement, and construction and maintenance of roads, bridges,
parks. But many also stress the educational value of national service in
promoting recognition of our common civic identity, our obligations to
each other and the community as a whole, in ways that may foster
greater civic virtue throughout most citizens' subsequent lives. Many
Americans probably want the best of both worlds: they want institutions, programs, and policies that will foster a sense of civic obligation
and a willingness to serve the common good in all, while also permitting all citizens to pursue their self-chosen courses as much as possible. But in keeping with the general predominance of liberal over civic
republican views in modern America, the second desire is most widely
expressed. Hence, voluntary, compensated national service proposals
have much more support than mandatory ones.

One further feature of the conventional debate between more liberal and more republican conceptions should be noted. Both sides
adhere to a shared explanation of how American citizenship came to
exist as a combinination of liberal and democratic or republican elements, with some important resulting tensions. This explanation usually involves an appeal to Alexis de Tocqueville's great work, *Democracy in America*. And though his views are actually more complicated,
the standard story of American civic identity does have a Tocquevillian
flavor. It holds that America was predominantly settled by European
colonists who brought with them Enlightenment ideals of liberty,
especially religious freedom. They were then shaped by the unusual
social conditions of the new country. Because land was plentiful, the
European aristocracy absent, and control by home officials weak,
Americans quickly became used to relatively equal economic and social statuses; considerable freedom in their religious, economic, and
personal lives; and considerable political self-governance, via town
meetings, local juries, and elected representative colonial assemblies.
And because they sought to grow in numbers, Americans were from

early on eager to embrace as fellow citizens anyone willing to support and participate in these ways of life, regardless of their backgrounds.

The colonists thus shaped eventually came to resent the way British imperial authorities infringed on their personal liberties, economic but also religious, and their long-established practices of political self-governance. Hence, they came to establish a new republican form of government, resting on popular sovereignty, favorable to commercial pursuits, and constructed with elaborate protections for individual rights. From at least the Revolution on, then, American citizenship was most shaped by the liberal and democratic commitments that ideology, geography, economics, culture, history, habits, and politics had conspired to produce. Or so the familiar story goes.

### The Missing Link

This standard view of American civic identity captures significant truths. But some crucial things are clearly missing, because there is a lot that this account does not explain. Why have Americans so often denied access to full citizenship to persons and groups who were perfectly willing to vouchsafe loyalty to American constitutional principles and to support themselves? Why were large subsets of citizens, including African-Americans and women, so long denied opportunities to participate in forms of public service, including military and jury duty, voting and office holding, even mandatory public schooling, on a fully equal and integrated basis? In these regards, the main lessons to be found in the conceptions of citizenship that Americans have written into their public laws are threefold.

First, though liberal and democratic notions have indeed been central, Americans also have defined both civic membership and the obligations and opportunities for national service extensively through appeal to a third family of conceptions that I term *Americanist*. *Americanism* holds that ascriptive characteristics, such as ethnicity, race, religion, gender, language, and cultural customs and heritage, are quite relevant for deciding who should be full American citizens. Specifically, American citizens should possess the characteristics of native-born WASP males or some none too distant approximation thereof. National institutions, including programs of public service, should promote the expression of such traits in all those capable of developing them, but traditionally Americanism has held that many could not reasonably be treated as having such potential. At times these less capable persons have included blacks, Native Americans, other ethnic minorities, and women. Americanism suggests such disparate groups should be assigned specialized and limited (though often arduous) forms of national service appropriate to their natural capacities. Some may be denied access to citizenship, and the central forms of civic service, altogether.

Second, analysts have underrated the importance of these Americanist notions in part because they have seen America through European eyes. They have focused on the lesser presence in the United States of the types of feudal political and economic class structures that have been central to European politics historically. Thus, they have not attended adequately to the forms of ascriptive hereditary hierarchy, racial, ethnic, sexual, cultural, and religious, that were in fact central, though frequently contested, constituents of American political development. Today we must reappraise American civic culture and its development from a standpoint which sees it as a common product shaped by all these ideological traditions and practices.

Third, Americanist conceptions have shown the power and tenacity they have because liberal and democratic conceptions of American civic identity, taken alone or in tandem, often have not seemed sufficient bases for senses of meaningful civic membership and both national and partisan political loyalties. Many Americans have regarded them as too demanding in terms of the individual efforts required to earn self-respect; too disruptive in terms of their implications for inherited, valued ways of life; and insufficiently affirming of Americans' inherent personal and social worth, as something validated by more transcendent historical, natural, and divine standards. Some Americans have gone so far as to renounce liberal conceptions of universal human rights and commitments to democratic self-governance. But most have tried to affirm liberal and democratic values while qualifying them by simultaneously affirming Americanist accounts that shortened the roster of those eligible to claim liberal rights and full democratic powers.

Americans, then, have generally not been pure liberals, democrats, or Americanists. Instead the nation's history, political parties and movements, and its laws, including its systems of national service, have displayed various blends of these elements, all with more or less severe internal tensions and inconsistencies. For many Americans, those tensions have been less important than the political, economic, and psychic benefits these combinations of beliefs and practices have provided. The tensions have, nonetheless, often spurred conflict and change.

Once we see American political culture and development as shaped not simply by the dynamics and tensions of liberal and republican traditions but also by the interaction of those values with Americanist ones, several important revisions in the standard narrative of American civic identity follow. In this view it appears normal, not aberrational, for Americans to blend apparently inconsistent principles in their institutions, such as equal rights for all and the subordination of women, African-Americans, and others to Anglo-Saxon males. It also seems predictable that many Americans will repeatedly seek to reinvent nonliberal, nondemocratic, often inegalitarian ideologies of civic identity as means of coping with discontents that liberal and democratic values have not addressed, and may indeed have fostered. We therefore also should not presume such reinventions are no longer possible today. The liberalizing and democratizing changes of the 1950s and 1960s prompted resurgent forms of Americanism in the late seventies and eighties, including political ads inflaming racial tensions and nativist calls for immigration restriction; and the trajectory of the nineties is not yet clear. And thus, we should see the contemporary challenge of American institutions, including programs of public service, as not simply a choice between more liberal and democratic conceptions. The quest for institutions that foster an appropriate balance between civic obligations and personal choices also compels us to find better ways to respond to the deep longings for less voluntaristic, more organic senses of civic identity that have so heavily, and often so oppressively, shaped national service and civic life in America.

With these basic points sketched, I examine in the rest of this essay some of the evidence that supports them. I especially note ways these various political traditions have been expressed in American systems of national service, primarily military service. Then I draw some lessons about how national service programs might be structured today to help bond the diverse modern American civic community while combating, rather than reinforcing, its traditional systems of civic inequality.

### Americanism, Civic Identity, and
### American National Service

The most frequent of many criticisms made against the claims just sketched is that they exaggerate the significance of nonliberal, inegalitarian ideologies and practices in American life. These have, many say, been real, but they have been recognized by most Americans as exceptional and marginal, and they have been slowly but steadily eliminated from American life throughout our history.

Perhaps so; but many facts speak powerfully the other way. Not just in exceptional periods but for over 80 percent of the nation's history, United States laws have declared most of the world's population to be ineligible for full American citizenship solely and explicitly because of their race, original nationality, or gender. For at least two-thirds of American history, a majority of the domestic adult population has also been ineligible for full citizenship for the same reasons. For persons of the wrong color, national background, or gender, it did not matter how "liberal," "democratic," "republican," or "pro-American" their views were, or how educated or prosperous they were.

Nor is it true that these patterns of civic exclusion, or assignment of second-class civic status, characterized the nation extensively at the outset and were gradually eroded. More women (though not many) legally had the vote in 1790 than in 1820. The civil rights of free blacks were better protected throughout the nation in 1790 than in 1850, and the rights of blacks were much more fully secured in 1870 than in 1920 (though they were not completely secured at any of these times). The legal rights of Native Americans also had more standing in American courts in 1790 than in 1850. The United States had no racial restrictions on immigration at all until 1882, and it did not adopt an elaborate, explicitly nationalistic quota system, designed to preserve the existing racial and ethnic makeup of the American citizenry, until 1924. "Two steps forward, one step back" is probably closer to the mark than slow but steady progress, but at times there have been two or three steps back.

The same patterns hold for national service in all its forms, including the preeminent form of civic service in United States history, membership in the armed forces. In keeping with liberal precepts, America has generally relied on volunteer armies as extensively as possible. In keeping with civic republican precepts, the nation relied on state militia much more than on a true national army through the nineteenth century, with state National Guard units remaining part of the national defense apparatus even today. But ascriptive Americanist elements have also always been visible. Until 1948, which is to say for just under 80 percent of United States history, African-Americans could officially serve only in segregated units, when they were allowed to serve at all. Although they have protested the restrictions much less, women, too, were denied opportunities for service in combat, a ban which continues today. And until very recently, top military posts were almost exclusively held by white men of northern European descent, while others frequently served in ethnically homogeneous units.

Other forms of national service exhibit the same patterns. Efforts to exclude African-Americans, Asian-Americans, Native Americans, and women from juries all have a long history and maintained considerable success up through the 1960s. All of these groups have also faced restrictions in access to the franchise and to electoral offices, forms of political participation valorized in civic republican traditions, at least, as aspects of public service. Public education, the oldest and most universal mandatory service program in the nation, long had an explicitly Protestant, Anglo-Saxon Americanist cultural content, and blacks and women frequently had distinct, limited educational opportunities designed to channel them into the low-skilled labor positions or the domestic roles that were considered to be their respective natural destinies. If, then, all major forms of national service, like so many other aspects of American life, prove on examination to have been structured in ways that express not only liberal and civic republican but also ascriptive Americanist precepts, the next question is why these often clashing elements have had such power in American life. There are many answers, but they include political problems present since the nation's founding. I wish to focus on these, because they are still relevant to issues of citizenship and national service today.

The acquisition and uses of political power are inevitably shaped by the senses of identity and value that existing populations possess, both because leaders must appeal to them to win support, and because these notions usually constitute in part the interests and ideals of the leaders themselves. Political aspirants often, however, seek to recraft existing senses of identity in ways that foster allegiance to their causes. Analyses of American civic institutions must begin, then, by recalling that the Europeans who came to colonial America believed themselves to be products of a superior civilization and bearers of the true religion. Some, indeed, saw themselves as people chosen by God to preserve true religion from corruption in Britain and Europe. From the outset, they gave religious and cultural, as well as economic, reasons to each other to explain why they were entitled to take land from the aboriginal tribes and to use Africans as chattel slaves.

When British colonists had overwhelmed Dutch, Swedish, and German immigrants and pushed French and Spanish populations, along with many tribes, to the margins of what is now the United States, they grew increasingly restive with many restraints imposed on them by British home authorities. But there was no massive groundswell for revolution; elites favoring that cause were faced with the political task of winning popular support for it. They could and did claim that Britain had become a corrupt, despotic monarchy, instead of a free mixed republic, and that it was violating their natural rights, as standard histories recount. But republicanism and liberal rights theories were not widely known or embraced among the more middling and lower classes of English-Americans. For many they did not provide a morally or politically compelling case for embracing membership in a new American nation. For most, they did not provide much assurance that this dangerous cause would prevail.

Hence, leaders also appealed to the American colonists' more broadly shared senses of religious and cultural identity. Americans were said to be a chosen people, destined to be a beacon of wholesome Protestant freedom, in contrast to decadent Britain and Europe and also to the savage American aborigines and barbaric, almost subhuman Africans. The forces of history, nature, and above all divine Providence could be counted on to ensure the success of their new endeavor. By elaborating this sense of themselves as possessing a religously sanctioned, superior, and freedom-favoring ethnocultural identity, Americans created Americanism.

This sense of American identity as something special but also something hereditary and ascribed, not chosen, helps explain one apparent anomaly in the policies of the Revolutionary leaders. Even as they proclaimed their natural right to throw off British rule and establish government by consent, the members of the Continental Congress insisted that all those native to or resident in the colonies owed allegiance to the rebellious colonial governments, regardless of their preferences. Hence, colonials could be tried for treason if they remained loyal to the king and refused to support the Revolutionary cause. The insistence that Americans possessed unchosen political obligations was fundamentally inconsistent with the doctrines of the Declaration of Independence, and it was undoubtedly prompted by the military exigencies of the moment. But notions of American identity as something bestowed by birth on a chosen few, who could not rightly reject the duties it implied, made the position at least initially tenable. Only later, when it was safe, did American courts decide that persons had possessed a "right of election" as to what government they would support during the Revolution; and high Federalists never accepted that idea.

In contrast to this ascriptive nationalism, during the war and the ensuing Confederation era, Congress consistently rejected the pleas of General George Washington and others to create a professional national army. Most leaders preferred to rely on volunteer civic militia that the states chose (or chose not) to contribute to national military actions. Within these militia troops often elected their officers, a democratic practice which would continue in the American military through the early years of the Civil War (when it was practiced on both sides). But most states did not permit blacks to join militia units, at least not until they were needed in wartime, and no one even considered service for women. They were to be "republican mothers," raising sons who would be good citizen-soldiers. Women always accompanied United States armies, but as nurses, cooks, laundresses, and official or unofficial sexual partners, never as civic equals. The native tribes and slaves were, of course, frequently the objects and never the subjects of American military service, for they were legally denied access to citizenship altogether.

The reasons Washington continued to fight for a truly national army went beyond military efficacy to the survival of the nation itself. He believed such an institution would help foster a sense of common national identity and strengthen American patriotism. His expectations were probably realistic, given the experiences of national military service that forged so many nationalistic leaders at Philadelphia in 1787. Their Constitution strengthened national military powers and gave the commander in chief authority to direct the militia in emergencies. But it reserved to the states the powers to appoint officers and organize the militia, powers reinforced by the 1792 Militia Act. Attachments to particular regions and to traditions of localistic republican self-governance were too strong for even Washington to overcome.

Apart from its recognition of slavery and the separate existence of the tribes, the Constitution appears fairly ethnoculturally neutral. But in fact this neutrality is an artifact of the ongoing difficulties of winning support for the new national government and for the new American nationality itself. The framers did not reject Americanist definitions of citizenship (though some had reservations about such views). The different regions disagreed too much on the proper variety of Protestant religiosity, on slavery, as well as on other issues, to permit any other national resolution of these ethnocultural controversies. Few thought women's status required any attention beyond better enforcement of the common law.

The first national administration nonetheless acted on behalf of Americanist conceptions of civic identity in several ways. It confined naturalization to "whites" in 1790, and it advanced or supported many other measures to maintain slavery, restrict rights of free blacks, expel the surviving tribes, and subordinate women's civic status to that of their husbands and fathers. The nation's political and intellectual leaders continued to expand on Revolutionary era doctrines of why American nationality was special, usually tilting their claims to support some leading party. Their sources were chiefly Protestant divines, buttressed by English historical works and continental Enlightenment theorists of racial difference. These elements were combined in various versions of the Anglo-Saxon myth, or what might be termed *Anglo-Saxon Americanism*: Americans were descended from northern European peoples, originally Teutonic, who had been shaped by their early history for Protestant spiritual and republican political freedom. Hence, God had placed them in the New World to be an example to more slavish peoples, religions, and cultures, peoples they might be wise to avoid, could choose to assimilate, but also could rightly dominate. The Constitution was divinely inspired as the vehicle for the realization of Americans' distinctive capacities.

The Federalists who enacted the Alien and Sedition Acts favored Anglo-Saxon origins but added an insistence on native birth for officeholders and voters. Nativity was said to indicate an upbringing shaped by America's special political culture. The Jeffersonians resisted this restrictive Americanism, correctly seeing it as an effort to limit their support from European immigrants. They were, however, the leading supporters of denials of equal citizenship to free blacks, Native Americans, and women. The Jeffersonians multiplied bans on blacks serving in militia, bearing arms, or even being postal carriers, out of fear that black freemen would lead slave insurrections.

In the later antebellum era, Anglo-Saxon Americanism was particularly visible in the Whigs' nationalistic rhetoric, which drew on British romantic poets and historians in order to foster patriotism and respect for property rights. The Whigs recruited popular Anglo-Saxon generals to run for president, thereby obtaining their major electoral successes, although their aging warhorses tended to die in the White House. Many Jacksonian leaders, who had Catholic and immigrant constituencies and who supported state powers to uphold slavery, opposed the Protestant Anglo-Saxonism and the New England abolitionist values they rightly saw as propagated by northern Whigs. But the Jacksonians had their own forms of Americanism blended in with their commitments to a democratic franchise and tolerance of religious and cultural differences among whites. They endorsed religious and scientific doctrines of racial difference, spelled out in the "American School of Ethnography," that served to justify the South's peculiar institution.

The Civil War and Reconstruction were dramatic reform eras that made the American Constitution and civic laws much more nationalistic, egalitarian, liberal, and inclusive. The Union did so, however, only by instituting conscription for the first time in United States history. Many found the case for mandatory service less than compelling. Outraged at the draft, working-class whites rioted in New York City in 1863, killing numerous African-Americans in their anger at being compelled to risk their lives to free slaves, especially when richer men were allowed to buy their way out. The North always feared compelling such conscripts to accept true equality with black soldiers. But while Union armies initially treated African-American slaves as war "contraband," only gradually allowed blacks to assume combat roles, and never created integrated units, granted equal pay, or permitted African-Americans to become officers, in the end the North relied so heavily on African-American troops that the war might not have been won without them. That military service, in turn, helped justify extending equal citizenship and voting rights to blacks during Reconstruction. Some Republicans even explained that it was their military service that had earned African-American men the franchise still denied to women, an argument which ignored how women had been denied any chance for a similar military role.

But like other Reconstruction reforms, this acceptance of African-Americans into the military not only failed to go as far or be as egalitarian as its most radical advocates wished; by and large it also ended with the triumphs of the southern white Redeemers. Blacks were again excluded from many state militia or National Guard units, and they held menial positions in the shrunken national army, if they served at all. Women's peacetime options to contribute to the nation through military service remained limited to republican motherhood.

By the end of the century Republicans and Democrats were both even more overtly nativistic, dividing labor movements and gaining native working-class votes via racial assaults on immigrant laborers, first the "Yellow Peril" of the Chinese, then southern and eastern Europeans. Many Republicans and some Democrats also used the narrative of Anglo-Saxon destiny to justify imperialism in the Caribbean and the Pacific in the late 1890s. The policies that resulted ended Chinese immigration and expanded an especially illiberal form of national service: American military governance of colonized "lower races," with the Phillipines and Puerto Rico added to American Indians (while moderate segregationists urged similar "tutelage" for blacks). Advocates of imperialism appealed to ongoing providentialist interpretations of United States history and also to the Darwinian racial theories and cognate historical theories of cultural evolution that then came to be embraced throughout intellectual life.

Matters began to change in the Progessive era, but none too rapidly. For most Americans, the emphasis in Progressive thought on society's evolutionary nature and the culturally shaped character of individuals only expressed and reinforced the concerns for civic racial, ethnic, and religious homogeneity visible in the late nineteenth century. Many Progressives supported Jim Crow, ethnically based immigration restrictions, colonialism, "protective" legislation for women that often denied them economic opportunities outside the home, and harsh "Americanization" policies designed to stamp out immigrants' original cultures. Progressives often advocated more modern national governmental institutions to accomplish these ends efficiently, achieving, for example, greater centralization and professionalization of the armed forces via the Dick Militia Act of 1903. But on into World War I, the armed forces remained reliant not only on state militia but on numerous ethnically organized units, such as homogeneous Irish-American and Italian-American companies. Though perhaps desirable as a means to promote esprit de corps, the design of such ethnic units also worked to preserve the predominance of Anglo-Saxon men in top leadership posts. The structure of the military thus still implicitly and explicitly reinforced the alleged superiority of northern European cultures and peoples. In the world wars not only blacks but southern and eastern European-Americans and eventually Asian-Americans often would be consigned to the least skilled and most dangerous military roles.

But in the Progressive years, Jane Addams, John Dewey, Randolph Bourne, Horace Kallen, and a few others developed different views. They looked at the American history just sketched and began reconceiving American civic identity in ways that had direct, if varying, implications for national service. Appalled at nativist and racist exclusionary policies and militant imperialism, they all argued for minimizing the importance of American national identity. Not that they minimized the importance of social identities: to the contrary, they all thought that the individualistic strains in American political culture, along with its crassly materialistic elements, naturally drove Americans to be attracted to doctrines preaching membership in some large community with higher aims, even if those doctrines were illiberal. Hence, they sought a public philosophy which would give greater weight to peoples' aspirations to belong to social units they saw as intrinsically meaningful. But those social units were not to be homogeneous nation-states.

They were, instead, to be more intimate, immediate, and sustaining human communities. The United States should be seen, they stressed, only as a confederation of smaller social groups, bound together by an ethic of mutual respect and tolerance for group differences and by the desire to achieve collectively certain limited goods on which the groups could agree, such as national peace, good health, and prosperity. All concurred, too, that public institutions should foster this tolerance and respect, as well as economic skills and the skills to participate in democratic processes through which these national common goods could be identified and pursued.

Here, however, Progressive thinkers parted company. Dewey conceived of all these smaller communities as voluntaristic, to be run via internally democratic procedures. Transforming civic republicanism in the direction of "strong" or "participatory democracy," Dewey believed government should foster democratic self-governance in every sphere of life. Kallen, in contrast, saw persons' primary community memberships as inherited and ascribed and as appropriately governed by hereditary customs and traditions, even if these were nondemocratic. Bourne sometimes echoed Kallen's stress on diverse hereditary cultural groups, but on balance he was inclined toward Dewey's democratic ethos. More than either, he urged that persons should feel free to embrace multiple memberships, large and small, in cosmopolitan fashion, including or even especially groups that transcended national boundaries. He praised "trans-national" Americanism and dual citizenships.

But as the nation moved toward World War I, many urged universal military service, both as a means of military preparedness and as training for citizenship. Bourne opposed that idea but agreed that some institutions had to foster a sense of national unity amidst the diversity he otherwise embraced. In order to avoid both militarism and exclusionary forms of Americanism, he modified a proposal by William James to create a national service program which would serve the nonmilitary goals that most Americans shared. James, a more politically conventional pragmatist, had sought to combat what he saw as the dangerous egoism of modern Americans by having all young American men undertake "the moral equivalent of war," hard manual labor in forests, mines, and fields, thereby learning the spirit of self-sacrifice. Bourne dismissed those tasks as "drudgery" and as unfairly competitive with American workers. He proposed instead to have both young men and women spend two years performing neglected public tasks, such as inspecting food and factories, teaching good health habits, helping with playgrounds, child care, and soup kitchens. Bourne's was in fact a form of national service aimed not at fostering traditional patriotism but at reducing class and gender differences and building a more humane social environment. Thus, like Dewey, he was really more concerned to transform restrictive hereditary social identities, including American identity, than he was to tolerate or assist them.

Both the James and Bourne proposals served as forerunners of New Deal nonmilitary service programs, such as the Civilian Conservation Corps, and Kennedy's Peace Corps. But Bourne had been far ahead of his time; the New Deal efforts were hardly free from the sorts of racial and gender hierachies that characterized the society at large. (The Peace Corps has, however, done much better in these regards.) With World War II a broader range of military roles, though not actual combat, opened up for women, and blacks and Asian-Americans served in greater numbers than ever before, though still largely in segregated units. The heroism of Japanese-American companies helped not only win the war but also to discredit the accusations of innate disloyalty that proved sufficient to consign many other Japanese-Americans to internment camps for the war's duration. In the wake of the war, the nation finally began desegregating what had at last become a permanent, professionalized national army. Both the exigencies of the Cold War and the ethos of national service that the New Deal and the war had reinforced made it politically possible to staff the military in part by ongoing conscription. The controversial Vietnam War destroyed that political support, however, and the nation moved to the all-volunteer force in place today. In the course of these developments, the United States made great strides in transforming American military service into much more open and inclusive systems at all levels, as Colin Powell's chairmanship of the Joint Chiefs of Staff vividly indicates.

But critics argue that the adoption of a volunteer professional army in place of the Selective Service System has modified but not ended the ways that the ethnocultural stratifications in American society are expressed in its programs of national service. Some contend that poor African-American and Hispanic-Americans are being driven by economic necessity to assume the more undesirable and risky forms of military service in disproportionate numbers. Ongoing disputes over women's ineligibility for combat, the Tailhook sexual harassment scandal, and other evidence of gender discrimination, as well as debates over whether openly gay Americans should be allowed to serve, all are further indications that controversial connections between the nation's military and its traditional social hierarchies are very much still with us.

Thus despite real progress, problems remain. The core difficulty is that liberal and democratic civic conceptions, by themselves, have rarely seemed to satisfy American leaders or voters. Broader, often religious, ethnic, patriarchal, and cultural senses of civic identity have virtually always also been built into national institutions and policies. The Progressive democratic reformers responded to this pattern, again, largely by trying to meet desires for stronger senses of community identity not at the level of the nation but within more intimate groups. Bourne modified that approach with his proposal for national service, but chiefly as a means to counter chauvinistic calls for military service. He, too, tried to craft a sense of national identity which would serve rather than override other group memberships. Although better than older nativist and racist policies, these Progressive conceptions still involve difficulties that the United States is currently exhibiting in practice.

One is the problem of whether Dewey or Kallen is right. Should we treat cultural groups, or even families, as voluntary associations, to be run democratically, or as traditional ascriptive memberships, to be run according to varying customs? A second problem is what the precise requirements of expressing mutual tolerance and respect are. Does tolerance require compulsorily integrated, democratic public institutions or permission for each religious and, possibly, ethnic, economic, or even racial group to set up its own separate institutions? These problems manifest themselves in regard to both the form and the content of a national service program. Should it be a voluntary option for citizens who always have rights to choose their commitments or a compulsory obligation rooted in their organic civic identities? Should national service programs exhibit ethnic, racial, religious, and economic integration at all levels, or is it both more efficacious and more just to assign persons to serve in their communities of origin? Should the tasks of national service be seen as assisting those communities in their current forms or as seeking to alter them in more democratic and inclusive directions?

Examining the problem of how we should conceive of American civic identity is a prerequisite for answering all those questions. Is it really a stable solution for a nation to tell itself that membership in the large political society is merely instrumental to the full communal lives that come only within more intimate associations? Will that sense of civic identity foster sufficient loyalty and attachment to the larger society? Will it encourage genuine respect and tolerance among quite different cultural groups, who feel themselves bound together only contingently, especially if some are faring much better than others economically? Or is this view of civic identity a formula for increasing fragmentation, Balkanization, and group hostility, as critics of "multiculturalism," assisted by affirmative action, contend?

If we assert instead that there is a national identity and a set of national purposes that deserve to trump the claims of more intimate groups, how do we define that identity and those purposes? Should we uproot all nonvoluntaristic and inegalitarian forms of association and group life in America, as Dewey and Bourne implied, using national service as one means to do so? What is the conception of the nation that can legitimate such demanding programs? Is it only some intellectuals' notion of a better, more "democratic" America, an ideal which has never existed and may, despite its democratic pretensions, lack much popular support?

### Some Suggestions

I do not have answers to those questions that fully satisfy me, but I am sure these issues are central to the problem of American national service today. And I think so because I do not believe that culturally pluralist Progressive conceptions of civic identity have ever laid to rest the appeal of the sorts of ascriptive Americanist notions of civic identity that have so pervasively shaped American development and national service programs. Today many Americans still want to feel they have a meaningful national identity, with common values, that is special in some fundamental way. At the same time older notions of that common nationality that were hierarchical and exclusionary are much less viable in national politics today, though far from absent. Their decline has meant that even many formerly dominant American groups are now withdrawing into their smaller ethnocultural and economic communities, since the presence of others in the common national culture threatens to disrupt or burden their accustomed ways of life. That is one reason why economic, racial, and religious re-segregation appear on the rise in many parts of the nation. But few are satisfied with this state of affairs.

Let me end, then, by fleshing out the lessons about citizenship and the appeal of ascriptive Americanist ideologies I draw from this history. They must be fully appreciated if the challenges they pose to national service are to be understood.

First, history confirms that Americanism has thrived in part because of its propagation by elites. American political leaders have sought to win support and loyalty to their partisan causes, sometimes including American nationality itself. They have therefore looked for ways to convince their core constituencies, and occasionally all Americans, that they are indeed part of some larger community that is specially endowed, divinely favored, a source of their worth and success and hence deserving of their loyalty. It is too mild to say that doctrines of racial, ethnic, religious, cultural, and gender identity and superiority have often served these political causes. The truth is that no successful American political leader or movement has failed to employ some such Americanist narrative as a rallying cry. Americanism has been particularly useful for summoning citizens to national military service, something liberalism and state-centered civic republicanism are less suited to, for different reasons.

But political appeals must fall on receptive ears. I think Americans have so often been receptive to Americanist arguments because taken seriously, both liberal and democratic commitments have always been subversive of many established social forms, and in tension with each other. Liberal notions of natural individual rights make a prima facie case that at least all those capable of developing powers of rational self-guidance should be treated as bearers of individual rights. Legal systems that automatically subordinate women, blacks, Native Americans, and non-Christian religious perspectives are therefore presumptively illegitimate. Strong democratic or republican emphases on civic participation can also have egalitarian implications, and at a minimum they militate against the claims of private religious, familial, and cultural groups, as well as individual conscientious choices, to justify failures to contribute to common civic endeavors. To have made the United States a purely liberal or purely democratic society in these senses would have seriously disrupted existing social and political hierarchies and customary ways of life. It still would do so.

Understandably, many who have been reasonably high up in those hierarchies or who found meaning in those ways of life regardless of their place within them have never been much attracted to the far-reaching transformations that liberal and republican principles, if followed fully, would have required. Many Americans wanted to keep slavery, or at least institutionalized white superiority; many tried to maintain only slightly modified traditional gender roles, to uphold Protestant Christianity in public life, and so on. They have reinforced these desires by embracing Americanist ideologies that went much beyond, and often against, liberal democratic principles.

The content of liberalism and republicanism as civic ideologies further fueled these desires for more and different civic views in at least two ways. The requirements that liberal and republican ide-ologies set for individuals to gain a secure sense of personal worth are rather high. Liberalism demands that individuals show themselves to be industrious, rational, and self-reliant, usually via economic produc-tivity. In times of economic distress, especially, many Americans have found it hard to meet those standards. Republicanism or strong de-mocracy calls for willingness to sacrifice to the public good and active contributions to public life, again demands that many have found burdensome and unrealistic, especially when they were struggling to survive in a competitive market economy. Neither doctrine, moreover, offers much reassurance that even most hardworking individuals will avoid ultimately being eclipsed by their own mortality. Good liberal individuals may be remembered by their families and businesses, a few republican heroes will be celebrated by the republics they helped maintain, but most will soon be lost to human memory.

It is thus not surprising that many Americans have often been at-tracted to accounts that designated them as intrinsically worthy be-cause of their social identities, as Anglo-Americans, as whites, as Christians, as men, regardless of their personal accomplishments or economic status. Persons are thus made to feel part of some larger, more enduring whole that will continue to flourish after they have perished, so that they will not have lived in vain. And according to reli-gious forms of Americanism, they may in fact have gained eternal life.

If these are the core, enduring problems of liberal and republican conceptions of civic identity as a basis for national community, it should be clear why the Progressive democratic notions have not entirely overcome the limitations of these older views. The voluntaris-tic view of human associations provided by Dewey and Bourne offers the comfort of ongoing association with generally like-minded fel-lows, but otherwise it reproduces all the greatest difficulties of tradi-tional liberal and democratic views. It provides no transcendental reassurance, it in fact challenges all traditional nonvoluntaristic asso-ciations, and it makes us work hard. Kallen's embrace of hereditary cultural groups as the primary locus of social identity fares better on these scores. It does so, however, only by endorsing an essentialism many find false, minimizing a national identity (and older civic hier-archies) which many wish to treasure, embracing particular traditions that many experience as confining if not oppressive, and by accepting considerable separatism that may foster all the ills of Balkanization.

Yet I would say that Kallen's vision still comes closest to describing the directions toward which American civic laws and civic education have been tending in this century, to the point where the problems of this view are now being more acutely experienced in everyday life. The reason that Kallen's view of American civic identity has gained force may well be precisely because it provides the more transcendent cultural identities and affirmations that people seek once older racist and nativist forms of Americanism have been admitted to be massively oppressive and unjust. It may be, however, that today the nation's acceptance of that vision has gone as far as it can go, given that it has assaulted older forms of Americanism and not replaced them with any very rich sense of why membership in the national community is intrinsically estimable. Many cry today not merely for mutual tolerance and respect and rich lives within particular communities but for a sense of common values uniting Americans. That, arguably, was one source of the appeal of the patriotic Republican presidential campaigns of the 1980s.

If these points are right, then the implications of the whole of American history up to the present remain pertinent. We cannot realistically discuss national service in terms of the contrast between liberal and democratic or civic republican conceptions alone. Americans have never been content to define their civic identities or construct their educational institutions without reference to the sorts of ethnocultural notions of membership that American traditions have conveyed. It is unlikely that they will be much more willing to do so in the future. How should those of us committed to the liberal and democratic traditions in American life respond?

Bourne's conception of national service may point the way. But we should begin by recognizing that his "trans-national" Americanism, which urged us to conceive of political identities as largely optional and unrestrictive, was in some ways unrealistic. In his aversion to bigoted forms of Americanism, Bourne gave insufficient weight to facts that a democratic pragmatist should have highlighted. American civic identity is not something natural. It is something human beings have constructed historically via great efforts and struggles. But it is, for that very reason, something both more real and more transcendent than any conceivable aggregate of unfettered personal choices in the here and now. It has been made concrete in a vast range of institutions, customs, and practices that have helped constitute the identities, interests, and moral commitments of many millions of people. In a world still chiefly organized into large states, it provides many with most of the resources and avenues they have to shape their lives in valuable ways, and it also imposes constraints on what they can realistically ever hope to be and do.

When persons are born Americans or choose to become Americans, then, they do indeed become part of something larger than themselves, something that preceded them and will almost certainly outlive them. They become part of a political community with a complex but finite history which will hereafter do much to shape the stories and the very meaning of their lives, even as they play parts in shaping its story and its meaning, out of the materials that history makes available to them. The same things are true, to be sure, of many other communities to which they belong. But however central any of those groups may feel to them, the laws, culture, economy, and conditions of physical security prevailing within the United States are all likely to have major impact on them, for good and ill, like it or not.

It is therefore on one level right to take Americanism as a larger order of which individual Americans are but temporary parts, an order which can infuse their lives with broader significance. But that significance is something over which they can exercise some choice—not unconstrained choice, because much that makes up America is deeply entrenched and both individual and collective human powers are limited—but genuine choice, about what cultural, political, economic, and religious traditions Americans today will seek to value and preserve in the society they have inherited, and what ones they will strive to end or transform. In making those choices Americans recurringly reshape both the content of the national narrative of which they are a part and the meaning of their own lives. They do so whether they choose to participate extensively in public affairs, to craft a society which honors private pursuits, or to take some other course. And however they choose, they knit the story of their nation and of their personal lives into a great tapestry of human history which will carry its meaning, and their meaning, into the future long after their work is done.

Thus conceived, American civic identity may well seem able to provide the sense of historical rootedness and intrinsic significance that many Americans have longed for, to far more people than purely liberal or civic republican notions have reached. American citizenship thus understood says little, however, about whether Americans should choose to strengthen the liberal and democratic aspects of their national identity or their other traditions. I hope Americans will persuade each other that the voluntaristic, inclusive features of American life are their most precious inheritances, ones that set standards for further progress. Others would decide differently.

But if they are to decide wisely, in this view all Americans are well advised to understand, as fully and as honestly as possible, the historical traditions and the current realities that characterize the society with which their own identity and significance are so deeply bound up. And that, in turn, is an important argument for certain kinds of national service. If, in the past, national service institutions such as armies, juries, and schools have reiterated the massive ethnocultural stratifications that have pervaded American life, then in the future national service programs might be effective ways for all Americans to get a richer understanding of the variety of conditions, histories, opportunities, and constraints that constitute the lives of the hugely diverse American citizenry of today. And with their civic understandings thus enriched, Americans might be better equipped to make judgments about how their national story can and should be continued or altered in, and by, their own lifetimes.

But if national service is to play this crucial role of enabling Americans to grasp and shape their shared existence better, it obviously should not simply rehearse its participants in the civic knowledge they already possess. That means, at a minimum, that it must not be designed to convey the message that the institutions, inequalities, and hierarchies that still exist are natural and unquestionable. Rather, service should help them perceive these features of their lives as ongoing American creations. Thus, a goal of enhancing understanding of the American civic community and the forces at work within it suggests that participants should not simply take up the tasks they know best, in the communities or regions of which they feel a part. But neither does it mean that everyone should be taught what manual drudgery feels like, in the manner of the Chinese Cultural Revolution, or that young people from more privileged backgrounds should instruct and assist the less fortunate, in a spirit of noblesse oblige or socioeconomic missionary work.

It means, instead, that national service should be a vehicle through which Americans learn to take seriously the problems, conditions, and

perspectives of Americans different from themselves. That goal requires a measure of egalitarianism in the internal organization of
national service programs, for people pay more attention to those who
work with them rather than for them. It also suggests that national
service should seek to provide people with meaningful work they can
usefully do in environments they do not usually encounter. That
formula may be misconstrued as a prescription for inefficiency, requiring that people be sent to communities they do not know to perform
tasks for which they lack skills. But national service programs concerned to enrich civic knowledge would not have to ignore the talents
of their participants. They should instead place participants where
they can use their skills in new contexts and new ways, assisting
others as they learn themselves. For example, recent economics grad-
uates would not have to become extra bedpan changers. Many might
more usefully be assigned to assist home buyers in applying for their
first mortgages, an experience which would probably be instructive in
how racially and economically homogeneous neighborhoods are
maintained. In contrast, an African-American woman who had recently graduated from an inner-city high school might serve as a
teaching assistant in suburban social studies courses, a role which
again might educate all involved.

The spirit of such a program would have much in common with
Bourne's hope for more inclusive national service programs that
would promote appreciation of the multiple communities that make
up America. But it would be premised on recognition of the practical
importance of their common civic identity to Americans' lives, instead
of implicitly minimizing that identity. And instead of directing participants to simple but socially valuable work that might assist the less
fortunate, it would strive to place participants where they could use
their special skills while learning about complex aspects of their civic
lives that they are not otherwise likely to comprehend.

Rather than Bourne's "trans-national" Americanism, national service thus conceived would promote a more *trans-America* nationalism
or civic identity. Its justification would clearly be as much educational
and integrative as economic, but it could in fact provide skilled workers to those who can use them productively but would otherwise lack
resources to gain access to them. I believe that, in contrast to past
systems of national service that further accustomed Americans to
accept their places in ascribed hierarchies, such programs might help

citizens to recognize the injustices that have so pervasively shaped American life, the ways that injustices are perpetuated today, and the practical means by which they can be combated. But at a minimum, national service crafted in these ways would give more Americans more insight into the realities of the civic identity they share, so they can better decide what American citizenship should mean now and in the future.

# 14   *DANIEL J.*
       *TICHENOR*

# Immigration and

# Political Community in

# the United States

Inasmuch as immigration policy entails decisions about which outsiders may share in all or part of the communal life of a society, it illuminates how a political community defines itself. As Michael Walzer and Frederick Whelan observe, the preservation of distinctive political communities requires the distribution of membership to be bounded in some fashion.[1] If bonds of mutual identification and responsibility among members are to be maintained, a degree of closure is necessary. Who is permitted to cross these boundaries (if anyone) sheds light on a society's conception of attachments and obligations to others, whether they be aliens or citizens. This conception involves not only criteria for alien admissions but a scale of membership goods available to noncitizens living within the territory of a political community.

Marc Landy, Deborah Stone, Lawrence Mead, James Q. Wilson, Robert Reich, Mary Ann Glendon, and other scholars have recognized that public policy has an enormous impact on the character of citizenship and public-spiritedness in liberal democracies.[2] In a similar vein, this chapter examines what recent United States immigration policy making tells us about membership and community in the modern

American state. I argue that the recent treatment of aliens by the American polity reveals both a promising inclusivity and a disquieting enervation of the responsibilities and perceived worth of citizenship. A central task of this chapter is to urge policy makers to be more attentive to local communities and the engagement of citizens in a policy realm dominated by nationalist and internationalist perspectives.

## Migratory Pressures of the 1970s and 1980s

Throughout the 1980s American policy makers wrestled with two daunting problems: dramatic increases in illegal immigration and the arrival of unprecedented numbers of "first asylum" refugees. These crises highlighted the extent to which national borders had become porous and inadequately regulated. They also underscored the fact that all forms of migration to the United States were now dominated by nonwhite newcomers from Asia, Latin America, and the Caribbean. Europe, once the origin of nearly all United States immigrants, has accounted for only 10 percent of total immigration since the 1970s.[3] The uninvited migration of illegal immigrants and asylum seekers prompted policy makers to begin a decade of debate over the entire structure of United States immigration and refugee policy. Two major immigration laws, the Immigration Reform and Control Act of 1986 (IRCA) and the Immigration Act of 1990, represent the culmination of this period of policy change. The character of immigration reform also was shaped by judicial and administrative policy making before and after this legislation was enacted.

## The Character of Immigration Policy Change

Public opinion polls throughout the 1970s and 1980s indicated that most Americans favored decreases in the number of immigrants and refugees allowed to enter the country.[4] Throughout American history policy makers have sought to restrict or bar the migration of outsiders of unfamiliar racial or ethnic origin. For example, Chinese exclusion in the 1880s and the national origins system of the 1920s were efforts to exclude all but northern and western European newcomers. Policy makers also historically have responded to worrisome illegal immigration by launching campaigns to seize and deport undocumented aliens en masse, with Mexicans as the most common target. Angst in the 1950s over illegal aliens emboldened dragnet raids, called Operation Wetback of 1954, that led to the expulsion of over one million Mexican aliens.[5] The Hart-Celler Act of 1965 was intended to strip away ethnic and racial quotas, but policy makers expected Third World applicants to compete for a very limited number of "independent" visas.[6] Thus, it was 1980s reformers who were the first to address the dominance of Asian, Latin American, and Caribbean migrants in United States immigration.

One of the most stunning outcomes of recent immigration reform, then, was that the 1986 and 1990 laws enabled nonwhite migrants from unfamiliar source countries to continue to dominate the nation's immigration. Not only did these laws not restrict "new immigration," but they produced powerful forces for significant increases in migration from these regions. With little support for internal enforcement, IRCA dealt with the illegal population residing in the country by granting legal status to over three million illegal aliens. The enforcement provisions of IRCA, which penalize employers who knowingly hire illegal aliens, never established a reliable identification system of employee eligibility. As a result, an underground industry of fraudulent documents permitted illegal immigration to return to pre-reform levels.[7] The Immigration Act of 1990 granted stays of deportation to family members of aliens legalized under IRCA. The 1990 law also established an increased cap on legal immigration that may be "pierced" for relatives of citizens. Several refugee groups received special protection as well.[8] These developments have prompted immigration scholars to tout the 1990s as "the decade of immigration," predicting a dramatic recasting of the nation's racial composition.[9] In short, immigration reforms expanded alien rights and increased migration to the United States although the original impetus for policy change was restrictionist.

### Rights, Global Labor Markets, and Immigration Reform

One of the most significant features of immigration reform politics was an ideological convergence in favor of sustained, if not increased, migration to the United States.[10] This development was undergirded by two important forces in American politics: the legacy of the civil rights movement and the resurgence of free-market philosophies in the 1980s. The first extensive federal regulations of immigration were enacted amid the drastic economic and social dislocations of the late nineteenth and early twentieth centuries.[11] As ties between members of the national community assumed greater importance, an agitated society directed its venom against those who it believed imperiled the American way of life: emancipated blacks and new immigrants from Asia and southern and eastern Europe.[12] Although the Jim Crow laws produced by this racially exclusive nationalism were perhaps more pernicious than the immigration restrictions, immigration policy was linked thereafter to the black struggle for full membership.

The crises of citizenship and race that now engulf western European states reached a high-water mark in the United States during the civil rights movement. The "programmatic liberalism" of the New Deal, the racist fascism of America's World War II foes, and the foreign policy imperatives of the Cold War underscored the glaring disparity between Jim Crowism and the nation's avowed liberal and egalitarian ideals. The national origins system that prevailed for most of this century presented a similar "American dilemma."[13] Continuing the work of John F. Kennedy, Lyndon Johnson and the other Great Society reformers explicitly linked the causes of civil rights and immigration reform. Although the Hart-Celler Act of 1965 was not intended to yield substantial increases in non-European immigration, it established the principle that immigration regulations should be free of racial and ethnic bias.

During the late 1960s and early 1970s the courts began to invalidate administrative policies and state laws limiting the legal rights and economic opportunities of aliens. In *Graham v. Richardson* (1971), for instance, the Supreme Court struck down statutes that limited welfare provision to citizens and legal residents of fifteen years.[14] The close association of immigration restriction with historical racial barriers imposed severe constraints on imposing new controls on immigration in the 1980s. Whereas illegal aliens of the 1950s were treated as criminals who were summarily seized and deported, the contemporary debate depicted them as a vulnerable population residing in the "shadows of American life" who deserved access to equal membership.[15] For many 1980s expansionists of the Left, the principal goal was to grant entry and new protection to powerless alien groups, particularly nonwhite illegal aliens and refugees. In recent immigration policy making, free-market expansionists viewed new immigration restrictions as unwelcome fetters on the free market, inhibiting the labor market demands of employers. Conservative think tanks and *Wall Street Journal* editorial pages encouraged the free movement of goods, technology, capital, and persons across borders.[16] For example, Stephen Moore of the Hudson Institute praised immigrants for "their propensity to start new businesses" and "their contribution in keeping U.S. businesses internationally competitive."[17] Industrial, commercial, and professional groups stressed that global competitors enjoyed easy access to the immigrant labor market and advocated more visas for immigrants with needed job skills or expertise. Employers of low-skilled workers, such as agricultural growers, the garment industry, and hotel and restaurant services, favored access to cheap alien labor. The key goals of the expansionist Right were to provide American businesses greater access to the immigrant labor market and relief from new regulations such as employer sanctions and job antidiscrimination protection for aliens.

Significantly, the ideological convergence in favor of sustaining robust immigration generated not consensual politics but new divisions within and between liberal and conservative coalitions. In the 1980s the restrictionist-expansionist axis often was less meaningful than a new divide between market-oriented and rights-oriented expansionists. That is, the locus of conflict seemed to shift from a question of whether there should be expansive immigration to a struggle over who should benefit from an opening of the gates. In the legislative arena free-market expansionists secured sharp increases in employer-sponsored and skilled-worker visas, as well as cheap alien labor for the agricultural, garment, restaurant, and hotel sectors. The disparate demands of rights-oriented expansionists included a generous amnesty program for illegal aliens, a new civil rights agency charged with combating job discrimination against aliens, elimination of exploitable temporary worker programs, legal status for previously excluded refugee groups, generous allocations of family reunification visas, and the removal of ideological and sexual orientation restrictions.

Obscured among these initiatives was the original purpose of reform: to curb illegal immigration and regain control of porous borders. Instead of representing the centerpiece of immigration reform, the enactment of an immigration control mechanism in 1986—employer sanctions—enabled an array of competing interests and policy goals to be realized in IRCA and the Immigration Act of 1990. While policy makers praised immigration reforms for addressing illegal immigration and responding to new demands for legal admissions, immigration control was clearly subordinate to expansionist designs. Civil rights activists and libertarians successfully opposed the creation of a new counterfeit- and tamper-resistant employee identification system. When a pilot program was proposed by Simpson in 1990 to use drivers' licenses in conjunction with employer sanctions, it was defeated on the House floor by members of the Hispanic Caucus who likened it to South Africa's former system of passbooks for blacks. Free-market expansionists exempted small businesses from employer sanctions and defended an "affirmative defense" clause that released employers of any obligation to verify the authenticity of documents presented to them. Lax enforcement of employer sanctions by the Reagan and Bush administrations, which viewed them as another regulatory burden on United States businesses, further undermined immigration control. Dampened briefly after IRCA was enacted, illegal immigration soon returned to the peak levels of the pre-reform era.[18]

The competing agendas of expansionists were pressed throughout the past decade in the administrative and judicial realms, where accountability was diminished. Republican executives were sometimes hostile or unsympathetic to the rights-oriented provisions of the 1986 and 1990 laws. Administrative politics could serve as a means of tempering or counteracting the expansion of alien rights in legislation. Charged with implementing the legalization of illegal aliens, the Reagan Justice Department denied eligibility to aliens who were deemed "likely to become a public charge" or who failed to meet its standards for "continuous residence," "timely filing," or "known to the government."[19] Fewer than 1 percent of Haitian and Salvadoran refugees were granted amnesty during the Reagan and Bush presidencies, and any noncitizen who carried the AIDS virus was denied admission to the country.[20] Finally, the Reagan White House served notice at IRCA's signing that it would interpret its antidiscrimination provision as placing the burden of proof on alien claimants.[21] The civil rights agency created by IRCA to prosecute these cases became a stepchild of the Justice Department, with a meager staff and only an answering machine to field discrimination claims.[22]

Humanitarian and civil rights groups generally turned to the judicial branch to challenge these administration policies. The courts were a familiar arena for aliens to make rights claims. Well before IRCA and the Immigration Act of 1990, immigration and civil rights activists pursued legal strategies to invalidate state and local laws imposing barriers to alien employment or access to welfare provision long before IRCA and the Immigration Act of 1990 were enacted.[23] Perhaps the most celebrated case of this sort, *Plyler v. Doe* (1982), successfully overturned a Texas law which prohibited the children of illegal aliens from attending public schools.[24] Groups like the Mexican-American Legal Defense Fund, active lobbyists in the legislative battles over immigration reform, mounted successful legal challenges to the Immigration and Naturalization Service (INS) eligibility rules for granting amnesty to illegal aliens.[25] With mixed success, refugee advocates sought judicial relief for Haitian and Salvadoran refugees denied due process hearings or routinely turned down for asylum.

Overall, political fragmentation and estrangement enabled policy makers and activists to play out conflicts in legislative struggles, the administrative process, and the courts. Immigration reform captures a defining feature of policy making in the American polity during the past quarter century: whereas the rise of the modern state has led to a centralization of power which insulates decision making from citizens, the decentralization and estrangement of national institutions has made policy making more permeable to a variety of policy entrepreneurs and advocacy groups. As a result, erratic, contentious policy making has yielded ambiguous outcomes and little political accountability.

### Aliens and the Inclusive Community: Comparing Membership Goods

The fact that the United States permitted increases in alien admissions and extended new membership goods to noncitizens is striking when compared to the political response of many western European nations to immigration and membership issues. During the past two decades, several western European states struggled between national identity and obligations owed to foreigners residing and working within their borders. In the midst of stunning postwar economic growth, Britain, France, Switzerland, West Germany, and other nations recruited millions of foreign guestworkers (from the Middle East and northern Africa) in the 1950s and 1960s to prevent labor shortages and to keep wages in check. Beginning in the 1970s anti-immigrant voices challenged the presence of guestworkers at a time of employment scarcity among citizens. The politicization of immigration was fueled further by waves of asylum seekers and illegal aliens seeking entry into these culturally homogenous societies. Conflict over immigration in Europe soon shifted from the economic impact of foreign workers to debates about whether European civic cultures could assimilate new ethnic and racial groups. New restrictionists in Europe made "overforeign-ization" their watchword, warning that aliens undermined sentiments of solidarity and loyalty that common historical experience and eth-nicity engendered.[26] As Kay Hailbronner notes, Germans "think of their nation not as a political unit but as a cultural, linguistic, and ethnic unit."[27]

Several political parties emerged as standard-bearers of this new breed of nationalist politics, most notably the National Front parties of France and Great Britain and the Republikaner party in Germany. "These movements were built, not surprisingly, on the edifice of anti-immigrant, racist and xenophobic appeals," James Hollifield notes.[28] Jean-Marie Le Pen, leader of the French National Front, garnered at least 10 percent of the vote in elections throughout the 1980s, sound-ing the battle cry "La France aux Français." His consistent appeal, drawing on nationalist subcultures of Jacobinism on the Left and Gaullism on the Right, prompted other parties in France to redefine their immigration position.[29]

A strong two-party system and stout resistance from Margaret Thatcher weakened the National Front in Britain, but largely because Conservatives embraced its anti-immigrant position.[30] The 1981 Na-tionality Act addressed the legacy of colonialism by establishing gra-dations of membership that took the form of territorially differentiated citizenship. It also marked a transition from simple to conditional jus soli (birthright citizenship): children born in Britain to parents without permanent residency status were no longer guaranteed full member-ship. Even in Sweden and Denmark, known for their generosity to refugees, strict denial rates were imposed on asylum seekers. As Lawrence Fuchs notes, "Europeans generally [have] asked about for-eigners, How can we get these outsiders to go home? or, failing that, How can we keep them outside the polity a while longer even as they work among us?"[31] Significantly, the resurgence of restrictive national-ism occurred when most of the migrants seeking membership were nonwhites.

Today's newspaper headlines remind us of the conflagrant character of immigration politics in a newly unified Germany, vividly captured by violent flashes of xenophobia in economically depressed eastern Germany. As German leadership moves to rescind generous asylum laws, Gypsies may be only the first of many groups interned or deported as a solution to the "foreigner problem."[32] The breakdown of the Soviet empire has unleashed formidable nativist and ethnic impulses. Integrating forces in modern world politics are complemented by a new ethnic nationalism and fragmentation that poses formidable challenges to Third World immigrants and refugees.

American immigration reform has had a distinctive tone, one that contrasts sharply with the citizenship crises of Europe. Like Europe, the United States has absorbed a "new immigration" of nonwhite, Third World nationals during the past quarter century. Yet nativist voices reminiscent of the Know-Nothings, American Protective Association, and the Immigration Restriction League have been largely muted or marginalized in American politics during the past quarter century. Indeed, it is telling from a comparative perspective that United States immigration policy on the whole expanded rather than limited alien admissions and rights. Whereas 1980s European policy makers restricted the flow of immigrants and refugees to their countries, summarily deported illegal aliens and asylum seekers, and denied full membership to foreign guestworkers (regardless of how long these "guests" have lived and labored in their societies), their American counterparts increased alien admissions, made citizenship easier to gain, and expanded the opportunities and protection of the most vulnerable persons in our society: illegal aliens and temporary workers.

One can overstate the generosity of pro-immigration reforms. After all, free-market expansionists were more concerned with labor market demands than with the well-being of newcomers. Reflecting on the religiosity of Americans in the Jacksonian era, Alexis de Tocqueville suggested that it was the head rather than the heart that brought so many to the altar.[33] The expansive terms of alien admissions and membership in the modern American polity seem to be the offspring of both head and heart. For example, millions of illegal aliens were granted amnesty because they were perceived as a vulnerable subclass with established ties in their communities. Because they were participants in the life of American society, albeit clandestine, policy makers decided to bestow legal status on their de facto membership. Antidiscrimination rights, new opportunities and protection for temporary foreign workers, and increases in visas for reuniting families were all justified as humanitarian. But this responsiveness to the moral claims of outsiders was matched by market-based goals. Temporary workers, especially in the agricultural sector, were welcomed as a cheap supply of labor. New emphasis on skilled laborers and foreign investors represented an effort to create more domestic jobs and spur economic growth. In short, pro-immigration reforms reflect both an inclusive vision of membership and self-interested economic calculations.

These distinct rationales for expansive immigration are hardly novel. In his *Report on Manufactures*, Alexander Hamilton noted that it was in the national interest "to open every possible avenue to emigration from abroad." Consistent with his vision of a commercial empire, he perceived aliens as "an important resource, not only for extending the population, and with it the useful and productive labor of the country, but likewise for the prosecution of manufactures."[34] Almost a century later Andrew Carnegie praised open immigration as "a golden stream which flows into the country each year." He added crassly, "These adults are surely worth $1500 each—for in former days an efficient slave sold for that sum."[35] Economic growth, they believed, was tied closely to expansive immigration.

Whereas Hamilton emphasized the financial empire to be reaped from open immigration, Thomas Jefferson's enlightened idealism expressed a special obligation to newcomers. Although he had opposed immigration as a young man, Jefferson wrote in 1817 that the United States should be a new Canaan where outsiders would be "received as brothers and secured against . . . oppression by participation in . . . self-government."[36] According to Hans Kohn, this declaration exemplified "Jefferson's faith in America's national mission as mankind's vanguard in the fight for individual liberty." In contrast to Carnegie's economic pragmatism, Ralph Waldo Emerson exalted in 1878 that "our whole history appears like a last effort of the Divine Providence in behalf of the human race." He extolled American opportunity—"opportunity to civil rights, of education, of personal power"—which he saw as an "invitation to every nation, to every race and skin."[37]

The American political community is often characterized as lagging well behind industrial democracies of Europe in terms of the distribution of membership goods. In particular, welfare state scholars emphasize that the American framers' penchant for dividing political authority has produced an attenuated, even anemic system of social welfare which pales in comparison to its European counterparts.[38] "Against the backdrop of European welfare states," Ann Shola Orloff writes, "the American system of public social provision seems incomplete and belated."[39]

Hugh Heclo, Theodore Marmor, Jerry Mashaw, Philip Harvey, and R. Shep Melnick emphasize that the American welfare state is not so much incomplete as sui generis.[40] But for our purposes, a comparison of immigration and citizenship policies more generally highlights the extent to which the distribution of membership goods take distinctive forms on opposite sides of the Atlantic. The issue of how a nation treats those from outside of its boundaries—hence, those with the weakest claims—reminds us that inclusivity and benevolence encompass but are not limited to welfare provision. Rather than applying a European model of the welfare state as the litmus test of political justice, might it not be more useful to examine how a wider range of membership goods are distributed by political communities?

For much of this century, ethnic and racial exclusion prevailed in American immigration policy. But while early twentieth-century policy changes codified hostilities toward new immigrant groups, recent reforms sustained the immigration of Third World migrants. Not only were expansive alien admissions policies enacted, but aliens in American society were granted an unprecedented panoply of rights including access to full membership. A residual effect of the civil rights movement is a political culture less threatened by new ethnic and racial immigrant groups.

### Rights, Markets, and Citizen-Strangers: The Enduring Cleavage of Race

If the recent expansion of alien admissions and rights demonstrated a promising inclusivity which encompassed outsiders, it also captured a troubling enervation of the bonds between American citizens. During the Great Depression, John Dewey defended the construction of a regulatory administrative state to an "uneasy" society still devoted to the "autonomous individual."[41] True liberalism, he wrote, must celebrate the "full freedom of the human spirit" by recognizing that "the content of the individual and freedom change with time." Freedom in the twentieth century required government to secure not only the natural rights of individuals but also the economic well-being of citizens from the vagaries of the market and other uncertainties of modern life.[42] Franklin Roosevelt would seize upon these themes both as a presidential aspirant in 1932 and an aging statesman in 1944, calling for an "economic constitutional order" to reinvigorate the "old social contract."[43] The recasting of American liberalism in fact demanded a sense of communal responsibility, one in which citizens share in, or at least support, the enterprise of attaining a basic standard of economic integration for all members.

This new "social contract" raises the question of whether certain obligations owed to disadvantaged members of a political community must be met before newcomers are granted admission and membership goods. Joseph Carens has observed that the steady influx of poor, needy aliens erodes the communal bonds and mutual identification that make the welfare state politically possible.[44] Yet the American political community never has embraced fully the extension of Roosevelt's economic bill of rights to the nation's poorest citizens. It is telling that admission to the United States is probably easier to attain for aliens than social citizenship is for an indigenous economic "underclass."[45] Welcoming outsiders to membership in the American community corresponds well with a nineteenth-century notion of offering temporary assistance to individuals whose future success depends on participation in a "work-based system."[46]

To some extent the expansive alien admissions and membership policies that recently emerged in the United States demonstrate an inclusive vision of political community. Yet in a society in which many citizens are economically excluded, they also expose the impoverishment of attachments and obligations among citizens. This can be accounted for in part by the limitations that rights and markets—the driving forces of immigration reform—place on political deliberation and choice.

The agenda of rights-oriented expansionists focused resolutely on certain egalitarian and humanitarian goals, such as giving legal status to millions of illegal aliens or granting asylum to more refugees. Concern about how increases in alien admissions would affect disadvantaged citizens was expressed by the Select Commission on Immigration and Refugee Policy, but hardly fazed rights-oriented expansionists who drew attention to the compelling needs of individual aliens.[47] The courts often focused on how state and INS policies influenced the rights of aliens. That is, judicial rulings also centered on the moral force of individual appeals.

My point is not that extending new protection to vulnerable non-citizens was an unworthy goal, but that the policy-making process instead focused attention on certain rights claims while marginalizing others. At its most absurd extreme, Senator Edward Kennedy employed the language of the civil rights movement to characterize Irish aliens as disadvantaged by the nation's immigration laws. Melnick observes that for the past quarter century, the United States polity has tended to define nearly every public policy issue in terms of individual rights.[48] As a result, rights claims pervade our political discourse, offering few opportunities to consider policy costs or important trade-offs. The absoluteness of rights-based arguments often derails meaningful deliberation of contending claims.

Free-market expansionists emphasized that opening the immigrant labor market for employers would spur United States economic growth. Allowing companies to transfer personnel across borders with greater ease and dramatically increasing visas for aliens with needed job skills were viewed as efficient means of enhancing American economic competitiveness. The supply of cheap, unskilled alien workers to fill jobs in agriculture, the garment industry, and hotel and restaurant services was justified for two reasons: lower prices for American consumers and the fact that the vast majority of these jobs were deemed unattractive to most citizens. The virtue of a market-driven allocation of visas, so the argument goes, is both its flexibility in meeting the labor needs of United States businesses (which bolsters the nation's economic health) and the benefits it provides hardworking aliens.

Absent from this calculus is any serious consideration of whether the presence of numerous unskilled and vulnerable foreign workers perpetuates a segmented labor force, forcing unskilled domestic workers to choose between low-wage jobs with poor working conditions or unemployment. Would a restricted labor force and/or new regulatory standards make many of the unskilled jobs assigned to foreign workers more attractive to unskilled domestic workers? This is a question that never figured prominently in policy debate. Nor were the civic merits of having United States companies or the state train or retrain citizens to fill skilled positions fully weighed by policy makers; an imported labor force was preferred instead.[49]

While immigration policy change was responsive to the needs of aliens and American employers—though in a manner which gener-

ated contradictions and cross-purposes in policy—it ignored how reforms affected many native blacks. Indeed, many Americans seemed
more partial to Asian, Central American, European and Mexican newcomers than to urban black citizens. For example, William Julius Wilson found in a 1992 study that the loss of manufacturing jobs in
Chicago affected blacks and new immigrant groups very differently.
Although less formally educated than black workers, Mexican and
other immigrants lost jobs at a lower rate. When they were displaced
from blue-collar jobs, immigrant workers had greater success in finding new employment. Wilson discovered in interviews with Chicago-
area employers that there was a disparity in how these groups were
perceived. Whereas inner-city blacks (especially young black males)
were viewed by employers as "uneducated, unstable, uncooperative,
and dishonest," Mexicans and other Third World immigrants were
"perceived to exhibit better 'work ethics' than native workers" largely
because they endured poor work conditions, meager pay, and few
opportunities to advance.[50] He suggests that the unwillingness of
many native blacks to tolerate these wages and conditions has shaped
employer attitudes. His findings are supported by a General Accounting Office report that janitorial firms in Los Angeles replaced union-
ized black workers with nonunionized immigrants.[51] Tellingly, the
preference for immigrant labor is not a new development. More than a
century ago Frederick Douglass lamented that "every hour sees the
black man elbowed out of employment by some newly arrived immigrant." Stanley Lieberson's study of job competition in expanding
urban labor markets of the late nineteenth century suggests that new
immigrants were preferred over blacks who had migrated from the
South.[52]

Competition for employment is compounded by the fact that immigrants place special strains on the government services of major cities
and metropolitan areas. Six major cities and metropolitan areas account for the settlement of three-quarters of current immigration: New
York, Los Angeles, San Francisco, Chicago, Miami, and Houston (earlier waves settled in industrial cities across the Northeast and Mid-
west).[53] Since the migration of blacks from the South to northern cities
earlier this century, the problems of urban America—school decline,
limited tax revenues, crumbling infrastructure, an economic underclass—have been largely the problems of black America. While studies
indicate that immigrants pay more in taxes than they cost in govern-

ment services, newcomers have placed the greatest burdens on services such as education and emergency health care for which city and state governments bear considerable responsibility. Thomas Muller and Thomas Espenshade estimate that state and local benefits outweighed taxes paid by a margin of roughly two to one for Mexicans in Los Angeles County.[54] The Los Angeles County Board of Commissioners found that providing services to legal immigrants, amnesty aliens, and illegal aliens represented an estimated 30.9 percent of the county's costs in 1991–92.[55] And San Diego County officials discovered that two-thirds of emergency medical funds for the poor were spent on aliens.[56]

Although immigration reform drew much of its energy from the civil rights movement, policy making ironically showed a profound inattention to the most intractable problems of black citizens. Indeed, the character of immigration policy making seems to exemplify a political community of citizen-strangers in which many white members express a greater affinity and identification toward newcomers than for fellow black members. This estrangement of citizens is reinforced by the flight of white citizens from cities to fortress communities that offer safe haven from urban problems, now including immigrant burdens on services. It is worth adding that aliens whom black citizens most hoped to see admitted—Haitian refugees and African immigrants—benefited the least from immigration reform.

All this is not to say that new immigration has to represent a zero-sum game in which the economic and political ends of newcomers are at odds with native blacks. Alliances between black and Hispanic leaders may produce important economic and political cooperation. But what is disturbing about immigration policy making is that so many fundamental questions about how policy outcomes might affect the nation's urban poor, especially black citizens, were never examined. Tragically, a new openness to alien newcomers in the United States has coincided with a troubling enervation of the bonds of citizenship.

### Language, Culture, and Decline
### of Political Community

With Third World migrants dominating United States immigration totals, some observers see this latest wave of newcomers as a formidable threat to American culture. Richard Lamm and Gary Imhoff warn that ethnic, racial, and religious differences may become "pathological": "they can grow, fester, and eventually splinter a society."[57] Likewise, Leon Bouvier believes "it is not too far-fetched to depict a scenario where the major groups—Anglo, Black, Latino, Asian—remain separate from one another," and "where cultures and values differ significantly among groups."[58] When these studies provide specific illustrations of cultural cleavages caused by recent immigrants and refugees, however, they concentrate almost exclusively on Latin Americans. Indeed, there is little or no mention of newcomers from Asia or Europe failing to assimilate into American society. The most compelling problem brought to light by these studies is not the danger of greater racial and ethnic heterogeneity but a new cultural separatism exemplified by Latinos in several American cities and the Southwest.

More than any other group of Third World migrants, communities of Mexican-Americans, Cubans, and other Latin American nationals have been described as resistant to embracing the nation's language, its political institutions and values, and other aspects of American culture. In a study of Mexican-American children in Texas, James LaMare found that none preferred the label "American" over labels denoting their national origin.[59] Morris Janowitz suggests that Mexican-American migrants are exceptional because they are returning to territory once controlled by Mexico. "Such a Chicano does not see himself as breaking with the homeland but looks forward to close linkage with it, or even return," he notes.[60] In cities like Miami large immigrant enclaves have remained linguistically and culturally distinct for decades.

Americans long have been suspicious of newcomers who have sought to maintain the languages and traditions of their homelands. Benjamin Franklin expressed hostility toward Germans living in Pennsylvania in 1751, lamenting that they "will never adopt our language or customs anymore than they will acquire our complexion."[61] Successive waves of Irish, Chinese, Korean, Japanese, Italian, Slavic, Russian, and other aliens of the nineteenth and early twentieth centuries prompted similar angst among American natives.[62] But whereas earlier immigrant groups sought protection to observe their cultural traditions in private associations such as places of worship or foreign-language schools, some Latin American groups have demanded that the language and culture of their homelands also be protected in the public sphere.[63]

Language policy has become the volatile focus of political debate over the cultural separatism espoused by some Hispanic-Americans. While many Hispanic-American advocacy groups have favored bilingual education, services, and ballots, political opponents have lobbied for English to be established as the official national language. In the view of English-only activists, such as the United States English movement organized in the 1980s, national unity requires a common public language. One of the movement's leaders, former California senator S. I. Hayakawa, emphasizes that "the language we share is at the core of our identity as citizens, and our ticket to full participation in American political life."[64] By contrast, the League of United Latin American Citizens, the National Council of La Raza, and other Hispanic-American advocacy groups have supported bilingual programs as a means of preserving their own non-English culture and language. They have viewed bilingual education, for instance, not as a transitional program to integrate children of immigrant families into English-speaking classes but as a method of cultural maintenance. In short, the agenda of these Hispanic-American activists is unprecedented in seeking to make all aspects of public life officially bilingual.[65] Scholars have pointed to a number of other characteristics which suggest that many Latin American immigrants are disconnected from American society. High dropout rates among young Puerto Ricans and Mexican-Americans, Lawrence Fuchs worries, may have created "a class of persons identified by ethnicity and language deficiency who were doomed to function outside of the dominant, primary labor markets and civic culture."[66] Whether because some bilingual education programs have segregated Hispanic students or because lower-income children have been isolated in urban school districts, the children of many Latin American immigrants are marginalized from the economic and cultural mainstream of the United States.

The concept of consensual citizenship has been imperiled in the United States, according to Peter Schuck and Rogers Smith, by dramatically low naturalization levels among new immigrants, especially Latin Americans. Today a significant portion of resident aliens either naturalize well after they become eligible or forgo citizenship altogether. Some of these newcomers surely hope to return to their native country. But as Schuck and Smith suggest, this development seems to be closely related to the expansion of services and protection available to persons in the United States without regard to citizenship status.

Both Congress and the courts have invalidated administrative policies and state laws limiting the legal rights and economic opportunities of aliens.[67] As the rights of noncitizens living in the United States have accumulated, the incentives for acquiring full membership concomitantly have declined. Similarly, Peter Skerry finds that affirmative action programs and civil rights reforms have encouraged Third World immigrants to "see themselves as victims of deprivation and discrimination," producing policies "frequently inappropriate" to their assimilation.[68] The United States is one of only a few countries to require candidates for citizenship to demonstrate familiarity and support for its political institutions.[69] Ironically, a substantial number of today's newcomers see little reason either to subject themselves to such examinations or to become full participating members of the American political community.

Throughout American history natural-born citizens have assigned blame to new immigrants groups for failing to become fully integrated members of society. Rodolfo de la Garza offers an alternative explanation for why Mexican-Americans and perhaps other Latinos have been slow to embrace American culture: "Mexican Americans have retained a 'Mexicanness' only because they were so long denied access to American institutions."[70] Significantly, many Latin Americans gained access to these institutions amid a dramatic expansion of individual and group rights which transformed the political culture, shaping the character of their involvement in the national community. For most of the nineteenth century, new immigrants were incorporated into the political community by Martin Van Buren's compromise between republican virtue and modern democracy: decentralized political parties. These imperfect "civic associations," to borrow Wilson Carey McWilliams's phrase, linked the interests of immigrants to something larger than themselves.[71] The civic education of today's immigrants, by contrast, has been provided by a rights-based regime which teaches little about obligations and the value of participation.

### Conclusion: Recovering Local and Participatory Citizenship

Scholarly debates concerning alien admissions and rights generally have oscillated between national and global perspectives, either challenging or vindicating the sovereign right of nation-states to control their borders. Local, participatory citizenship is all but neglected in theories that center on immigration, aliens, and political community. Joseph Carens, Judith Lichtenberg, and other proponents of an internationalist view have stressed that the equal moral worth of individuals discards distinctions between aliens and citizens.[72] Because nationality (and statelessness) is arbitrary, they argue, closure of political communities cannot be justified. Many of these theories follow the lead of Charles Beitz and Brian Barry in applying Rawlsian principles of justice on a global scale. Strikingly, the obligations owed by wealthy nation-states to poorer ones do not figure as prominently in their arguments.[73]

Michael Walzer, Bruce Ackerman, and Mark Gibney have offered disparate defenses for national control of borders.[74] They argue with varying ardor that open borders would render communal life meaningless, sacrificing essential bonds and duties between national citizens. Total equality between citizens and aliens in effect bankrupts citizenship. According to Walzer, boundary setting is an inevitable element of social groupings; families, neighborhoods, clubs, and nations are given meaning by the distinctions between members and nonmembers. National political communities must set criteria for excluding at least some outsiders if special commitments among members are to be sustained.

Recent immigration reform exposes an American political community with remarkably weak ties and obligations among citizens. Fragmentation of national institutions accentuated divisions between policy makers, producing contradictions and cross-purposes in policy outcomes. Centralization and insulation of political power distanced the policy-making process from most citizens. Finally, the most definitive boundary setting in the American community occurred between citizen-strangers by race and income.

Some may view the willingness of national policy makers and activists to advance reforms that conflicted with public opinion as bold leadership. By insulating policy making from the views of the public, a constriction of alien admissions and alien rights was averted. Yet the failure to engage citizens and localities in policy making may carry a high cost which the champions of expansive reforms did not anticipate: a strong political backlash producing severe restrictions. Sustained illegal immigration—given visibility by the Los Angeles riots, Zoe Baird's confirmation hearing, and the bombing of the World Trade

Center—threatens recent expansions in alien admissions and rights. The vulnerability of reforms is compounded by the fact that new immigration has placed the greatest strain on key electoral states: Florida, Texas, California, Illinois, and New York.[75] Indeed, Governor Pete Wilson of California has reawakened immigration reform impulses with well-publicized recommendations for federal action to stem illegal immigration: linking immigration control and the North American Free Trade Agreement, limiting birthright citizenship to exclude children of illegal aliens, and halting federal benefits to illegal aliens.[76] Recent polls indicate that at least 60 percent of the American public shares a new antipathy toward immigration.[77] By insulating meaningful policy making from local communities and public deliberation, national decision makers have unintentionally provided a window of opportunity for irresponsible politicians to translate xenophobic appeals into votes. The new volatility of American immigration politics has increased the likelihood of dramatic policy changes in the next few years as political pressure for new restrictions builds.

Requiring immigration policy makers to be attentive to the concerns of citizens and local communities might bring important costs and trade-offs to the surface, providing an opportunity for public officials and citizens to educate one another. It also gives aliens a greater incentive to pursue cultural and political membership so that they may participate in a meaningful deliberative process. For instance, the common goal of most proponents of English-only and bilingual education—to help immigrant children gain proficiency in the nation's dominant public language—would be even more critical if public communication among citizen-members had an impact on government policies. As Marc Landy stresses, the nurturance of citizenship in the modern state requires public leaders to be civic educators who seek to enhance citizen capacities for "judgement and deliberation."[78] Responsible political leaders ultimately need to be more attentive to integrating Third World immigrants into the national community, even as they introduce immigration in a way which is sensitive to local communities.

American political life can be revitalized by enlivening local and participatory citizenship. Walzer and Jane Mansbridge write that citizenship and community are best cultivated by decentralizing political processes.[79] Yet the isolation of urban problems by metropolitan fragmentation raises daunting problems for decentralization. In the

United States zoning laws and other measures have empowered local communities to select who may live within their borders and what businesses may operate there. Local political jurisdictions have set boundaries that in effect exclude by income and race.[80] Citizen-strangers and fortress communities exemplify the weakness of the American political community. One solution to these dilemmas, advanced by Theda Skocpol and William Julius Wilson, is to make policies more universal by addressing the mutual concerns of the middle class and the poor.[81] Such a political strategy alone, however, cannot achieve this very public objective. If these internal barriers are to be overcome, it will also require political processes—deliberation, civic education, and party politics—that engage citizens in balancing self-interest and the public good. Such an effort, however elusive, may enable American political communities to respond to the needs of citizens and newcomers of diverse ethnic and racial groups without diffusing the special commitments and obligations that foster attachments among members.

NOTES

ABOUT THE AUTHORS

INDEX

# NOTES

## Introduction

1. This book has a companion volume entitled *Rights and the Common Good: The Communitarian Perspective* (forthcoming New York, 1995). Communitarians of all stripes were invited to participate in one of the two volumes. A few, who were not available for one reason or another, will be found elsewhere (and we hope in future editions of these books), and so will communitarian writings from earlier generations. Most are represented in these twin volumes.

## Old Chestnuts and New Spurs

In drafting this essay I greatly benefited from the comments of William Galston, Hans Joas, and W. Bradford Wilcox.

1. "Liberals" refers both to classical liberals such as John Locke and contemporary liberals such as Bruce Ackerman and Downs.

2. For a discussion of this point from a Catholic perspective, see Oliver F. Williams, "Catholic Social Teaching: A Communitarian Democratic Capitalism for the New World Order," in Oliver F. Williams and John W. Houck, eds., *Catholic Social Thought and the New World Order* (Notre Dame, Ind., 1993), pp. 5–28.

3. Markate Daly, *Communitarianism: A New Public Ethics* (Belmont, Calif., 1994), p. ix.

4. For a communitarian critique of liberalism on this count, see Michael Sandel, "The Procedural Republic and the Unencumbered Self," *Political Theory* 12 (1984): 81–96. For an example of this kind of liberal community, see David Gauthier, "The Liberal Individual," in Shlomo Avineri and Avner de-Shalit, eds., *Communitarianism and Individualism* (New York, 1992).

5. Martin Buber, *I and Thou*, trans. Ronald Gregory Smith (New York, 1937).

6. For a review of early communitarian ideas, see Frank Iacobucci, "The Evolution of Constitutional Rights and Corresponding Duties: The Leon Ladner Lecture," *University of British Columbia Law Review*, 1992, pp. 1–19.

7. Robert Bellah et al., *Habits of the Heart: Individualism and Commitment in American Life* (Berkeley, Calif., 1985). See various articles in the communitarian quarterly, The *Responsive Community*.

8. Iacobucci, "Constitutional Rights," p. 1.

9. Dallin Oaks, "Rights and Responsibilities," *Responsive Community* 1 (Winter 1990/1991): 41.

10. Christopher D. Stone, *Should Trees Have Standing?* (Los Altos, Calif., 1974),

p. 17; Katherine E. Stone and Benjamin Kaufman, "Sand Rights: A Legal System to Protect the "Shores of the Sea,'" *Shore and Beach* 56 (July 1988): 8–14.

11. See Amitai Etzioni, "Too Many Rights, Too Few Responsibilities," *Society*, Jan./Feb. 1991, pp. 41–48; Etzioni, *The Spirit of Community* (New York, 1993), pp. 163–91.

12. Tony Mauro, " 'Communitarians' Want to Share the Stage," *USA Today*, 18 Nov. 1992, p. 4A.

13. Mary Ann Glendon, *Rights Talk* (New York, 1991), p. 77.

14. See William Kornhauser, *The Politics of Mass Society* (Glencoe,Ill., 1959); Eric Fromm, *Escape from Freedom* (New York, 1941).

15. See Tibor Machan, "The Communitarian Manifesto," *Orange County Register*, 12 May 1991.

16. Glasser cited in Amitai Etzioni, "What Fascists?" *Responsive Community* 1 (Winter 1990/1991): 13.

17. Charles Derber, "Communitarianism and Its Limits," *Tikkun*, July/Aug. 1993, p. 29.

18. Arthur Schlesinger, Jr., *The Disuniting of America: Reflections on a Multicultural Society* (New York, 1991); Dinesh D'Souza, *Illiberal Education* (New York, 1991).

19. For further discussion of community, see David E. Price, *The "Quest for Community" and Public Policy* (Bloomington, Ind., 1977).

20. Stephen Holmes, *The Anatomy of Antiliberalism* (Cambridge, Mass., 1993), p. 178.

21. For more discussion, see Etzioni, *The Spirit of Community*, pp. 116–60.

22. For a discussion of community definition and the accordant scope of obligation, see David Price, "Community, 'Mediating Structures,' and Public Policy," *Soundings* 62, no. 4 (Winter 1979): 369–94.

23. Stephen Elkin, *City and Regime in the American Republic* (Chicago, 1987), p. 11.

24. See Samuel H. Beer, *To Make a Nation: The Rediscovery of American Federalism* (Cambridge, Mass., 1993).

25. Mark Blitz, "What Are We to Conserve?" *Hudson Briefing Paper*, no. 152 (May 1993): 1.

26. Harry C. Boyte, "Community vs. Public?" *Responsive Community* 2 (Fall 1992): 75.

27. See Etzioni, *The Moral Dimension*.

28. See Michael Walzer, *Spheres of Justice: A Defense of Pluralism and Equality* (New York, 1983).

29. Robert Nisbet, *The Quest for Community* (New York, 1953), p. 278.

30. Clint Bolick, *Grassroots Tyranny: The Limits of Federalism* (Washington, D.C., 1993).

31. Personal communication with Charles Taylor. See also John Rawls, "Kantian Constructivism in Moral Theory: The Dewey Lectures 1980," *Journal of Philosophy* 77 (1980): 515–72; Rawls, "A Revival of Natural Law?" *Wilson Quarterly*, Summer 1992, pp. 142–43.

32. This is not say that communitarian thinking does not acknowledge the important and distinctive liberty guarantees that the Constitution provides for religious groups. In fact, in the two cases at hand a communitarian might frame the issue a bit differently. One could argue, for instance, that the societal value accorded to the "free exercise" of religion was at stake in both of these cases and that the local communities of Oregon and Hialeah had disregarded that societal value. The point, though, is to illustrate the fact that there often tensions between particular communities—be they religious or local—and societywide values and that these tensions need to be negotiated by an overarching set of values. One interesting approach to this kind of dilemma comes from Os Guiness, *The American Hour* (New York, 1993), pp. 239–57.

33. For a discussion of deontological approaches, see Tom L. Beauchamp, *Philosophical Ethics: An Introduction to Moral Philosophy* (New York, 1982).

34. Richard Rorty, *Contingency, Irony, and Solidarity* (Cambridge, Eng., 1989), p. 50.

35. Alison Jaggar, *Feminist Politics and Human Nature* (Towata, N.J., 1983), p. 130.

36. Iacobucci, "Constitutional Rights," p. 12.

37. See Alex Inkeles and David H. Smith, *Becoming Modern: Individual Change in Six Developing Countries* (Cambridge, Mass., 1974).

38. For a discussion of the issue and references to the literature, see Etzioni, *The Moral Dimension.*

39. William A. Galston, "Clinton and the Promise of Communitarianism," *Chronicle of Higher Education*, 2 Dec. 1992, p. A52.

## 1. Communitarian Liberalism

1. Herbert Butterfield, *The Origins of Modern Science* (New York, 1962), esp. chap. 2, "The Conservatism of Copernicus."

2. For an account of this pattern in an early subversive modern thinker—albeit not a prototypical liberal one—see my essay "David Hume's Experimental Science of Morals and the Natural Law Tradition," in Francis Canavan, ed., *The Ethical Bases of Political Life* (Durham, N.C., 1983).

3. For an excellent analysis of some of these distortions in the case of Locke, see Steven M. Dworetz, *The Unvarnished Doctrine: Locke, Liberalism, and the American Revolution* (Durham, N.C., 1990), esp. chap. 4.

4. See John Dunn, *The Political Thought of John Locke* (Cambridge, Eng., 1969), and Nathan Tarcov, *Locke's Education for Liberty* (Chicago, 1984).

5. These are Richard Hooker's words, but they are cited as authoritative by Locke in one of his many reliances upon the Anglican divine, in *Second Treatise*, sec. 135.

6. Patrick Riley, *Will and Political Legitimacy* (Cambridge, Mass., 1982), p. 63.

7. Marie Jean Antoine Nicolas Caritat de Condorcet, *Sketch for a Historical Picture of the Progress of the Human Mind*, trans. June Barraclough (London, 1955), p. 192.

8. Jean-Paul Sartre, "The Flies," in *No Exit and Three Other Plays*, trans. S. Gilbert (New York, 1949), p. 122.

9. Condorcet, *Progress of the Human Mind*, p. 180.

10. Robert Nozick, *Anarchy, State, and Utopia* (New York, 1974).

11. Milton Friedman, *Capitalism and Freedom* (Chicago, 1962), p. 195.

12. These moral premises and their consequences receive lucid and sophisticated expression in John Rawls, *A Theory of Justice* (Cambridge, Mass., 1971).

13. Friedman, *Capitalism and Freedom*, p. 12.

14. John Rawls, for example, argues that a "plan of life" which consists solely in counting blades of grass should be valued on a par with any other. And Bruce Ackerman proscribes any contestation about the human good from liberal dialogue. See *Social Justice in the Liberal State* (New Haven, 1980).

15. Rawls's account of "social union," for example, embodies the dubious belief that people can adhere to a common conception of justice and be motivated to sacrifice for their fellow citizens even if they have wholly incompatible and incommensurable notions of the good. In this respect, he shares Kant's excessive faith in the power of pure practical reason.

16. I have elsewhere characterized this problem as one of trying to put old wine into new wineskins. See *The Irony of Liberal Reason* (Chicago, 1981), pp. 70–75, 198–203. Alasdair MacIntyre has offered a parallel analysis of these difficulties in his account of "why the Enlightenment project had to fail." See *After Virtue* (Notre Dame, Ind., 1981), pp. 49ff.

17. William Galston, "Liberal Virtues," *American Political Science Review* 76 (1982): 621–29.

18. See Alan Wolfe, *Whose Keeper?: Social Science and Moral Obligation* (Berkeley and Los Angeles, Calif., 1989).

19. See Mary Ann Glendon, *Rights Talk* (New York, 1991).

20. See James Fishkin, *Democracy and Deliberation* (New Haven, 1991), and Benjamin Barber, *Strong Democracy* (Berkeley and Los Angeles, Calif., 1984).

## 2. The Communitarian Critique of Liberalism

1. Karl Marx, "On the Jewish Question," in *Early Writings*, ed. T. B. Bottomore (London, 1963), p. 26.

2. Alasdair MacIntyre, *After Virtue* (Notre Dame, Ind., 1981).

3. Thomas Hobbes, *The Elements of Law*, pt. 1, chap. 9, para. 21. I have noticed

that the two favorite writers of communitarian critics of this first kind are Hobbes and Sartre. Is it possible that the essence of liberalism is best revealed by these two, who were not, in the usual sense of the term, liberals at all?

4. See Albert Hirschman's *Exit, Voice, and Loyalty* (Cambridge, Mass., 1970).

5. MacIntyre, *After Virtue*, chaps. 2, 17.

6. This is Richard Rorty's summary of Sandel's argument: "The Priority of Democracy to Philosophy," in Merrill D. Peterson and Robert C. Vaughan, eds., *The Virginia Statute for Religious Freedom: Its Evolution and Consequences in American History*, (Cambridge, Eng., and New York, 1988), p. 273; see Sandel, *Liberalism and the Limits of Justice* (Cambridge, Eng., 1982).

7. Thomas Hobbes, *De Cive*, ed. Howard Warrender (Oxford, 1983), pt. 1, chap. 1.

8. Robert Bellah et al., *Habits of the Heart: Individualism and Commitment in American Life* (Berkeley, Calif., 1985), pp. 21, 290; see Rorty's comment, "Priority of Democracy," p. 275 n.12.

9. And also its practical working out, in the career open to talents, the right of free movement, legal divorce, and so on.

10. See A. Campbell et al., *The American Voter* (New York, 1960), pp. 147–48.

11. See the evocation of King in Bellah et al., *Habits of the Heart*, pp. 249, 252.

12. Roberto Mangabeira Unger, *The Critical Legal Studies Movement* (Cambridge, Mass., 1986), p. 41.

13. Cf. Buff-Coat (Robert Everard) in the Putney debates: "Whatsoever . . . obligations I should be bound unto, if afterwards God should reveal himself, I would break it speedily, if it were an hundred a day" (in *Puritanism and Liberty*, ed. A. S. P. Woodhouse [London, 1938], p. 34). Is Buff-Coat the first superliberal or Unger a latter-day Puritan saint?

14. I do not intend a determinist argument here. We mostly move around within inherited worlds because we find such worlds comfortable and even life-enhancing; but we also move out when we find them cramped, and liberalism makes the escape much easier than it was in preliberal societies.

15. I describe how free-ridership works in ethnic groups in "Pluralism: A Political Perspective," in Stephan Thernstrom, ed., *Harvard Encyclopedia of American Ethnic Groups* (Cambridge, Mass., 1980), pp. 781–87.

16. John Rawls, *A Theory of Justice* (Cambridge, Mass., 1971), pp. 527ff.

17. See the argument for a modest "perfectionism" (rather than neutrality) in Joseph Raz, *The Morality of Freedom* (Oxford, chaps. 5, 6).

18. Irving Bernstein, *Turbulent Years: A History of the American Worker, 1933–1941* (Boston, 1970), chap. 7.

19. See my essay on "Socializing the Welfare State," in Amy Gutmann, ed., *Democracy and the Welfare State* (Princeton, N.J., 1988), pp. 13–26.

20. John Dewey, *The Public and Its Problems* (Athens, Ohio, 1985), pp. 71–72.

21. This kind of pluralist republicanism is also likely to advance the prospects of

what I called "complex equality" in *Spheres of Justice* (New York, 1983). I cannot pursue this question here, but it is worth noting that both liberalism and communitarianism can take egalitarian and non- or antiegalitarian forms. Similarly, the communitarian correction of liberalism can strengthen the old inequalities of traditionalist ways of life, or it can counteract the new inequalities of the liberal market and the bureaucratic state. The "republic of republics" is likely, though by no means certain, to have effects of the second sort.

22. The issue is starkly posed in Sandel, *Liberalism and the Limits of Justice*; much of the recent discussion is a commentary on or an argument with Sandel's book.

23. See Will Kymlicka, "Liberalism and Communitarianism," *Canadian Journal of Philosophy*, June 1988, pp. 181–204.

24. Horace Kallen, *Culture and Democracy in the United States* (New York, 1924).

## 3. Moral Argument and Liberal Toleration: Abortion and Homosexuality

1. I do not defend the stronger claim that the morality (or immorality) of a practice is the only relevant reason in deciding whether there should be a law against it.

2. *Roe v. Wade*, 410 U.S. 113 (1973).

3. *Bowers v. Hardwick*, 478 U.S. 186 (1986).

4. *Roe*, 410 U.S. 113, 162 (1973).

5. Id. at 153.

6. *Thornburgh v. American College of Obstetricians & Gynecologists*, 476 U.S. 747, 777 (1986) (Stevens, J., concurring).

7. Eichbaum, "Towards an Autonomy-Based Theory of Constitutional Privacy: Beyond the Ideology of Familial Privacy," *Harvard C.R.-C.L. Law Review* 14 (1979): 361, 362, 365.

8. Richards, "The Individual, the Family, and the Constitution: A Jurisprudential Perspective," *New York University Law Review* 55 (1980): 1, 31.

9. Karst, "The Freedom of Intimate Association," *Yale Law Journal* 89 (1980): 624, 641. For articles discussing the connection between privacy and autonomy rights, see also Henkin, "Privacy and Autonomy," *Columbia Law Review* 74 (1974): 1410; Smith, "The Constitution and Autonomy," *Texas Law Review* 175 (1982); Wilkinson III and White, "Constitutional Protection for Personal Lifestyles, *Cornell Law Review*, 1977, p. 563.

10. Karst, "Intimate Association," p. 641.

11. *Carey v. Population Services International*, 431 U.S. 678, 687 (1977).

12. *Thornburgh*, 476 U.S. 747, 772 (1986).

13. *Doe v. Bolton*, 410 U.S. 179, 211 (1973) (Douglas, J., concurring) (emphasis omitted).

14. *Kelley v. Johnson*, 425 U.S. 238, 251 (1976) (Marshall, J., dissenting).

15. *Bowers*, 478 U.S. 186, 205 (1986) (Blackmun, J., dissenting).

16. *Whalen v. Roe*, 429 U.S. 589, 599–600 (1977).

17. *Roberts v. United States Jaycees*, 468 U.S. 609, 618–19 (1984).

18. Id. at 619.

19. Samuel Warren and Louis Brandeis, "The Right to Privacy," *Harvard Law Review* 4 (1890): 193.

20. Ibid., pp. 195–96.

21. Prosser, "Privacy," *California Law Review* 48 (1960): 383 (discussing the ensuing recognition and development of a right to privacy).

22. *Poe v. Ullman*, 367 U.S. 497 (1961).

23. Id. at 509.

24. Id. at 519–21 (Douglas, J., dissenting).

25. Id. at 519.

26. Id. at 545 (Harlan, J. dissenting).

27. Id. at 545–46.

28. Id. at 553.

29. Id. at 554.

30. *Griswold v. Connecticut*, 381 U.S. 479 (1965).

31. Id. at 485–86.

32. Id. at 486.

33. *Eisenstadt v. Baird*, 405 U.S. 438 (1972).

34. In fact, the case arose when a man was convicted for giving away a contraceptive device at a public lecture. Id. at 440.

35. Id. at 453.

36. *Griswold*, 381 U.S. at 485.

37. *Eisenstadt*, 405 U.S. at 453. The Court's opinion in *Eisenstadt* camouflages the shift from the old privacy to the new with a false hypothetical premise: "If under Griswold the distribution of contraceptives to married person cannot be prohibited, a ban on distribution to unmarried persons would be equally impermissible." Id. But *Griswold* did not hold that distribution to married persons cannot be prohibited.

38. *Roe*, 410 U.S. 113 (1973).

39. Id. at 153.

40. *Planned Parenthood of Missouri v. Danforth*, 428 U.S. 52 (1976).

41. Id. at 69, 75.

42. *Carey*, 431 U.S. 678 (1977).

43. Id. at 687.

44. Id.

45. Id. (quoting *Eisenstadt*, 405 U.S. at 453) (emphasis added in *Carey*).

46. Id. (quoting *Roe*, 410 U.S. at 153) (emphasis added in *Carey*).

47. Id.

48. *Thornburgh*, 776 U.S. 747, 772 (1986).

49. *Bowers*, 478 U.S. 186, 190–91 (1986).

50. Id. at 196.

51. Id.

52. Id. at 204 (Blackmun, J., dissenting) (quoting *Thornburgh*, 476 U.S. at 777 n.5 [Stevens, J., concurring] [quoting Fried, correspondence, *Philosophy and Public Affairs*, 1977, pp. 288–89]).

53. Id. at 205.

54. Id.

55. Id. at 211.

56. Id. In striking down a similar sodomy law, the New York Court of Appeals clearly expressed the idea that government must be neutral among competing conception of the good. "It is not the function of Penal Law in our governmental policy to provide either a medium for the articulation or the apparatus for the intended enforcement of moral or theological values." *People v. Onofore*, 51 N.Y.2d 476, 488 n.3, 415 N.E.2d 936, 940 n.3, 434 N.Y.S.2d 947,951 n.3 (1980), cert. denied, 451 U.S. 987 (1981).

57. Rawls, "Justice as Fairness: Political Not Metaphysical," *Philosophy and Public Affairs* 14 (1985): 223, 245; Rorty, "The Priority of Democracy to Philosophy," in Merrill D. Peterson and Robert C. Vaughan, eds., *The Virginia Statute for Religious Freedom: Its Evolution and Consequences in American History* (Cambridge, Eng., and New York, 1988), p. 257.

58. *Roe*, 410 U.S. 113 (1973).

59. Id. at 159.

60. Id.

61. Id. at 160–62.

62. Id. at 162.

63. Id.

64. Id. at 163.

65. *Thornburgh*, 476 U.S. 747 (1986).

66. Id. at 797 (White, J., dissenting).

67. Id. at 796.

68. Id. at 790. Justice Harlan suggested a similar way of bracketing the moral controversy over contraception in *Poe v. Ullman*, 367 U.S. 497, 547 (1961) (Harlan, J., dissenting): "The very controversial nature of these questions would, I think, require us to hesitate long before concluding that the Constitution precluded Connecticut from choosing as it has among these various views."

69. Id. at 777 (Stevens, J., concurring).

70. Id. at 777–78 (quoting id. at 794 [White, J. dissenting]).

71. *Bowers*, 478 U.S. 186 (1986).

72. Id. at 191.

73. The phrases are from *Griswold*, 381 U.S. 479, 486 (1965).

74. 478 U.S. at 205 (Blackmun, J. dissenting).

75. Id. at 206.

76. Id. at 217 (Stevens, J., dissenting) (quoting *Fitzgerald v. Porter Memorial Hospital*, 523 F.2d 716, 719–20 (7th Cir. 1975), cert. denied, 425 U.S. 916 (1976)).

77. Id. at 218–19.

78. *Hardwick v. Bowers*, 760 F.2d 1202 (11th Cir. 1985), reviewed, 476 U.S. 747 (1986).

79. Id. at 1211–12.

80. Id. at 1212 (quoting *Griswold*, 381 U.S. 479, 486 (1965)).

81. Id. at 1212.

82. For individualist readings of *Griswold*, see *Eisenstadt*, 405 U.S. 438, 453 (1972), and *Carey*, 431 U.S. 678, 687 (1977).

83. *Stanley v. Georgia*, 394 U.S. 557 (1969).

84. Id. at 564–66, 568 ("This right to receive information and ideas, regardless of their social worth, is fundamental to our free society. . . . [T]he States retain broad power to regulate obscenity; that power simply does not extend to mere possession by the individual in the privacy of his own home") (citation omitted).

85. *People v. Onofre*, 51 N.Y.2d 476, 415 N.E.2d 936, 434 N.Y.S.2d 947 (1980), cert. denied, 451 U.S. 987 (1981).

86. Id. at 487–88, 415 N.E.2d at 939–41, 434 N.Y.S.2d at 950–51.

87. Id. at 488 n.3, 415 N.E.2d at 940 n.3, 434 N.Y.S.2d at 951 n.3.

88. Id.

89. *Bowers*, 478 U.S. 186, 191.

## 4. Community: Reflections on Definition

1. For a more elaborate discussion of community, see my *The Dance with Community: The Contemporary Debate in American Political Thought* (Lawrence, Kans., 1991).

2. A rather different approach than mine is embodied in the concept of communities understood entirely as "communities of practice" as conceptualized well by such thinkers as Charles Anderson, *Pragmatic Liberalism* (Chicago, 1990), and Alasdair MacIntyre, *After Virtue* (Notre Dame, Ind., 1984). Their approach to community is far more inclusive and usually less public than is mine. It is also less a discussion directed to American political intellectuals than a description of actual communities "of practice" (such as the scientific community) somewhat uneasily combined with what is a normative argument for their value. Another interesting treatment of many of the current issues is Allen E. Buchanan, "Assessing the Communitarian Critique of Liberalism," *Ethics*, July 1989, pp. 852–82.

3. Benjamin Barber, *Strong Democracy: Participatory Politics for a New Age* (Berkeley, Calif., 1984), pp. 173, 132.

4. Carole Pateman is the best exponent of this perspective. See her *Participation and Democratic Theory* (Cambridge, Eng., 1970).

5. J. G. A. Pocock, *The Machiavellian Moment: Florentine Political Thought and the*

*Atlantic Republic Tradition* (Princeton, N.J., 1975); for a significant dissent, see Joyce Appleby, *Capitalism and a New Social Order: The Republican Vision of the 1790s* (New York, 1984).

6. See, for a discussion of the issues, history, and otherwise: Don Herzog, "Some Questions for Republicans," *Political Theory* 14 (Aug. 1986); Richard Beeman, Stephen Botein, and Edward C. Carter II, *Beyond Confederation: Origins of the Constitution and American National Identity* (Chapel Hill, N.C., 1987); Russell Hanson, *The Democratic Imagination in America* (Princeton, N.J., 1985).

7. For a skeptical view, see Appleby, *New Social Order*.

8. See n. 11.

9. For example: Benedict Anderson, *Imagined Communities: Reflections on the Origins and Spread of Nationalism* (New York, 1991), and Ernest Gellner, *Culture, Identity, and Politics* (New York, 1987).

10. Bob Pepperman Taylor is a welcome current exception. See his *Our Limits Transgressed: Environmental Political Thought in America* (Lawrence, Kans., 1992).

11. Two classic expositions: Robert Heilbroner, *An Inquiry into the Human Prospect* (New York, 1974); Jonathan Schell, *The Fate of the Earth* (New York, 1982).

12. For example: Kirkpatrick Sale, *Human Scale* (New York, 1980); Murray Bookchin, *Municipalization: Community Ownership of the Economy* (Burlington, Vt., 1986); Bruce Stokes, *Helping Ourselves: Local Solutions to Global Problems* (New York, 1981).

13. Leo Strauss, *What Is Political Philosophy and Other Studies* (Glencoe, Ill., 1959); Allan Bloom, *The Closing of the American Mind* (New York, 1987).

14. Bloom, *Closing of the American Mind*, p. 85.

15. Ibid., pp. 167–72.

16. Two interesting treatments: Christopher Lasch, *Haven in a Heartless World: The Family Besieged* (New York, 1977); Robert Bellah et al., *Habits of the Heart: Individualism and Commitment in American Life* (Berkeley, Calif., 1985), chaps. 4, 5.

17. See, for example, discussions by Parker Palmer, *The Company of Strangers* (New York, 1981); Jim Wallis, *The Soul of Politics: A Practical and Prophetic Vision for Change* (New York, 1994).

18. Robert Wuthnow, *The Restructuring of American Religion: Society and Faith since World War II* (Princeton, N.J., 1988).

19. Bellah et al., *Habits of the Heart*; Stanley Hauerwas, *A Community of Character* (Notre Dame, Ind., 1981); Richard J. Neuhaus, *The Naked Public Square* (Grand Rapids, Mich., 1984); Rosemary Radford Ruether, *Gaia and God* (New York, 1992).

20. Glenn Tinder, *Community: Reflections on a Tragic Ideal* (Baton Rouge, La., 1980), pp. 85, 199; John Patrick Diggins, *The Lost Soul of American Politics* (Chicago, 1984).

21. Wallis, *The Soul of Politics*; Palmer, *Company of Strangers*.

22. For example: Peter Clecak, *America's Quest for the Ideal Self* (New York, 1983).

23. Michael Walzer, *Spheres of Justice: A Defense of Pluralism and Equality* (New York, 1983).

24. Nancy J. Rosenblum, *Another Liberalism: Romanticism and the Reconstruction of Liberal Thought* (Cambridge, Mass., 1987); Bellah et al., *Habits of the Heart*; Michael Sandel, *Liberalism and the Limits of Justice* (Cambridge, Eng., 1982); Tinder, *Community*.

25. As explicated in the famous *Federalist* no. 10.

26. Tinder, *Community*, p. 2.

27. Glenn Tinder, "Can We Be Good without God?" *Atlantic Monthly*, Dec. 1989, pp. 69–85; Clarke Cochran, *Character, Community, and Politics* (University, Ala., 1982). Wilson Carey McWilliams seems a good candidate here: *The Idea of Fraternity in America* (Berkeley, Calif., 1974). Two classics are: Albert Camus, *The Plague*, trans. Stuart Gilbert (New York, 1972), and Martin Buber, *The Writings of Martin Buber*, ed. Will Herberg (New York, 1956)

28. Rosenblum, *Another Liberalism*.

29. Plato, "The Republic," in *The Portable Plato*, trans. Benjamin Jowett (New York, 1984), pp. 656–57.

30. Cochran, *Community, Character, and Politics*, p. 155.

31. Iris Marion Young, *Justice and the Politics of Difference* (Princeton, N.J., 1990).

## 5. The Communitarian Individual

1. P. D. James, *The Children of Men* (New York, l992).

2. Mary Midgley, *Can't We Make Moral Judgements?* (New York, l99l).

3. Arthur Kornhaber, M.D., and Kenneth L. Woodward, *Grandparents/Grandchildren: The Vital Connection* (New York, l980).

4. Harry Boyte, *The Backyard Revolution* (Philadelphia, l980).

5. From a forthcoming book of that title.

## 6. Personhood and Moral Obligation

1. See Peter Singer, *The Expanding Circle: Ethics and Sociobiology* (New York, 1981), chap. 4.

2. Thomas Nagel, *The Possibility of Altruism* (Princeton, N.J., 1970), p. 145.

3. Universalism/particularism is one of the "pattern variables" introduced by Parsons and Shils (Talcott Parsons and Edward A. Shils, eds., *Toward a General Theory of Action: Theoretical Foundations for the Social Sciences* [New York, 1951], pp. 76–91) and Parsons (Talcott Parsons, *The Social System* [Glencoe, Ill., 1951], pp. 45–67). Others include ascription/achievement, instrumental/expressive, specificity/diffuseness. These contrasts have long been familiar in sociology, e.g., as implicit in the theory of gemeinschaft and gesellschaft.

4. George Eliot, *Middlemarch: A Study of Provincial Life* (1872; rept., New York, 1964), p. 601.

5. H. L. A. Hart, "Who Can Tell Right from Wrong?" *New York Review of Books*, 17 July 1986, p. 52.

6. Singer, *Expanding Circle*, p. 157.

7. Ibid.

8. Therefore, our aim should be to reduce the psychic distance between those who inflict harm, for whatever reason, and their victims. See also Charles Fried, *Right and Wrong* (Cambridge, Mass., 1978), chap. 2.

9. This does not mean that only what is unique to that person matters, rather than what is shared with other persons. But in the process of attending to someone's needs, which may be similar to other people's needs, the person is treated as a distinctive bearer of intrinsic worth. See Lawrence A. Blum, *Friendship, Altruism, and Morality* (London, 1980), p. 95.

10. Paul Ramsey, *Basic Christian Ethics* (Chicago, 1950), p. 94f.

11. *Homage to Catalonia* (1938; rept., London, 1974), pp. 230ff.

12. Charles Dickens, *Bleak House* (1853; rept., Harmondsworth, Eng., 1971), p. 85.

13. David Hume, *A Treatise of Human Nature* (1740), ed. L. A. Selby-Bigge (Oxford, 1955), p. 519.

14. Ibid., pp. 488ff.

15. Ibid.

16. Robert E. Goodin, *Protecting the Vulnerable: A Reanalysis of Our Social Responsibilities* (Chicago, 1985), p. 9.

17. Ibid., p. 11.

18. Ibid., p. 206.

19. Ibid., p. 119.

20. To perform a role is to act in the light of governing norms. Therefore, to some extent this ground of obligation introduces an element of univeralism. The immediacy of the relation reinforces the obligation but is not its ground. Furthermore, as the role is generalized—fellow citizen, fellow human, fellow creature—responsibility for particular others is attenuated.

21. Blum, *Friendship*, p. 70.

22. For a history of *person*, see Adolf Trendelenburg, "A Contribution to the History of the Word *Person*," *Monist* 20 (1910): 336–63.

23. See Jacques Maritain, *The Person and the Common Good* (New York, 1947); Steven Lukes, *Individualism* (Oxford, 1973), chap. 20; J. S. La Fontaine, "Person and Individual: Some Anthropological Reflections," in Michael Corrithers, Steven Collins, and Steven Lukes, eds., *The Category of the Person: Anthropology, Philosophy, History* (Cambridge, Eng., 1985), pp. 123–40.

24. Trendelenburg, "The Word *Person*," p. 345.

25. Henry Sumner Maine, *Ancient Law* (1861; rept., Boston, 1963), p. 165. On

the limits of Maine's formula, see my *Law, Society, and Industrial Justice* (New York, 1969), pp. 61ff.

26. Lukes, *Individualism*, p. 148.

27. Bernard Williams, *Moral Luck* (Cambridge, Eng., 1981), p. 14.

## 7. Human Nature and the Quest for Community

1. Robert Bellah et al., *Habits of the Heart: Individualism and Commitment in American Life* (Berkeley, Calif., 1985); Bellah et al., *The Good Society* (New York, 1991); Amitai Etzioni, *The Moral Dimension: Towards a New Economics* (New York, 1988) and *The Spirit of Community: Rights, Responsibilities, and the Communitarian Agenda* (New York, 1993); Alan Wolfe, *Whose Keeper?: Social Science and Moral Obligation* (Berkeley and Los Angeles, Calif., 1989); Philip Selznick, *The Moral Commonwealth: Social Theory and the Promise of Community* (Berkeley and Los Angeles, Calif., 1992); James Q. Wilson, *The Moral Sense* (New York, 1993).

2. Ronald Dworkin, *Taking Rights Seriously* (Cambridge, Mass., 1977), pp. 184–205.

3. J. Baird Callicot, *In Defense of the Land Ethic: Essays in Environmental Philosophy* (Albany, 1986); Bill Devall and George Sessions, *Deep Ecology: Living As If Nature Mattered* (Salt Lake City, 1985); Donna Haraway, *Primate Visions: Gender, Race, and Nature in the World of Modern Science* (New York and London, 1989); Bill McKibben, *The End of Nature* (New York, 1989).

4. For a liberal response to ecological viewpoints, see Luc Ferry, *Le nouvel ordre ecologique: L'arbre, l'animal, et l'homme* (Paris, 1992).

5. Elinor Ostrom, *Governing the Commons: The Evolution of Institutions for Collective Action* (Cambridge, Eng., 1990).

6. Greta Jones, *Social Darwinism and English Thought: The Interaction between Biological and Social Theory* (Sussex, Eng., 1980).

7. Stephen Horigan, *Nature and Culture in Western Discourses* (London, 1988).

8. Thomas Sowell, *A Conflict of Visions: Ideological Origins of Political Struggles* (New York, 1987).

9. Milton Friedman, *Capitalism and Freedom* (Chicago, 1962).

10. Kenneth Dyson, *The State Tradition in Western Europe* (New York, 1980).

11. Oliver Williamson, *Markets and Hierarchies: Analysis and Anti-Trust Implications: A Study in the Economics of Internal Organizations* (New York, 1975).

12. Robert Ardrey, *The Territorial Imperative: A Personal Inquiry into the Animal Origins of Property and Nations* (New York, 1966); Konrad Lorenz, *On Aggression* (New York, 1966).

13. Frans de Waal, *Peacemaking among Primates* (Cambridge, Mass., 1989).

14. For just a few examples, see Dorothy L. Cheney and Robert M. Seyfarth, *How Monkeys See the World* (Chicago, 1990); John Tyler Bonner, *The Evolution of Culture in Animals* (Princeton, N.J., 1980); Edward O. Wilson, *The Insect Societies*

(Cambridge, Mass., 1971); Thomas Sebeok, ed., *How Animals Communicate* (Bloomington, Ind., 1977).

15. Wilson, *The Moral Sense*.

16. Donald Worster, *Nature's Economy: The Roots of Ecology* (San Francisco, 1977).

17. Derek L. Phillips, *Towards a Just Social Order* (Princeton, N.J., 1986).

18. James Lovelock, *Gaia: A New Look at Life on Earth* (New York, 1979).

19. Hillel Levine and Lawrence Harmon, *The Death of an American Jewish Community: A Tragedy of Good Intentions* (New York, 1992). However, Claude Fischer, in *To Dwell among Friends* (Chicago, 1982), argues that most notions about community decline are not true.

20. David Popenoe, *Disturbing the Nest: Family Change and Decline in Modern Societies* (New York, 1988); Sylvia Ann Hewlitt, *When the Bough Breaks: The Cost of Neglecting Our Children* (New York, 1991).

21. Julian L. Simon and Aaron Wildavsky, "Facts, Not Species, Are Threatened," *New York Times*, 13 May 1993, p. A23.

22. Arlene Skolnick, *Embattled Paradise: The American Family in an Age of Uncertainty* (New York, 1991); Stephanie Coontz, *The Way We Never Were: American Families and the Nostalgia Trap* (New York, 1992).

23. Albert O. Hirschman, in *The Rhetoric of Reaction: Perversity, Futility, Jeopardy* (Cambridge, Mass., 1991), calls this the "futility" trope of conservative rhetoric.

24. Stephen Mintz and Susan Kellogg, *Domestic Revolutions: A Social History of American Family Life* (New York, 1988).

25. Hannah Arendt, *Between Past and Future: Eight Exercises in Political Thought*, 2d ed. (New York, 1968), p. 211.

26. Ernst Mayr, *One Long Argument: Charles Darwin and the Genesis of Modern Evolutionary Thought* (Cambridge, Mass., 1991).

27. N. Blurton Jones and Melvin J. Konner, "!Kung Knowledge of Animal Behavior," in Richard B. Lee and Irven DeVore, eds., *Kalahari Hunter-Gatherers* (Cambridge, Mass., 1976), p. 341.

28. Wilson, *The Moral Sense*.

29. Michael E. Lamb, "The Bonding Phenomenon: Misinterpretations and Their Implications," *Journal of Pediatrics* 191 (Feb. 1982): 555–57.

30. Diane Eyer, *Mother-Infant Bonding: A Scientific Fiction* (New Haven, 1992).

31. Philip Lieberman, *Uniquely Human: The Evolution of Speech, Thought, and Selfless Behavior* (Cambridge, Mass., 1991).

32. Wolfe, *Whose Keeper?*

## 8. Virtue, the Common Good, and Democracy

1. The argument presented here is a development and adaptation of ideas I have expressed elsewhere in "The Common Good Revisited," *Theological Studies* 50 (1989): 70–94; "Contexts of the Political Role of Religion: Civil Society and Culture,"

*San Diego Law Review* 30(1993): 877–901; and "Afterword: A Community of Freedom," in R. Bruce Douglass and David Hollenbach, eds., *Catholicism and Liberalism: Contributions to American Public Philosophy* (Cambridge, Eng., and New York, 1994).

2. John Rawls, "The Idea of an Overlapping Consensus," *Oxford Journal of Legal Studies* 7 (1987): 4.

3. Ibid. See note 7 of Rawls's essay for a sketch of the presuppositions of this "common sense sociology."

4. Ibid., pp. 12–13.

5. Ibid., p. 13.

6. Ibid., p. 15.

7. Richard Rorty, "The Priority of Democracy to Philosophy," in Merrill D. Peterson and Robert C. Vaughan, eds., *The Virginia Statute for Religious Freedom: Its Evolution and Consequences in American History* (Cambridge, Eng., and New York, 1988), p. 263.

8. The phrase is from Robert J. Pranger, *The Eclipse of Citizenship: Power and Participation in Contemporary Politics* (New York, 1968). See also Michael Walzer, "The Problem of Citizenship," in *Obligations: Essays on Disobedience, War, and Citizenship* (Cambridge, Mass., 1970), pp. 203–28.

9. E. J. Dionne, Jr., *Why Americans Hate Politics* (New York, 1991).

10. National Conference of Catholic Bishops, *Economic Justice for All: Pastoral Letter on Catholic Social Teaching and the U.S. Economy* (Washington, D.C., 1986).

11. Robert Bellah et al., *Habits of the Heart: Individualism and Commitment in American Life* (Berkeley, Calif., 1985), p. 277.

12. Peter L. Berger, Brigitte Berger, and Hansfried Kellner, *The Homeless Mind: Modernization and Consciousness* (New York, 1973), pp. 77–78.

13. The term is taken from Peter L. Berger and Richard John Neuhaus, *To Empower People: The Role of Mediating Structures in Public Policy* (Washington, D.C., 1977), p. 2.

14. Alan Wolfe, *Whose Keeper? Social Science and Moral Obligation* (Berkeley, Calif., 1989), p. 20 and passim.

15. Ibid., p. 20.

16. For analysis of this adversarial relationship of Catholicism and democracy and its transformation over the past half century, see Douglass and Hollenbach, *Catholicism and Liberalism*.

17. For evidence of the strong alliance of Catholicism and democracy that has developed since the Second Vatican Council, see Samuel P. Huntington, "Religion and the Third Wave," *National Interest* 24 (Summer 1991): 29–42. This article is excerpted from Huntington, *The Third Wave: Democratization in the Late Twentieth Century* (Norman, Okla., 1991).

18. Pope Pius XI, *Quadragesimo Anno* (Washington, D.C., 1942).

19. John A. Coleman, "Religious Liberty in America and Mediating Structures," in Coleman, *An American Strategic Theology* (New York, 1982), p. 226.

20. See Aristotle, *Nicomachean Ethics* 1167a, b.

21. Pope John Paul II, *Sollicitudo Rei Socialis*, no. 38 in David J. O'Brien and Thomas A. Shannon, eds., *Catholic Social Thought: The Documentary Heritage* (Maryknoll, N.Y., 1992).

22. Aristotle, *Politics* 1253a.

23. Benjamin R. Barber, *Strong Democracy: Participatory Politics for a New Age* (Berkeley, Calif., 1984), p. 106.

24. Rawls, "Overlapping Consensus," p. 8.

## 9. The Virtues of Democratic Self-Constraint

1. Jean-Jacques Rousseau, *The Social Contract*, bk. 3, chap. 15.

2. George Kateb emphasizes the importance of eternal vigilance as a democratic virtue. For an insightful account of a democratic culture which can cultivate eternal vigilance along with other democratic virtues, see George Kateb, *The Inner Ocean: Individualism and Democratic Culture* (Ithaca, N.Y., 1992), esp. introduction and chaps. 1–3.

3. Compare Samuel Freeman's important interpretation of judicial review as "a shared precommitment by free and equal citizens to maintain the conditions of their sovereignty." On Freeman's view of democracy, as I understand it, judicial review is no more (or less) democratic if citizens and public officials deliberatively consent to it. The precommitment is built into the democratic ideal and need not actually be acknowledged by citizens. See Samuel Freeman, "Constitutional Democracy and the Legitimacy of Judicial Review," *Law and Philosophy* 9 (1990): 327–70.

4. For more about deliberation and constitutional democracy, see Cass Sunstein, *The Partial Constitution* (Cambridge, Mass., 1993), esp. pp. 133–45.

5. Frank I. Michelman, "Welfare Rights in a Constitutional Democracy," *Washington University Law Quarterly*, Summer 1979, pp. 659–93; Michelman, "In Pursuit of Constitutional Welfare Rights: One View of Rawls' Theory of Justice," *University of Pennsylvania Law Review* 121 (1973): 962–1019.

6. For a complementary account of democratic citizenship which emphasizes the importance of persuasive argument in democratic decision making, see Michael Walzer, *Spheres of Justice: A Defense of Pluralism and Equality* (New York, 1983), pp. 303–11. Walzer does not discuss deliberation per se, but his view of democratic citizenship clearly points in this direction.

7. Ibid., pp. 309–10.

8. I concentrate on the convergence of liberal and democratic rationales for nonrepression and nondiscrimination in "How Liberal Is Democracy?" in Douglas MacLean and Claudia Mills, eds., *Liberalism Reconsidered* (Totowa, N.J., 1983), pp. 25–50.

9. A more detailed defense of this conclusion, and its political implications, can be found in *Democratic Education* (Princeton, N.J., 1987).

10. For a defense of this democratic perspective, see Amy Gutmann and Dennis Thompson, "Moral Conflict and Political Consensus," *Ethics* 101 (Oct. 1990): 64–88.

11. Diane Ravitch, *The Schools We Deserve: Reflections on the Educational Crises of Our Times* (New York, 1985), p. 288.

12. William Galston, *Liberal Purposes: Goods, Virtues, and Diversity in the Liberal State* (Cambridge, Eng., 1991), p. 252.

13. Ibid., pp. 254–55, 252.

14. Ibid., pp. 253–55.

15. Ibid., p. 255.

16. *Bob Mozert et al. v. Hawkins County Public Schools et al.*, 827 F.2d. 1058 (6th Cir. 1987).

17. Greg Stankiewicz, "The Controversial Curriculum," case study, Woodrow Wilson School, Princeton, N.J., 1991.

18. "It is in the case of children," John Stuart Mill wrote, "that misapplied notions of liberty are a real obstacle to the fulfillment by the State of its duties. One would almost think that a man's children were supposed to be literally, and not metaphorically, a part of himself" (Mill, *On Liberty*, chap. 5, para. 12).

19. Galston notes that parents cannot in practice "seal their children off from knowledge of other ways of life," but the argument concerns whether they have the right to do so (and the state a duty to let them so do) as far as is possible even if this comes at the expense of lessons in democratic deliberation (Galston, *Liberal Purposes*, p. 253).

20. Thomas Nagel's excellent essay, "Moral Conflicts and Political Legitimacy," *Philosophy and Public Affairs* 16 (1987), introduced me to Robert Frost's characterization of a liberal.

21. Galston, *Liberal Purposes*, p. 253.

22. For two well-informed and well-argued but distinctive positions on distributive justice in health care, see Norman Daniels, *Just Health Care* (Cambridge, Eng., 1985), and Ezekiel J. Emanuel, *The Ends of Human Life: Medical Ethics in a Liberal Polity* (Cambridge, Mass., 1991).

23. For an insightful account of this contractarian standard, see T. M. Scanlon, "Contractualism and Utilitarianism," in *Utilitarianism and Beyond* (Cambridge, Eng., 1982), pp. 103–29.

## 10. Institutions as the Infrastructure of Democracy

1. I have attempted to describe the common themes of this philosophic liberalism as it has affected American public discourse in *Reconstructing Public Philosophy* (Berkeley and Los Angeles, Calif., 1982). For a provocative comparative discussion of the role of liberal theory in American legal thought, see Mary Ann Glendon, *Abortion and Divorce in Western Law: American Failures, European Challenges* (Cambridge, Mass., 1987), pp. 119–42.

2. See, for example, Alan Wolfe, *Whose Keeper? Social Science and Moral Obligation* (Berkeley and Los Angeles, Calif., 1989).

3. See Alasdair MacIntyre, *After Virtue: A Study in Moral Theory*, 2d ed. (Notre Dame, Ind., 1984).

4. See the landmark study by Robert A. Putnam, *Making Democracy Work: Civic Traditions in Modern Italy* (Princeton, N.J., 1993), pp. 109–14.

5. Charles Taylor has highlighted this mutual implication of agency and context. He has argued against the notion of freedom as unconstrained self-creation that agency only becomes possible and meaningful when choices are perceived as possessing value independent of subjective choice, as existing within "horizons of value." These horizons, not individual will or consciousness, represent the actual starting points for the achievement of identity and free agency. That is, freedom and identity, agency itself, can only be realized as embedded within ongoing community life, a life shaped by distinctions of value. See Charles Taylor, *Sources of the Self: The Making of the Modern Identity* (Cambridge, Mass., 1989), esp. pp. 3–54, 91–110.

6. This definition and the following discussion of institutions draws directly upon Robert N. Bellah et al., *The Good Society* (New York, 1991), esp. pp. 4–18.

7. This important insight has been developed by Douglass C. North, *Institutions, Institutional Change, and Economic Performance* (New York, 1990), esp. pp. 73–83.

8. Jerome H. Skolnick and David H. Bayley, *Community Policing: Issues and Practices around the World* (Washington, D.C., 1988), p. 3, quoted in Philip Selznick, *The Moral Commonwealth: Social Theory and the Promise of Community* (Berkeley and Los Angeles, Calif., 1993), p. 514.

9. This is the development documented by Robert Putnam among the more prosperous and integrated regions of northern Italy. See Putnam, *Making Democracy Work*.

## 11. Liberal Politics and the Public Sphere

1. John Stuart Mill, "On Liberty," in *Three Essays* (Oxford, 1975), p. 74.

2. I have discussed this in "Invoking Civil Society," a paper presented to a Castel Gandolfo seminar and published in German translation, as "Die Beschwörung der civil society," in Krzysztof Michalski, ed., *Europa und die Folgen* (Stuttgart, 1988).

3. Jurgen Habermas, *The Structural Transformation of the Public Sphere*, trans. Thomas Burger (Cambridge, Mass., 1989).

4. Michael Warner, *The Letters of the Republic* (Cambridge, Mass., 1990).

5. Habermas, *Structural Transformation*, p. 91, refers to Locke in this connection.

6. Warner, *Letters*, chap. 1.

7. This indicates how far the late eighteenth-century notion of public opinion is from what is the object of poll research today. The phenomenon that "public opinion research" aims to measure is, in terms of my above distinction, a convergent unity, and doesn't need to emerge from discussion. It is analogous to the opinion of mankind. The ideal underlying the eighteenth century version emerges in this passage from Burke, quoted by Habermas (*Structural Transformation*, pp. 117–18): "In a free country, every man thinks he has a concern in all public matters; that he has a right to form and deliver an opinion on them. They sift, examine and discuss them. They are curious, eager, attentive and jealous; and by making such matters the daily subjects of their thoughts and discoveries, vast numbers contract a very tolerable knowledge of them, and some a very considerable one. Whereas in other countries none but men who office calls them to it having much care or thought about public affairs, and not daring to try the force of their opinions with one another, ability of this sort is extremely rare in any station of life. In free countries, there is often found more real public wisdom and sagacity in shops and manufactories than in cabinets of princes in countries where none dares to have an opinion until he comes to them."

8. Habermas, *Structural Transformation*, p. 119.

9. Warner, *Letters*, p. 41.

10. See Fox's speech, quoted in Habermas, *Structural Transformation*, pp. 65–66: "It is certainly right and prudent to consult the public opinion. . . . If the public opinion did not happen to square with mine; if, after pointing out to them the danger, they did not see it in the same light with me, or if they conceived that another remedy was preferable to mine, I should consider it as my due to my king, due to my Country, due to my honour to retire, that they might pursue the plan which they thought better, by a fit instrument, that is by a man who thought with them. . . . but one thing is most clear, that I ought to give the public the means of forming an opinion."

11. Cited in ibid., p. 117.

12. Ibid., p. 82.

13. See Warner, *Letters*, pp. 40–42. Warner also points to the relationship with the impersonal agency of modern capitalism (pp. 62–63), as well as the closeness of fit between the impersonal stance and the battle against imperial corruption that was so central a theme in the colonies (pp. 65–66), in the framing of this highly overdetermined mode.

14. Ibid., p. 46.

15. See E. Kantorowicz, *The King's Two Bodies* (Princeton, N.J., 1957).

16. For an extra-European example of this kind of thing, see Clifford Geertz's *Negara* (Princeton, N.J., 1980), where the pre-Conquest Balinese state is described.

17. As a matter of fact, excluding the religious dimension is not even a necessary condition of my concept of *secular* here, let alone a sufficient one. A secular

association is one grounded purely on common action, and this excludes any dividing grounding for this association, but nothing prevents the people so associated from continuing a religious form of life; indeed, this form may even require that, e.g., political associations be purely secular. There are for instance religious motives for espousing a separation of church and state.

18. Benedict Anderson, *Imagined Communities* (London, 1983), pp. 28–31.

19. Anderson borrows a term from Benjamin to describe modern profane time. He sees it as a "homogenous, empty time." "Homogeneity" captures the aspect I am describing here, that all events now fall into the same kind of time; but the "emptiness" of time takes us into another issue: the way in which both space and time come to be seen as "containers" which things and events contigently fill, rather than as constituted by what fills them. This latter step is part of the metaphysical imagination of modern physics, as we can see with Newton. But it is the step to homogeneity which is crucial for secularization, as I am conceiving it.

The step to emptiness is part of the objectification of time that has been so important a part of the outlook of the modern subject of instrumental reason. Time has been in a sense "spatialized." Heidegger has mounted a strong attack on this whole conception in his understanding of temporality; see especially *Sein und Zeit* (Tubingen, 1926), div. 2. But distinguishing secularity from the objectification of time allows us to situate Heidegger on the modern side of the divine. Heideggerian temporality is also a mode of secular time.

20. Mircea Eliade, *The Sacred and the Profane* (New York, 1959), pp. 8off.

21. See, especially, Joseph Schumpeter, *Capitalism, Socialism, and Democracy* (New York, 1950), for an eloquent statement of this view.

22. See Noam Chomsky, *Deterring Democracy* (London, 1991), for one of the most hard-hitting criticisms of this range.

23. I have discussed the background to the "politics of recognition" in a paper of that name (forthcoming).

24. Mary Ann Glendon, *Abortion and Divorce in Western Law* (Cambridge, Mass., 1987), has shown this has made a difference to American decisions on this issue, as compared with those in other comparable Western societies.

25. I have raised the issue about democratic stability in "Cross-Purposes: The Liberal-Communitarian Debate," in Nancy Rosenblum, ed., *Liberalism and the Moral Life* (Cambridge, Mass., 1989). There is a good discussion of the slide toward this lopsided package in American politics in Michael Sandel, "The Procedural Republic and the Unencumbered Self," *Political Theory* 12 (Feb. 1984). I have compared the American and Canadian systems in this respect in "Alternative Futures," in Alan Cairns and Cynthia Williams, eds., *Constitutionalism, Citizenship, and Society in Canada* (Toronto, 1985). There is a good critique of this American political culture in Robert Bellah et al., *Habits of the Heart: Individualism and Commitment in American Life* (Berkeley, Calif., 1985) and *The Good Society* (New York, 1991).

## 12. Free Speech and Free Press: A Communitarian Perspective

1. Jeffrey B. Abramson, F. Christopher Arterton, and Gary Orren, *The Electronic Commonwealth: The Impact of New Media Technologies on Democratic Politics* (New York, 1988), p. 240. The analysis of free press issues in this chapter draws on the co-author's previous writings in *The Electronic Commonwealth*.

2. *See, e.g., Abrams v. United States*, 250 U.S. 616, 629 (1919), where Justice Holmes in dissent characterizes the suppressed leaflets as the work of "puny anonymities."

3. Laurence Tribe, *American Constitutional Law* (Mineola, N.Y., 1978), p. 578.

4. Thomas Emerson, *The System of Freedom of Expression* (New York, 1970), p. 6.

5. *Police Department of Chicago v. Mosley*, 408 U.S. 92, 95 (1972).

6. *Miller v. California*, 413 U.S. 15 (1973).

7. *Stanley v. Georgia*, 394 U.S. 557, 564 (1969).

8. 47 U.S.C. sec. 301; see also the Radio Act of 1927, 44 Stat. 1162.

9. Robert D. Hershey, Jr., "F.C.C. Votes Down Fairness Doctrine in a 4–0 Decision," *New York Times*, 5 Aug. 1987, p. A1.

10. James Madison, *Writings of James Madison* 9:103, quoted in *Board of Education, Island Trees Union Free School District v. Pico*, 457 U.S. 853, 867 (1982).

11. Alexander Meiklejohn, *Free Speech and Its Relation to Self-Government* (New York, 1948), pp. 88, 89.

12. Harry Kalven, Jr., *The Negro and the First Amendment* (Columbus, Ohio, 1965), p. 16.

13. *Cohen v. California*, 403 U.S. 15 (1971).

14. Id. at 24, 25.

15. *See, e.g., Gitlow v. New York*, 268 U.S. 652 (1925) and *Dennis v. United States*, 341 U.S. 494 (1951).

16. *Buckley v. Valeo*, 424 U.S. 1, 19 (1976).

17. Id.

18. The Court did approve limits on presidential campaign expenditures conditioned upon the candidate's acceptance of public financing.

19. *FEC v. National Conservative PAC*, 470 U.S. 480 (1985)

20. *Buckley*, 424 U.S. at 48–49.

21. Id. at 49.

22. Rogers Smith, *Liberalism and American Constitutional Law* (Cambridge, Mass., 1985), p. 248.

23. Ibid.

24. John Rawls, *Political Liberalism* (New York, 1993), p. 361.

25. We owe this point to Rawls, ibid., p. 362.

26. *Lochner v. New York*, 198 U.S. 45 (1905).

27. *Red Lion Broadcasting Co. v. F.C.C.*, 395 U.S. 367, 390 (1969).

28. Id. at 390.

29. Hershey, "F.C.C. Votes Down Fairness Doctrine," p. A1.

30. "Excerpts from F.C.C. Statement," *New York Times*, 5 Aug. 1987, p. C26.

31. *Miami Herald Publishing Co. v. Tornillo*, 418 U.S. 241 (1974).

32. Abramson et al., *The Electronic Commonwealth*, p. 283.

33. Ibid., p. 284.

34. Peter Kerr, "Cable TV Pressing Free-Speech Issue," *New York Times*, 5 April 1984, p. C22.

35. Sheldon Wolin, "What Revolutionary Action Means Today," *Democracy* 2 (1982): 18.

36. Ronald Beiner, *Political Judgment* (Chicago, 1983), p. 138.

37. Wolin, "Revolutionary Action," pp. 20–21.

## 14. Immigration and Political Community in the United States

1. Michael Walzer, "The Distribution of Membership," in Peter Brown and Henry Shue, eds., *Boundaries: National Autonomy and Its Limits* (Totowa, N.J., 1981), pp. 1–36; Frederick Whelan, "Citizenship and Freedom of Movement: An Open Admission Policy?" in Mark Gibney, ed., *Open Borders? Closed Societies?* (New York, 1988), pp. 3–40.

2. Marc Landy, "Citizen First: Public Policy and Self Government," *Responsive Community*, Spring 1991, pp. 56–64; Deborah Stone, *Policy Paradox and Political Reason* (Glenview, Ill., 1988); Lawrence Mead, *Beyond Entitlement: The Social Obligations of Citizenship* (New York, 1986); James Q. Wilson, "The Rediscovery of Character: Private Virtue and Public Policy," *Public Interest*, Fall 1985, pp. 3–16; Robert Reich, ed., *The Power of Public Ideas* (Cambridge, Mass., 1988); Mary Ann Glendon, *Rights Talk: The Impoverishment of Political Discourse* (New York, 1991).

3. U.S. Immigration and Naturalization Service, *Statistical Yearbook of the Immigration and Naturalization Service, 1991* (Washington, D.C., 1992), pp. 14–21.

4. Rita Simon, "Immigration and American Attitudes," *Public Opinion* 10 (1987): 47–50; Edwin Harwood, "American Public Opinion and U.S. Immigration Policy," *Annals of the American Academy of Political and Social Science*, Sept. 1986, pp. 201–12.

5. Juan Garcia, *Operation Wetback: The Mass Deportation of Undocumented Mexican Workers in 1954* (Westport, Conn., 1980).

6. David Reimers, "An Unintended Reform: The 1965 Immigration Act and Third World Immigration to the United States," *Journal of American Ethnic History*, Fall 1993, pp. 9–28, and Reimers, *Still the Golden Door: The Third World Comes to America* (New York, 1985). See also Abba Schwartz, *The Open Society* (New York, 1968); Edward Kennedy, "The Immigration Act of 1965," *Annals of the American Academy of Political and Social Science*, Sept. 1966, pp. 137–49.

7. *New York Times*, 13 Dec. 1991.

8. For instance, Rep. Joe Moakley (D-Mass.) succeeded in gaining a special protective status for Salvadoran refugees under the 1990 act.

9. Alejandro Portes, "Immigration and the Reshaping of America," *Baltimore Sun*, 13 May 1992; David Reimers, "History of Recent Immigration Regulation," *Proceedings of the American Philosophical Society* 130 (1992).

10. See Peter Schuck on new sources of consensus in American immigration politics in "The Politics of Rapid Legal Change: Immigration Policy in the 1980s," *Studies in American Political Development* 6 (1992): 37–92. This superb analysis understates the degree to which new political divisions emerged, however.

11. Ronald Weibe, *The Search for Order, 1877–1920* (New York, 1967); Barry Karl, *The Uneasy State: The United States from 1915–1945* (Chicago, 1983).

12. Morton Keller, *Affairs of State* (Cambridge, Mass., 1977); Barbara Miller Solomon, *Ancestors and Immigrants* (Cambridge, Mass., 1956); C. Vann Woodward, *The Strange Career of Jim Crow*, 3d rev. ed. (New York, 1974); John Higham, *Strangers in the Land* (New York, 1974).

13. Gunnar Myrdal, *An American Dilemma* (New York, 1944).

14. *Graham v. Richardson*, 403 U.S. 365 (1971).

15. See House debate, *Congressional Record*, 99th Cong., 2d sess. (15 Oct. 1986), pp. H10583–99; Senate debate, *Congressional Record*, 99th Cong., 2d sess. (17 Oct. 1986), pp. S16879–915; *Papers of the Select Commission on Immigration and Refugee Policy* (Frederick, Md., 1984), reel 1, p. 69.

16. The *Wall Street Journal*'s chief commentator on immigration is Julian Simon. On the economic benefits of unregulated immigration, see his *The Economic Consequences of Immigration* (Cambridge, Eng., 1989).

17. Stephen Moore, "Who Should America Welcome?" *Society*, July/Aug., 1990, p. 55.

18. Frank Bean, Barry Edmonston, and Jeffrey Passel, eds., *Undocumented Migration to the United States* (Washington, D.C., 1990); Barry Chiswick, "Illegal Immigration and Immigration Control," in Francisco Rivera-Batiz, Ira Gang, and Selig Sechzer, eds., *U.S. Immigration Policy Reform in the 1980s* (New York, 1991), pp. 45–64.

19. *Federal Register* 52, no. 84 (1 May 1987): 16211–12; ibid., 54, no. 132 (12 July 1989): 29450. For thoughtful discussion of legalization implementation, see Zdenka Griswold, "*Ayuda v. Thornburgh*: Did Congress Give the Executive Branch Free Rein to Define the Scope of Legalization?" *Fordham International Law Journal*, 1990, pp. 361–89; Susan Gonzalez Baker, *The Cautious Welcome: The Legalization Programs of the Immigration Reform and Control Act* (Washington, D.C., 1990).

20. Lawyers Committee for Human Rights, Refugee Project, "A Survey and Report," Sept. 1992.

21. "President's Statement on Signing S.1200 into Law," *Weekly Compilation of Presidential Documents*, 6 Nov. 1986, pp. 1534–37. The provision's sponsor, Barney Frank, called Reagan's interpretation "dishonest" and "mean-spirited" (*New York Times*, 23 Nov. 1986, p. 1).

22. "Orphan Agency to Combat Bias," *National Journal*, 27 Oct. 1990, p. 193.

23. For a superb review of cases prior to recent reforms, see Schuck, "The Transformation of Immigration Law," *Columbia Law Review* 84 (1984): 14–86.

24. *Plyler v. Doe*, 457 U.S. 202 (1982).

25. See Baker, *The Cautious Welcome*, pp. 81–118.

26. James Hollifield, *Immigrants, Markets, and Rights* (Cambridge, Mass., 1992); Gary Freeman, *Immigrant Labor and Racial Conflict in Industrial Societies* (Princeton, N.J., 1979).

27. Kay Hailbronner, "Citizenship and Nationhood in Germany," in William Rogers Brubaker, ed., *Immigration and the Politics of Citizenship in Europe and North America* (New York, 1989), p. 74.

28. Hollifield, *Immigrants, Markets, and Rights*, p. 171.

29. Ibid.

30. Zig Layton-Henry, *The Politics of Race in Britain* (London, 1984); Anthony Messina, "Race and Party Competition in Britain," *Parliamentary Affairs*, 1985, pp. 423–36.

31. Lawrence Fuchs, *The American Kaleidoscope: Race, Ethnicity, and the Civic Culture* (Middletown, Conn., 1990), p. 477.

32. *New York Times*, 2 Nov. 1992.

33. Alexis de Tocqueville, *Democracy in America*, ed. J. P. Mayer (New York, 1966), pp. 529–30.

34. Alexander Hamilton, *Papers on Public Credit, Commerce, and Finance*, ed. Samuel McKee (New York, 1957), pp. 194–95.

35. Andrew Carnegie, *Triumphant Democracy, or Fifty Years of the Republic* (New York, 1887), pp. 34–35.

36. Jefferson to George Flower, *The Writings of Thomas Jefferson*, ed. A. A. Lipscomb and A. E. Bergh (New York, 1903), 15:139–42. James Madison emphasized both the economic and humanitarian appeal of generally open immigration and easy naturalization, see his "Speeches in the First Congress," *The Writings of James Madison*, ed. Gaillard Hunt (New York, 1904), 5:436–37, and "Population and Emigration," *National Gazette*, 21 Nov. 1791, ibid., 6:65.

37. Hans Kohn, *American Nationalism: An Interpretive Essay* (New York, 1961), pp. 143–44.

38. See John Palmer, "Philosophy, Policy, and Politics," in Palmer, ed., *Perspectives on the Reagan Years* (Washington, D.C., 1986), pp. 186–90, and the essays, especially Ann Shola Orloff, "The Political Origins of America's Belated Welfare State," in Margaret Weir, Ann Shola Orloff, and Theda Skocpol, eds., *The Politics of Social Policy in the United States* (Princeton, N.J., 1988), pp. 37–80.

39. Orloff, "Political Origins," p. 37.

40. Hugh Heclo, "General Welfare and Two American Political Traditions," *Political Science Quarterly*, 1986, no. 2, p. 182; Theodore Marmor, Jerry Mashaw, and Philip Harvey, *America's Misunderstood Welfare State* (New York, 1990); R. Shep Melnick, "The Courts, Congress, and Programmatic Rights," in Richard Harris and Sidney Milkis, eds., *Remaking American Politics* (Boulder, Colo., 1989), p. 209.

41. Karl, *The Uneasy State*.

42. John Dewey, "The Future of Liberalism," *Journal of Philosophy*, 25 April 1935, pp. 226–27, 230.

43. Franklin D. Roosevelt, "Commonwealth Club Address," *Public Papers and Addresses* (New York, 1938), 1:756; Roosevelt's State of the Union Address of 1944, 28 Oct. 1944.

44. Joseph Carens, "Immigration and the Welfare State," in Amy Gutmann, *Democracy and the Welfare State* (Princeton, N.J., 1988), p. 211.

45. The development of this concept is discussed by Nicholas Lemann, "The Origins of the Urban Underclass," *Atlantic*, June/July 1986, pp. 31–43, 54–68, and William Julius Wilson, *The Truly Disadvantaged* (Chicago, 1987).

46. Deborah Stone, *The Disabled State* (London, 1984).

47. Select Commission on Immigration and Refugee Policy, *U.S. Immigration Policy and the National Interest* (Washington, D.C., 1981); interview of Lawrence Fuchs by the author.

48. Melnick, "The Courts, Congress, and Programmatic Rights."

49. In contrast to United States employers and politicians, economists were divided over the effects of immigration on domestic labor. Compare John Kenneth Galbraith, testimony to the Select Commission, Boston, Mass., Nov. 19, 1979; Simon, *The Economic Consequences of Immigration*; and Michael Piore, *Birds of Passage* (Cambridge, Eng., 1979); to Vernon Briggs, "Mexican Workers in the U.S. Labor Market," *International Labor Review*, 1975, pp. 351–68, and George Borjas, *Friends or Strangers* (New York, 1990). Select Commission on Immigration and Refugee Policy Report, Appendix D (1981), offers a synthesis of additional economists' views.

50. William Julius Wilson, "The Plight of Black Male Job-Seekers," *Focus*, Sept. 1992, pp. 7–8.

51. The GAO report is discussed in Jack Miles, "Blacks vs. Browns," *Atlantic Monthly*, Oct. 1992, p. 41.

52. Stanley Lieberson, *A Piece of the Pie: Blacks and White Immigrants since 1880* (Berkeley, Calif., 1980); see also Arnold Shankman, *Ambivalent Friends* (Westport, Conn., 1982).

53. Nathan Glazer, "The New Immigration and the American City," in Donald L. Horowitz and Gérard Noiriel, eds., *Immigrants in Two Democracies: French and American Experience* (New York, 1992), pp. 268–70.

54. Thomas Espenshade and Thomas Muller, *The Fourth Wave: California's Newest Immigrants* (Washington, D.C., 1985).

55. Los Angeles County Board of Supervisors, *Impact of Undocumented Persons and Other Immigrants on Costs in Los Angeles County*, 6 Nov. 1992.

56. "Health Funds Go to Migrants," *San Diego Union*, 3 Feb. 1993.

57. Richard Lamm and Gary Imhoff, *The Immigration Time Bomb* (New York, 1985), p. 77.

58. Leon Bouvier, *Peaceful Invasions: Immigration and Changing America* (New York, 1992), p. 178.

59. James LaMare, "The Political Integration of Mexican-American Children: A Generational Analysis," *International Migration Review* 16 (1981): 173.

60. Morris Janowitz, *The Reconstruction of Patriotism* (Chicago, 1983), p. 130.

61. Benjamin Franklin, "Observations concerning the Increase of Mankind," *The Papers of Benjamin Franklin*, ed. Leondard Labaree (New Haven, 1959), 4:234.

62. Antihyphenism and Americanization campaigns during the first decades of the twentieth century emboldened federal and state governments, trade unions, businesses, and voluntary associations to sponsor thousands of civics courses for southern and eastern European immigrants. Much of the antiforeign feeling of this period was spurred by World War I and the Red Scare. On this topic, see John F. McClymer, "The Americanization Movement and the Education of the Foreign-Born Adult, 1914–1925," in Bernard Weiss, ed., *American Education and the European Immigrant, 1840–1940* (Urbana, Ill., 1982), pp. 96–116; Robert Carlson, *The Quest for Uniformity: Americanization through Education* (New York, 1975).

63. Lawrence Fuchs discusses this public-private distinction in his chapter "Respecting Diversity, Promoting Unity: The Language Issue," in *The American Kaleidoscope*, pp. 458–73.

64. Hayakawa is quoted in Lamm and Imhoff, *The Immigration Time Bomb*, p. 113.

65. Peter Skerry, *Mexican Americans: The Ambivalent Minority* (New York, 1993), pp. 283–91; Bouvier, *Peaceful Invasions*, pp. 177–94; Fuchs, *The American Kaleidoscope*, pp. 460–69; and the essays in Richard Lambert, ed., "English Plus: Issues in Bilingual Education," *Annals of the American Academy of Political and Social Science*, March 1990.

66. Fuchs, *The American Kaleidoscope*, p. 472.

67. Peter Schuck and Rogers Smith, *Citizenship without Consent* (New Haven, 1985), pp. 90–115.

68. Peter Skerry, "Borders and Quotas: Immigrants and the Affirmative Action State," *Public Interest*, Summer 1989, p. 102.

69. Canada and Germany have similar naturalization requirements; see William Rogers Brubaker, "Citizenship and Naturalization: Policies and Politics," in Brubaker, *Immigration and the Politics of Citizenship in Europe and North America*, pp. 109–12.

70. Rodolfo de la Garza, "Mexican Americans, Mexican Immigrants, and Immigration Reform," in Nathan Glazer, ed., *Clamor at the Gates* (San Francisco, 1985), p. 99.

71. Wilson Carey McWilliams, "Parties as Civic Associations," in Gerald Pomper, ed., *Party Renewal in America* (New York, 1980), pp. 51–68.

72. Joseph Carens, "Aliens and Citizens: The Case for Open Borders," *Review of Politics* 49 (Spring 1987): 251–73, and "Immigration and the Welfare State," in Amy

Gutmann, *Democracy and the Welfare State* (Princeton, N.J., 1988); Judith Lichtenberg, "National Boundaries and Moral Boundaries: A Cosmopolitan View," in Brown and Shue, *Boundaries: National Autonomy and Its Limits*, pp. 70–100.

73. Charles Keely argues that aliens could be assisted with aid other than admission. He notes that "a development approach will do more to relieve human suffering and advance permanent solutions for refugees than . . . third-country resettlement" (Keely, *Global Refugee Policy: The Case for a Development-Oriented Strategy* [New York, 1981]).

74. Walzer, "The Distribution of Membership"; Bruce Ackerman, *Social Justice in the Liberal State* (New Haven, 1980); Mark Gibney, *Strangers or Friends: Principles for a New Alien Admissions Policy* (New York, 1986).

75. Consider that California's Republican governor, Pete Wilson, blamed his state's fiscal woes on immigration reforms and is threatening to sue the federal government for reimbursement (*San Diego Union*, 29 Sept. 1991). Florida's Democratic governor, Lawton Chiles, persuaded the Clinton White House to abandon a campaign pledge to lift the blockade on Haitian passage to United States shores. In the wake of hurricane damage, he warned that his state could not absorb an influx of Haitians comparable to the 1980 Marielitos.

76. "A Governor's Brave Stand on Illegal Aliens," *New York Times*, 23 Aug. 1993.

77. For a glimpse of recent survey results, see *Newsweek*, 9 Aug. 1993, p. 19, and William Schneider, "Americans Turn against Immigration," *National Journal*, 24 July 1993, p. 1900.

78. Landy, "Public Policy and Citizenship."

79. Walzer, "Civility and Civic Virtue in Contemporary America," *Radical Principles* (New York, 1980), pp. 54–72; Jane Mansbridge, *Beyond Adversary Democracy* (New York, 1980), p. 289.

80. Michael Danielson, *The Politics of Exclusion* (New York, 1976); Edward Mills, "Non-Urban Policies as Urban Policies," *Urban Studies*, 1987, pp. 562–63; Paul Peterson, ed., *The New Urban Reality* (Washington, D.C., 1985).

81. Wilson, *The Truly Disadvantaged*; Theda Skocpol, "Fighting Poverty without Poverty Programs," *American Prospect*, Summer 1990, pp. 58–70.

JEFFREY ABRAMSON is Professor of Politics at Brandeis University and ELIZABETH BUSSIERE is Assistant Professor of Political Science at the University of Massachusetts at Boston.

JEAN BETHKE ELSHTAIN is the Laura Spelman Rockefeller Professor of Social and Political Ethics at the University of Chicago.

ROBERT BOOTH FOWLER is Hawkins Professor of Political Science, University of Wisconsin-Madison

AMY GUTMANN is Laurance S. Rockefeller University Professor at Princeton University.

DAVID HOLLENBACH, S.J., is Flatley Professor of Theology at Boston College.

MICHAEL SANDEL is Professor of Government at Harvard University.

PHILIP SELZNICK is Professor Emeritus of Law and Sociology at the University of California, Berkeley.

ROGERS M. SMITH is Professor of Political Science at Yale University.

DANIEL TICHENOR is a Research Fellow at the Gordon Center at Brandeis University.

THOMAS A. SPRAGENS, JR., is Professor of Political Science at Duke University.

WILLIAM M. SULLIVAN is Professor of Philosophy at La Salle University.

CHARLES TAYLOR is Professor of Philosophy at McGill University.

MICHAEL WALZER is UPS Foundation Professor of Social Science at the Institute for Advanced Study in Princeton, New Jersey.

ALAN WOLFE is University Professor of Sociology at Boston University.

# INDEX

Addams, Jane, 247
*Americanism*, 237–58
Anderson, Benedict, 24, 197, 198
Ardrey, Robert, 129
Aristotle, 150, 151
autonomy, 28, 40–42, 73–87, 124–25,
    148, 162–63

Barber, Benjamin, 50, 89, 151
Beer, Samuel H., 26
Bellah, Robert, 92, 146
Berger, Peter, 146
Blackmun, Harry, 79–80, 84
Blitz, Mark, 26
Bloom, Allan, 91
Bolick, Clint, 28
Bourne, Randolph, 69, 247, 248–49,
    250, 253, 254
Bouvier, Leon, 274
Boyte, Harry, 26, 108
Brandeis, Louis, 75
Brennan, William J., 78
Buber, Martin, 18
Burger, Warren, 224

Carlyle, Thomas, 47
civic friendship, 49–50
civil society, 49, 67–68, 147–48, 150–53,
    170–80, 183–217
Coleman, John, 148
community
    of crisis, 89–90
    definition, 24–26, 88–95
    of ideas, 88–89
    of memory, 90–92
    natural vs. social, 130
    values of a, 28–31
Condorcet, Jean, 40–41, 43
Copernicus, Nicolaus, 39

Daly, Markate, 18
deliberation, 27–28, 50, 160–69, 223–
    24, 228–29, 270–71, 278–79
Derber, Charles, 22
Dewey, John, 66–67, 69, 247–48, 250,
    251, 253, 269
Dionne, E. J., 145
Douglas, Stephen, 74, 75, 76–77, 82
D'Souza, Dinesh, 24
Dworkin, Ronald, 116, 126
Durkheim, Emile, 130

Elkin, Stephen L., 26
Emerson, Ralph Waldo, 268
Engels, Friedrich, 127
Eyer, Diane, 135

First Amendment, 23–24, 29–31, 165–
    66, 218–29
    and campaign expenditures, 222–24
    and community, 228–29
    and the "fairness doctrine," 225–26
Fishkin, James, 50
Friedman, Milton, 44
Fuchs, Lawrence, 266, 275

Galston, William, 48, 163–65, 167
Garza, Rodolfo de la, 276
Glasser, Ira, 22
Glendon, Mary Ann, 21
Goodin, Robert E., 119

Habermas, Jurgen, 187, 191, 192
Hailbronner, Kay, 266
Harlan, John Marshall, 75, 76
Harvey, Philip, 269
Hauerwas, Stanley, 92
Heclo, Hugh, 269
Hegel, Georg, 32

Hentoff, Nat, 24
Hobbes, Thomas, 45, 128, 134
Hollifield, James, 266
Holmes, Steven, 25
human nature, 31–34, 126–40
    and animal nature, 129
    and biology, 126–40
Hume, David, 42, 118

Iacobucci, Frank, 20, 33
Imhoff, Gary, 274
immigration, 240, 259–79
    and language, 273–76
    and race, 269–73
    restrictions on, 261–69
individualism, 19–21, 37–40, 43, 122–
        25, 146
    vs. institutions, 170–80
    possessive, 104
    radical, 104–5
interdependence, 146, 149–50, 153

Jagger, Alison, 33
James, P. D., 100, 103, 105
James, William, 248
Janowitz, Morris, 274
Jefferson, Thomas, 43, 268
Johnson, Lyndon, 262

Kallen, Horace, 69, 247, 248, 250, 253–
        54
Kalven, Harry, Jr., 221
Kant, Immanuel, 32, 190
Kennedy, John F., 21, 262
King, Martin Luther, 61
Kornhaber, Arthur, 102–3, 106

LaMare, James, 274
Lamm, Richard, 274
Landy, Marc, 278
liberalism
    history of, 39–44
    practice of, 53–56
    theory of, 56–57
Lieberson, Stanley, 272

Locke, John, 19, 40, 43, 46
Lorenz, Konrad, 129

MacIntyre, Alasdair, 54–55, 61, 174
Madison, James, 94
Maine, Henry Sumner, 124
majoritarianism, 22–24, 50, 154, 156
Mansbridge, Jane, 278
Maritain, Jacques, 148
Marmor, Theodore, 269
Marshall, Thurgood, 74
Marx, Karl, 33, 47, 54, 92
Mashaw, Jerry, 269
Meiklejohn, Alexander, 220, 221
Melnick, R. Shep, 269, 271
Mercier, Louis Sebastian, 190
Michelman, Frank, 158–59
Midgely, Mary, 101, 103
Mill, John Stuart, 40, 41–42, 43–44, 46,
        48, 64, 68, 184
mobility, 57–61
Murray, John Courtney, 148

Neuhaus, Richard, 92
neutrality, 67–68, 73–87, 219, 222
Nisbet, Robert, 28
Nozick, Robert, 44

Oakeshott, Michael, 62
Oaks, Dallin, 20
obligation, 115, 118–22
ordered liberty, 16, 20–24, 154–56
Orloff, Ann Shola, 269
Orwell, George, 117

Paine, Thomas, 43
Parsons, Talcott, 130
personal responsibility, 110–25, 175
pluralism, 144, 150
Pocock, J. G. A., 89
Pope John Paul II, 150
Pope Pius XI, 148
privacy, 73–87, 148–49

Ravitch, Diane, 163
Rawls, John, 63, 67, 69, 151

Reagan, Ronald, 225, 264
Rehnquist, William, 224
Reuther, Rosemary Radford, 92
Rorty, Richard, 32

Sandel, Michael, 25, 56
Schlesinger, Arthur M., Jr., 24
Schuck, Peter, 275
self-constraint, 154, 156–58, 165–69
Singer, Peter, 115
Skerry, Peter, 276
Smith, Adam, 19, 43, 128, 134
Smith, Rogers, 275
social bonds, 62–64
social compact, 105–8
social contract, 103–4
social responsibility, 139–40, 149–53,
    172–74, 177, 180
  vs. individual rights, 20–22
  and the media, 218–22
solidarity, 145, 148–53
Spencer, Herbert, 43, 127
Stevens, John Paul, 82–83
Strauss, Leo, 91
Strossen, Nadine, 21
subsidiarity, 148–49

Tocqueville, Alexis de, 22, 50, 173, 201,
    207, 210–11, 215, 267
tolerance, 144–45, 149, 173–74, 245–48,
    250, 254

Unger, Roberto, 62
universalism vs. particularism, 110–
    25

Walzer, Michael, 93, 161–62, 259,
    277
Warner, Michael, 187, 191
Warren, Samuel, 75
Washington, George, 243
Weber, Max, 92
Whelan, Frederick, 259
White, Byron, 82–83
Will, George, 24
Williams, Bernard, 125
Wilson, James Q., 135–36, 137
Wilson, William Julius, 272
Wolin, Sheldon, 108
Woodward, Kenneth L., 102–3,
    106

Young, Iris Marion, 95